Parallels and Convergences

Parallels and Convergences: Mormon Thought and Engineering Vision

Edited by
A. Scott Howe
Richard L. Bushman

Greg Kofford Books
Salt Lake City 2012

Copyright © Greg Kofford Books
Cover design copyright © 2012 Greg Kofford Books, Inc.

Cover design by Loyd Ericson. "The Blue Marble" courtesy of NASA.

Published in the USA.

All rights reserved. No part of this volume may be reproduced in any form without written permission from the publisher, Greg Kofford Books. The views expressed herein are the responsibility of the authors and do not necessarily represent the position of Greg Kofford Books, Inc.

Greg Kofford Books
P.O. Box 1362
Draper, UT 84020
www. koffordbooks.com

2015   14   13   12   11   5   4   3   2   1

Library of Congress Cataloging-in-Publication Data

Parallels and convergences : Mormon thought and engineering vision / edited by A. Scott Howe, Richard L. Bushman.
   pages cm
  Includes index.
  ISBN 978-1-58958-187-6
  1. Religion and science. 2. Church of Jesus Christ of Latter-day Saints--Doctrines. 3. Mormon Church--Doctrines. I. Howe, A. Scott, editor. II. Bushman, Richard L., editor.
  BL241.P37 2011
  261.5'5--dc23
                                     2011052415

Contents

Foreword, v
Richard Lyman Bushman

Introduction: No Small and Cramped Eternities:
Parley Pratt and the Foundations of Mormon Cosmology, vii
Terryl L. Givens

Section 1
Parallels in Mormon Thought:
Physics and Engineering

1. Models of Spirit Matter, 3
   Adam N. Davis

2. A Standard Physics Model of Spirit, 17
   A. Scott Howe

3. A Technical Interpretation of Mormon Physics and Physiology, 29
   Lincoln Cannon and A. Scott Howe

4. Materialism, Free Will, and Mormonism, 43
   Adam N. Davis

Section 2
Parallels in Mormon Thought:
Philosophy and Engineering

5. God, the Perfect Engineer, 57
   Allen W. Leigh

6. Complementary Aspects of Mormonism and Transhumanism, 67
   Brent Allsop, Christopher Bradford, Lincoln Cannon, Andrew West, A. Joseph West, and Carl A. Youngblood

7. Quantified Morality, 93
   A. Scott Howe

8. Theological Implications of the New God Argument, 111
   Lincoln Cannon and A. Joseph West

Section 3
Parallels in Mormon Thought: Practice and Engineering

9. Gaia, Mormonism, and Paradisiacal Earth, 125
   Roger D. Hansen

10. Spiritual Underpinnings for a Space Program, 135
    William R. Pickett, A. Scott Howe, and James W. Young

11. Welcome to the Twenty-First Century: The Uncharted Future Ahead, 157
    David H. Bailey

Contributors, 175
Scripture Index, 179
Index, 181

Foreword

Richard Lyman Bushman

The Claremont Mormon Studies conference on "Mormon Thought and Engineering Vision" had its origins in a casual conversation. I met Scott Howe at a talk I gave on the progress of the Mormon studies program at Claremont Graduate University. Howe, an engineer at the NASA Jet Propulsion laboratory in Pasadena, approached me with a question: Had I ever contemplated the links between engineering and Mormon theology? We talk all the time about science and theology; what about engineering and theology? Howe pointed out that science is based on the idea that pure chance rules the universe. Life emerges, according the scientific view, out of the random juncture of elemental particles. Engineering, by contrast, is based on purposeful design. Engineers construct useful instruments for achieving worthy ends. Isn't God more like an engineer than a scientist?

A few minutes of conversation convinced me that Latter-day Saint engineers had reason to engage in theological discussion. How did the exponential growth of engineering knowledge and capacity relate to the Latter-day Saint idea of humans growing into godhood? How does the constantly increasing control of the human environment relate to the godly ability to create worlds? I asked Howe if he thought Latter-day Saint engineers would benefit from coming together to explore some of these questions. He not only said yes but agreed to organize a meeting to be held at Claremont Graduate University. The essays in this volume come out of that conference held March 6-7, 2009.

Howe rapidly assembled a committee of LDS engineers from around the country in a variety of fields ranging from artificial intelligence to moon settlements, his own specialty. I was fearful their discussions would be geared to an audience with high technical proficiency—engineers talking to engineers. At the conference, my fears were allayed. Every paper engaged my attention. There was some technical talk, certainly, and some allusions I could not fully appreciate, but the presenters clearly wanted to speak to a general audience.

And what is the message? I took it to be that Mormon theology leads us to see eternal implications in engineering. Engineers enable us to make the world more comfortable and to perform incredible feats of movement and communication. But their work may go beyond the amelioration of the human condition. The end point of engineering knowledge may be divine knowledge. Mormon theology permits us to think of God and humans as collaborators in bringing to pass the immortality and eternal life of man. Engineers may be preparing the way for humans to act more like gods in managing the world.

Kindliness, wise parenting, righteousness, and service are probably more fundamental in leading humans toward eternal life. But improving our physical world serves divine purposes, too. In constructing better worlds, engineers may be learning godly skills. From a Latter-day Saint perspective, they may be incipient creators.

The chapters in this volume capture the thought of a group of LDS engineers exploring the interactions of their work and their belief at the beginning of the twenty-first century. Ideally these essays will launch a discussion that will continue for many years to come.

Introduction

No Small and Cramped Eternities: Parley Pratt and the Foundations of Mormon Cosmology

Terryl L. Givens

In his book on *The Everlasting Man*, the great Christian apologist G. K. Chesterton resists the diminution of man consequent upon a thoroughly Darwinized universe. He writes:

> No philosopher denies that a mystery still attaches to the two great transitions: the origin of the universe itself and the origin of the principle of life itself. Most philosophers have the enlightenment to add that a third mystery attaches to the origin of man himself. In other words, a third bridge was built across a third abyss of the unthinkable when there came into the world what we call reason and what we call will. Man is not merely an evolution, but rather a revolution.
>
> It is the simple truth [he continues] that man differs from the brutes in kind and not in degree; and the proof of it is here; that it sounds like a truism to say that the most primitive man drew a picture of a monkey and that it sounds like a joke to say that the most intelligent monkey drew a picture of a man. Something of division and disproportion has appeared; and it is unique.... This creature was truly different from all other creatures; because he was a creator as well as a creature.[1]

I want to explore the implications of this last phrase, for in defining man as Homo erector, rather than Homo sapiens, we find a potent link between what this volume calls "Mormon Thought and Engineering Vision."

When Church Father Origen wrote one of the earliest treatises on Christian belief in the early third century, he noted that some articles of the faith were "delivered ... with the utmost clearness on certain points

---

1. Gilbert K. Chesterton, *Everlasting Man* (San Francisco, Calif.: Ignatius Press, 1993 printing), 26, 34-35.

which they believed to be *necessary to every one*."[2] Ever since, theology has largely been concerned with articulating and elaborating those foundational tenets of religious faith. Such tenets consist of "the character and attributes of God, . . . the doctrines we are to believe, and the duties we are to practice," according to the 1828 Webster's definition of theology. A more recent authority, surveying the historical scope of theology, describes its purview as "the whole complex of the Divine dispensation from the Fall of Adam to the Redemption through Christ and its mediation to men by His Church."[3] The limitations of theology are implicit in that formulation (fall through redemption) but are made more explicit in the greatest Christian epic in the West, Milton's *Paradise Lost*. Milton pushed the boundaries of "God-science" further than most—at least he claimed he did—when he determined to soar "above th' Aonian Mount," in order to pursue "Things unattempted yet in Prose or Rhime." Yet even in his audacious claim to "justifie the wayes of God to men," he knew when to recognize the limits of appropriate inquiry. God sends the angel Raphael to impart further light and knowledge to Adam, but ends by counseling the over-curious human,

> Sollicit not thy thoughts with matters hid,
> . . . Heav'n is for thee too high
> To know what passes there; be lowlie wise:
> Think onely what concernes thee and thy being;
> Dream not of other Worlds, what Creatures there
> Live, in what state, condition, or degree,
> Contented [with what] thus farr hath been reveal'd.[4]

The questions that Christian theology has by and large resisted the urge to adjudicate are legion. What of the time *before* Creation? What was God doing then? Preparing Hell for those who would ask such impudent questions, Augustine was tempted to respond.[5] What of God's other dominions? Another mystery it falls not to theology to explain. Why is there man at all? For Milton, the boldest exponent of theodicy before Parley Pratt, it was to deprive Satan of bragging rights in having suborned a third of heaven's angels. The scriptures, however, are silent. What of human des-

---

2. Origen, *De Principiis*, Preface, 3, translated by F. Crombie, in A. Roberts and J. Donaldson, eds., *The Ante-Nicene Fathers* (Grand Rapids, Mich,: Eerdmans, 1978), 4:239.

3. "Theology," in F. L. Cross and E. A. Livingstone, eds., *Oxford Dictionary of the Christian Church* (Oxford, England: Oxford University Press, 1997), 1,604.

4. John Milton, *Paradise Lost*, Bk. 8, ll. 167-177.

5. Augustine, *Confessions*, Bk. 11, chap. 12. Tempted, because he actually thought the question was meaningless, since time began with Creation.

tiny in the worlds beyond? What is man being saved *for*? Dante thought a state of eternal, rapturous contemplation, and few have proffered more specifics than that. Post-redemption theology is an oxymoron. So *traditional* theology, in other words, confines itself to defining the terms and conditions of a very limited concept of salvation, of a soul of unknown beginnings, from an evil of unknown origin, to prepare for a future of unknown nature, all in accordance with the inscrutable will of a God who is beyond human comprehending. What it *does* elaborate are the articles of faith demanding assent and the sacraments necessary to comply with in the course of human life. The focus is decidedly, emphatically, on the time frame and the personal transformations that lead "from the Fall of Adam to the Redemption through Christ."

Against this conservative Christian background, Parley Pratt's major work stands in sharp relief. No Mormon thinker, Pratt included, would exceed Smith's own audacity as a Christian iconoclast. Speculating on heavenly councils, Gods that were once human, and humans that could attain to Godhood—these and other doctrines blasted asunder the creedal conceptions of God and Man alike. But it fell to Pratt to assemble these ideas for the first time in something like a systematic form—in some cases apparently giving public expression to them before Smith. Here is perhaps the prime instance of Pratt playing Paul to Joseph's Jesus. If Smith was the instigator of Mormonism's essential beliefs, Pratt organized them, elaborated them, and defended them in a manner that gave them the enduring life and the complexion they had in the early church. Pratt was, in this sense, the first theologian of Mormonism.

Precedents for Pratt's atypically boundless theologizing were recent. Thomas Dick defended his *Philosophy of a Future State* as consistent with, if not affirmed by, Holy Writ and took his fellow theologians to task for their reticence in plumbing "the nature of heavenly felicity, and the employments of the future world." He lamented "the vague and indefinite manner in which such subjects have been hitherto treated" and "the want of those expansive views of the Divine operations which the professors of Christianity should endeavor to attain." Like Pratt, Dick was consumed by the spectacle of a scientific juggernaut that was already opening worlds both immense and minute to human knowledge, and which would leave in its wake any theology too timid to follow. "Consider the boundless extent of the starry firmament," Dick rhapsodized, "the scenes of grandeur it displays, the new luminaries, which, in the course of ages, appear to be gradually augmenting its splendour, and the countless myriads of exalted intelligences which doubtless people its expansive regions." In regard to the latter, he felt ennobled rather than diminished by the titanic scope of creation involved. "And if the multiplicity of objects in one world overwhelms our powers of conception and computation," he wrote, "how much more the number and variety of beings and operations connected with the economy of millions of worlds!" At a bare minimum, he concluded, men and angels in a future state would continue their intellectual progress in the realms of mathematics and astronomy, as a simple precondition for understanding the glory and majesty of the heavens they inherit. But why stop with those two disciplines? And Dick goes on to enumerate natural philosophy, anatomy and physiology, history, and other subjects as "some of those branches of science which will be recognized [and studied] by the righteous in a future state."[6]

This was heady doctrine, and Pratt's own work only reaffirmed and expanded upon it in at least two key regards. He wrote on the basis of what he believed was authoritative revelation rather than simple inference. And he wedded his system to a young but flourishing institution, which assured its dissemination and survival.

The real key to understanding Pratt's great synthetic work, consummated in his *Key to the Science of Theology*, is in the implications he draws from one of Mormonism's most radical claims. "Jesus Christ and his Father [are] in possession of not merely an organized spirit but also a glorious immortal body of flesh and bones." Such extreme anthropomorphosizing is startling in and of itself. But the inference that follows is what shatters the boundaries of traditional theologizing. If the Father and Son have physical tabernacles, he reasons, then they are "subject to the laws that govern, of necessity, even the most refined order of physical existence." Because "all physical element, however embodied, quickened, or refined, is subject to the general laws necessary to all existence."[7]

What this means is that, by naturalizing Deity, the entire universe of God and humankind, heaven and hell, body and spirit, the eternal and the mundane—all are collapsed into one sphere. The paradigm to which this breathtaking view of things stands in opposition is neatly formulated by Pratt's contemporary and most famous amateur theologian, Samuel Taylor Coleridge, who stated the matter simply: "The very ground of all Miracle," he proclaimed, is "the heterogeneity of Spirit and Matter."[8] On that distinction

---

6. Thomas Dick, *Philosophy of a Future State* (Philadelphia, Pa.: Biddle, 1845), v, 136, 145, 166.

7. Parley P. Pratt, *Key to the Science of Theology* (1855; rpt. Salt Lake City, Utah: Deseret News, 1893), 23.

8. Samuel Taylor Coleridge, *Notebooks*, edited by H. J. Jackson (Oxford, England: Oxford University Press, 1985), 555.

stand the viability of miracles, the sacred, and God's immunity to the Babel tower of scientific materialism and the hubris of philosophical materialism.

Pratt not only declares the distinction erased and the spheres conflated into one, but he also insists that that sphere is governed by laws fully conformable to and accessible by human reason. In the aftermath of Sir Isaac Newton's momentous decipherment of the laws of the universe, the French scientist Pierre-Simon de Laplace famously told Napoleon, in his philosophical euphoria, that he no longer had need of God to make sense of creation. Secular science could henceforth exile God from his universe. In Pratt's theological euphoria, God was reinscribed in the universe, but as a part of it, rather than outside it. For this reason, it would be more accurate to say that for Pratt, science encompassed theology rather than simply coexisting harmoniously with it. That is the sense in which Pratt's title must be understood: "Key to the Science of Theology."

In an earlier work, "The World Turned Upside Down," Pratt had already signaled his intention to reinterpret all theology within the construct of a kind of scientific materialism. "Matter and spirit are the two great principles of all existence," he had written there. Both constitute the eternal—and material—constituents of the universe. The resulting interaction between the physical and the spiritual, the earthly and the divine, was almost jarring. As the physical universe was directly affected by the fall of man, so must Christ's atonement be seen as entailing "the salvation and durability of the physical world, the renovation and regeneration of matter, and the restoration of the elements, to a state of eternal and unchangeable purity."[9]

This is more than simply innovation or heterodox speculation. Rather, it represents the most significant reconceptualizing of religious cosmology in Christian history. I am reminded in this regard of a much circulated essay by the iconoclastic theorist of computer science, Edsger W. Dijkstra. He wrote:

> The usual way in which we plan today for tomorrow is in yesterday's vocabulary. We do so, because we try to get away with the concepts that we are familiar with and that have acquired their meaning in our past experience.... It is the most common way of trying to cope with novelty: by means of metaphors and analogies we try to link the new to the old, the novel to the familiar.... In the case of a sharp discontinuity, however, the method breaks down: though we try to glorify it with the name "common sense," our past experience is no longer relevant.... One must consider one's own past, the experiences collected, and the habits formed in it as an unfortunate accident of history, and one has to approach the radical

---

9. Parley P. Pratt, *The World Turned Upside Down* (Liverpool, England: James and Woodburn, 1842), 5, 14.

novelty with a blank mind, consciously refusing to try to link it with the familiar, because the familiar is hopelessly inadequate.... Coming to grips with a radical novelty amounts to creating and learning a new foreign language that cannot be translated into one's mother tongue.[10]

This description applies perfectly to Mormonism, yet with an ironic qualifier: Mormonism's most striking discontinuity with Christian theology is in the radical continuity it establishes between the material and the eternal, the transcendent—even the supernatural. The result is a worldview that is shockingly—and refreshingly blithe—in its indifference to its own oddness. "When the elements melt with fervent heat," said Brigham Young, "the Lord Almighty will send forth his angels, who are well instructed in chemistry, and they will separate the elements and make new combinations thereof."[11] Orson Pratt would elaborate this view a few years later: "The study of science is the study of something eternal. If we study astronomy, we study the works of God. If we study chemistry, geology, optics, or any other branch of science, every new truth we come to the understanding of is eternal; it is a part of the great system of universal truth. It is truth that exists throughout universal nature; and God is the dispenser of all truth—scientific, religious, and political."[12] Humankind and God, building bridges and creating worlds, practicing chemistry and endowing the earth with its celestial glory—the mundane and the miraculous are but different degrees on an eternal scale of knowledge acquisition.

The most audacious Mormon principles followed inescapably from this monistic cosmology, and they pertained to the relationship between human beings and Deity. One of the most surprising aspects of Mormon culture was the ease with which early members, most from evangelical backgrounds, reared in strict Methodist, and Reformed Baptist traditions, transitioned into a faith that demolished some of Christendom's most sacred precepts. "An immortal man ... perfected in his attributes in all the fulness of celestial glory is called *a god*," wrote Pratt without apology. And then, without blinking, "It may then consistently be said that there are, in a subordinate sense, a plurality of Gods."[13] Even earlier, in 1838 (six years

---

10. Edsger W. Dijkstra, "On the Cruelty of Really Teaching Computing Science," E. W. Dijkstra Archive, http://userweb.cs.utexas.edu/users/EWD/transcriptions/EWD10/EWD1036.html (accessed February 2011).

11. Brigham Young, August 11, 1872, *Journal of Discourses*, 27 vols. (Liverpool, England: Franklin D. Richards and Samuel W. Richards, 1851-86; rpt. Salt Lake City, 1974), 15:127.

12. Orson Pratt, February 12, 1860, *Journal of Discourses*, 7:157.

13. Pratt, *Key to the Science of Theology*, 42.

before King Follett!) he had written that, because we will grow to have "the same knowledge that God has, [we] will have the same power. Hence the appropriateness of the appellation, 'Gods, even the sons of God.'"[14] Anglo-Saxon Protestantism had shown, since England's Toleration Act of 1689, a remarkable effort to countenance dissent and heterodoxy in Christian faith—within a few non-negotiable parameters. Notably, religious freedom was decreed in the 1689 Act for most dissenters from orthodoxy, providing they accepted the creedal definition of the Trinity. And here was Pratt, unabashedly professing Mormonism to be, in an essential regard, polytheistic. Certainly a case could be made, and has been made by Mormon leaders, that Latter-day Saints are monotheistic in the only way that matters—they worship God the Father in the name of Christ. The point is: Pratt did not stoop to make that claim, because he was not interested in passing muster with the guardians of Christian orthodoxy. It would have sounded too apologetic—and if there is one thing Pratt never condescended to, it was apologies for Mormon heterodoxy.

The fullest expression of this idea, of course, would come in Joseph Smith's famous discourse shortly before his death. King Follett presents us with two catastrophes for conventional theology—which may not be a bad thing. The first is the humanizing and temporalizing of God. I know thoughtful and faithful Mormons who rejoice that the King Follett discourse was never canonized for that reason. It does have one virtue, however—one that we will have the boldness perhaps to someday plumb, in that it lends itself to the world's best hope for a naturalistic theology. Stripped of all invocations of transcendent entities and transcendent eternities, such a universe should be at least potentially appealing to the hardcore materialists currently working the anti-God/anti-religion circuit.

One of Mormonism's greatest strengths, surely unexplored, untapped till now, is its potential to offer an alternative to the materialist/supernaturalist impasse that stymies productive discourse in this age of increasing polarization and rhetoric that reduces to caricature proponents of each cosmology. I would point out that positions that bridge the gap have been taken at times, by some of the more unconventional of the philosophically minded. Cambridge philosopher John McTaggart, for example, considered himself an atheist, insofar as he found nothing intellectually compelling about the God of religion east or west. The human soul, however, he found too powerful a paradigm to reject. In fact, he argues that there are better grounds for skepticism about the reality of matter and sensa, than to doubt

---

14. Parley P. Pratt, *Mormonism Unveiled: Zion's Watchman Unmasked* (New York: Pratt and Fordham, 1838), 27.

the reality of spirit.[15] And incidentally, he found its premortal existence vastly more compelling a belief than its purported immortality.

William James also famously proposed a religious paradigm that avoided the materialist/supernaturalist alternatives. Scientific naturalism is inadequate, he concludes, because "there are resources in us that naturalism with its literal and legal virtues never recks of, possibilities that take our breath away, of another kind of happiness and power ... and these seem to show a wider world than either physics or philistines can imagine." On the other hand, he argues, the problems with positing a God equivalent to the Absolute is utterly untenable. (Among other problems, satisfying as the concept of the absolute is, it satisfies only intellectual rationality. It does not successfully address what he labels aesthetic or moral rationality.) The only solution, he finds, would be a God who is in some sense Finite—that is, a God who is in the universe and subject to its laws. He believes, in accordance with biblical theism but at variance with creedal Christianity, that it would be hard to "conceive of anything more different from the absolute than the God, say, of David or of Isaiah," he wrote. "*That* God is an essentially finite being *in* the cosmos, not with the cosmos in him.... If it should prove probable that the absolute does not exist, it will not follow in the slightest degree that a God like that of David, Isaiah, or Jesus may not exist, or may not be the most important existence in the universe for us to acknowledge."[16]

And as a third example, I would point to the avowed atheist philosopher Thomas Nagel, who found both theism and scientific physicalism with its Darwinian evolution inadequate to the task of giving a general account of the human self. "I am denying," he writes, "that what rationality is can be understood through the theory of natural selection." To the question of what it is, he confesses, "I don't have a proper positive response.... [But] the physical story, without more, cannot explain the mental story, including consciousness and reason." He is loathe to invoke the specter of religious belief, and yet he concludes, after his wrestle with the non-God, "We are simple examples of minds, and ... the existence of mind is certainly a *datum* for the construction of any world picture: At the very least, its *possibility* must be explained. And it hardly seems credible that its appearance should be a natural accident, like the fact that there are mammals."[17]

---

15. John McTaggart and E. McTaggart, *The Nature of Existence*, edited by C. D. Broad (Cambridge, England: Cambridge University Press 1927), 2:87ff.

16. William James, *A Pluralistic Universe* (Cambridge, Mass.: Harvard University Press, 1977), 305-54.

17. Thomas Nagel, *The Last Word* (New York: Oxford University Press, 1997), 132-38.

Positions like these should be of acute interest to Mormons, it seems to me. Because all of them begin with what Nagel calls the datum of the human soul in a universe where a transcendent God is not an a priori condition. Reversing the usual sequence, the soul is, in these cases, not the emanation, not the temporal or logical consequence of a creator God. It is the starting point for the development of a cosmology, as it is in the King Follett address.

The second of the King Follett assaults on orthodoxy, of course, is its premise that a human being can become a god. This I find the most exciting prospect Mormonism holds out to us. It is also, of course, the most feared theological tenet in the whole history of Christendom—and even beyond. In the earliest creation myth of which we have record—the Mesopotamian *Atrahasis*—the man created at the instigation of a Divine Assembly is made to forget his origin in the heavens, lest he aspire to return to his place among the gods. The Church Father Tertullian in the early third century, gave fullest expression to the horror with which guardians of God's sanctity faced down the possibilities of theosis. In these early Christian centuries, the premortal soul provided by far the most compelling solution to numerous dilemmas associated with incarnation, but in preexistence lurked a cardinal danger as well. Tertullian attributed the idea to the pagan philosopher Plato. And Plato, he wrote, has conceded to the soul

> so large an amount of divine quality as to put it on a par with God. He makes it unborn, which single attribute I might apply as a sufficient attestation of its perfect divinity; he then adds that the soul is immortal, incorruptible, incorporeal—since he believed God to be the same—invisible, incapable of delineation, uniform, supreme, rational, and intellectual. What more could he attribute to the soul, [he asked in outrage,] if he wanted to call it God? We, however, who allow no appendage to God (in the sense of equality), by this very fact reckon the soul as very far below God: for we suppose it to be born.[18]

Like much else in Mormonism, the prospect of theosis can appeal to vainglorious and ignoble reasons, as well as to more pure-hearted ones. Of course, given the context of Enoch's weeping God and the Christ of Gethsemane, we know that acquiring the divine nature is more about infinite vulnerability than infinite power (as my wife, Fiona, has spoken and written about so eloquently).

At the same time, I would argue, the God of Joseph Smith and Parley P. Pratt is a God of power, and unprecedented power at that. And here is why. The heavens are for Pratt, as they were for Jewish thinker Philo of

---

18. Tertullian, *Treatise on the Soul*, Bk. 24, in *Ante-Nicene Fathers*, 3:203.

Alexandria and for Church Father Origen, great defender of premortal existence, seething with activity, populous with humans, spirits, and gods, all going and coming, ascending and descending, like the angels on Jacob's ladder. The differences among them derive from "the varied grades of intelligence and purity and also in the variety of spheres occupied by each in the series of progressive being."[19] This is theology that comes fittingly out of the age of Thomas Malthus and G. W. F. Hegel, conformable to Darwin's universe of flux and agon and dynamism. If, by Pratt's day, the dour face of Puritanism had long been in retreat and Calvinism was fast becoming a "one-horse shay," the Christianity of yesteryear was not receding quickly enough to suit him. The gospel he taught and embraced was, like the age of progress, one of unfettered optimism and boundless possibilities, not one of guilt, rules, and hellfire. He urged upon his contemporary religionists the importance of "ceasing to teach and impress upon the youthful mind the gloomy thoughts of death, and the melancholy forebodings of a long slumber in the grave." The "wayward and buoyant spirits of youth," he continued, were already too "weighed down and oppressed," and he hated to see "the more cheerful faculties of the soul ... thus paralyzed."[20]

His embrace of human theosis, this "doctrine of equality," his more general application of the appellation "gods"—all are susceptible to the charge, if not of blasphemy, then of a dangerous collapse of sacred distance, a risky diminution of the grounds for reverence and awe that constitute reverence before God's transcendent holiness. But for Pratt, the invitation to fellowship with the gods was cause for unalloyed celebration of God's superabundance:

> What a glorious field of intelligence now lies before us, yet but partially explored. What a boundless expanse for contemplation and reflection now opens to our astonished vision. What an intellectual banquet spreads itself invitingly to our appetite, calling into lively exercise every power and faculty of the mind, and giving full scope to all the great and ennobling passions of the soul. ... All the virtuous principles of the human mind may here expand and grow, and flourish, unchecked by any painful emotions or gloomy fears.[21]

As for God's motive in giving earthly existence and eternal salvation to man, Pratt outlines the meaning and purpose of life in one eloquent paragraph, reminiscent of Plato's god described in *Timaeus*: "Wisdom in-

---

19. Pratt, *Key to the Science of Theology*, 21.
20. Parley P. Pratt, *The Millennium and Other Poems: To Which Is Annexed, a Treatise on the Regeneration and Eternal Duration of Matter* (New York: W. Molineux, 1840), 135-36.
21. Pratt, *The World Turned Upside Down*, 18-19.

spires the Gods to multiply their species and to lay the foundation for all the forms of life to increase in number and for each to enjoy himself in the sphere to which he is adapted, and in the possession and use of that portion of the elements necessary to his existence and happiness."[22] Plato, I will remind you, had said this about God and his motives. The creator "was good, and one who is good can never become jealous of anything. And so, being free of jealousy, he wanted everything to become as much like himself as was possible."[23] That's why he created the world and human souls to people it. Similarly with Pratt. God creates those conditions most favorable for the endless advance of his progeny "through every form of life, birth, change, and resurrection, and every form of progress in knowledge and experience." This great work of the Father, like the universe itself, will be "endless or eternally progressive.... While eternal charity endures, or eternity itself rolls its successive ages, the heavens will multiply and new worlds and more people will be added to the kingdoms of the Fathers. Thus, in the progress of events, unnumbered millions of worlds and of systems of worlds will necessarily be called into requisition and be filled by man, beast, fowl, tree, and all the vast varieties of beings and things ever budded and blossomed in Eden."[24]

"There is such a thing," Chesterton wrote, "as a small and cramped eternity. You may see it in many modern religions."[25] The cosmology of Joseph Smith, explicated by Parley Pratt, is no small and cramped eternity. And the possibilities it bestows upon humankind, the divine potential with which it endows a fallen race, is no blasphemy. It is in fact the highest tribute to God because it bespeaks the worship of a God as unencumbered by jealousies and insecurities as the capacious God of Plato. Such a conception of God should invite an equally unencumbered imaginative response.

---

22. Pratt, *Key to the Science of Theology*, 52.
23. Plato, *Timaeus* 29e, in *Plato: Complete Works*, translated by D J. Zeylm, A. Nehamas, and P. Woodruff, edited by J. M. Cooper (Indianapolis, Ind.: Hackett, 1997), 1,236.
24. Pratt, *Key to the Science of Theology*, 53.
25. Chesterton, *Orthodoxy*, 12.

Section 1
Parallels in Mormon Thought: Physics and Engineering

In the same way that each person should have the privilege of hearing the gospel in his or her own language, it might be important to consider that technical language is another mode of expression into which we ought to translate our most important concepts. The authors contributing to this volume certainly advocate such an approach and even show that what has been expressed in poetic ancient language by untechnical prophets in yesteryear often has a stunning visionary component that can be explained well in technical terms.

Physics is the study of properties and interactions of space, time, matter and energy (http://en.wiktionary.org/wiki/physics). If physics attempts to objectively lay bare the laws, engineering inserts intelligence into the equation in the conscious use of physical laws for a creative act. Perhaps we can define engineering as the manipulation of cause and effect in anticipation of some future outcome. The juxtaposition of physics and engineering may be applied to either the creator or the material used in the creation.

Adam Davis suggests as much in his "Models of Spirit Matter," where he introduces three interpretations that elaborate on the scriptural passage, "There is no such thing as immaterial matter. All spirit is matter, but it is more fine or pure, and can only be discerned by purer eyes" (D&C 131:7). LDS readers may recognize some of the ideas from their readings of early Church writers, namely, Parley P. Pratt, and some of the scenarios that Davis presents are not only entertaining but quite thought provoking.

Another interesting model is presented by Scott Howe in "A Standard Physics Model of Spirit." In the standard physics model, electromagnetic energy, light, and electrons are presented as possible candidates for spirit matter—though "we cannot see it" with our natural eyes, "when our bodies are purified we shall see that it is all matter" (D&C 131:8). Howe hints that our scientific instruments have gradually become sensitive or "pure" enough to observe spirit matter.

In "A Technical Interpretation of Mormon Physics and Physiology," Lincoln Cannon and Scott Howe argue that our salvation depends in part on learning about, governing, and organizing both the physical and the spiritual aspects of our universe. One interesting discussion illustrates parallels between Alma's discussion on faith (Alma 32) and the scientific method for creating knowledge.

In the last chapter under the topic of "Physics and Engineering," Adam Davis again provides an interesting discussion of intelligent matter in "Materialism, Free Will, and Mormonism." This chapter gives a logical argument about a potential relationship between Mormonism and materialism and includes thoughts on the possibility (or impossibility) of true artificial intelligence.

Regardless of the reader's interpretations of natural laws and how they square with the scriptures, this section on physics and engineering will provide fascinating reading.

1
Models of Spirit Matter

Adam N. Davis

Abstract

It is a well-grounded idea in Mormonism that there is much more to the universe than what we can see with our mortal eyes: the spirit realm. Despite that basic idea, very little is understood about spirit matter. I present three models of spirit matter and discuss their shortcomings. In doing so, we are left with the idea that spirit matter must be conceived of very differently than allowed by our usual conceptions about reality.

Introduction: What We Know

In many theologies, there is an idea that the world which we perceive with our physical senses is not the full extent of reality. Mormonism shares this idea, and spirit matter plays a fundamental role in it. While very little is known about spirit matter, our model of it should address what little we do know. I break down the items that each model of spirit matter must address into five basic topics:

- spirit matter as matter
- spirit bodies
- spirit worlds
- locality
- non-interaction

The first is that spirit matter is matter. This characteristic is established in the well-known scripture: "There is no such thing as immaterial matter. All spirit is matter, but is more fine or pure, and can only be discerned by purer eyes. We cannot see it, but when our bodies are purified, we shall see that it is all matter" (D&C 131:7–8). What is "more fine" and "more pure" is not so clearly established, and speculation is model specific.

The concept of spirit bodies is also established LDS doctrine. Not only do human beings have spirit bodies but so do all creatures:

> Q. What are we to understand by the four beasts, spoken of in the same verse? A. They are figurative expressions, used by the Revelator, John, in describing heaven, the paradise of God, the happiness of man, and of beasts, and of creeping things, and of the fowls of the air; that which is spiritual being in the likeness of that which is temporal; and that which is temporal in the likeness of that which is spiritual; the spirit of man in the likeness of his person, as also the spirit of the beast, and every other creature which God has created. (D&C 77:2)

Moreover, the spirit body is, at the very least, phenotypically similar to our physical body as evidenced by the experience of the brother of Jared: "Behold, this body, which ye now behold, is the body of my spirit; and man have I created after the body of my spirit; and even as I appear unto thee to be in the spirit will I appear unto my people in the flesh" (Ether 3:16).

In addition to the spirit bodies of living things is the concept of a spirit world inhabited by the spirit bodies. The spirit world is composed of a great many things that are in the likeness of things on earth—buildings, gardens, etc. At the funeral of Brigham Young's counselor Jedediah M. Grant, Heber C. Kimball, the other counselor, reported on a vision by the dying Grant:

> He also spoke of the buildings he saw there, remarking that the Lord gave Solomon wisdom and poured gold and silver into his hands that he might display his skill and ability, and said that the temple erected by Solomon was much inferior to the most ordinary buildings he saw in the spirit world.
>
> In regard to gardens, says brother Grant, "I have seen good gardens on this earth, but I never saw any to compare with those that were there. I saw flowers of numerous kinds, and some with from fifty to a hundred different colored flowers growing upon one stalk." We have many kinds of flowers on the earth, and I suppose those very articles came from heaven, or they would not be here.[1]

Whatever model of spirit matter that exists must accommodate not only living spirit bodies but a functional environment for the spirit bodies to exist.

---

1. Heber C. Kimball, December 4, 1856, *Journal of Discourses*, 26 vols. (London and Liverpool: LDS Booksellers Depot, 1855–86), 4:135–37, http://contentdm.lib.byu.edu/cdm4/browse.php?CISOROOT=%2FJournalOfDiscourses3 (accessed October 27, 2011).

As to the location of the spirit world and spirit bodies, Brigham Young taught that the spirit world was right here: "When you lay down this tabernacle, where are you going? Into the spiritual world. . . . Where is the spirit world? It is right here. Do the good and evil spirits go together? Yes they do. . . . Do they go beyond the boundaries of the organized earth? No, they do not. . . . Can you see it with your natural eyes? No. Can you see spirits in this room? No. Suppose the Lord should touch your eyes that you might see, could you then see the spirits? Yes, as plainly as you now see bodies."[2]

It is frequently assumed that the spirit body is located inside our physical body and that, as our physical body moves from place to place, the spirit body remains with it. This is consistent with patterns observed in reports of near-death experiences. Often the "dead" individual would be aware of his or her immediate surroundings.[3] It should be noted, however, that near-death experiences do not have a formal place in Mormonism and so, from that framework, constitute unreliable data.

Finally, it should be noted that the spirit world and the physical world do not readily interact. As mentioned in several of the citations above, the spirit world and its inhabitants are hidden from our natural eyes. Though the spirit world is co-local with our existence, it does not readily interact.

Being hidden from our eyes, however, has greater implications. Our physical eyes perceive photons of electromagnetic radiation. The nature of this interaction is essentially the same nature as the interaction of touch, taste, hearing, and smell—they are all electromagnetic interactions. Inherent in the concept of our physical bodies not being able to "see" spirit bodies is the idea that we can neither touch, taste, hear, nor smell them.

But there does seem to be some degree of interaction as evidenced by the possibility of spirits from the spirit world being able to possess the bodies of humans or animals. How this may occur would eventually have to be addressed by any serious model.

The Mirror Model

The mirror model is a modified version of a model taught by Parley P. Pratt. To him spirit matter and physical matter are gradations of matter:

---

2. Brigham Young, June 22, 1856, *Journal of Discourses*, 3: 362–75, http://contentdm.lib.byu.edu/cdm4/browse.php?CISOROOT=%2FJournalOfDiscourses3 (accessed October 27, 2011).

3. James Mauro, "Bright Lights, Big Mystery." *Psychology Today*, July 1992, http://www.psychologytoday.com/articles/200910/bright-lights-big-mystery (accessed January 2009).

> These elements have been separated, by philosophers, into two grand divisions, viz.—"physical and spiritual." To a mind matured, or quickened with a fulness of intelligence, so as to be conversant with all the elements of nature, there is no use for the distinction implied in such terms.
>
> To speak more philosophically, all the elements are spiritual, all are physical, all are material, tangible realities. Spirit is matter, and matter is full of spirit. Because all things which do exist are eternal realities, in their elementary existence.
>
> Who then can define the precise point, in the scale of elementary existence, which divides between the physical and spiritual kingdoms? There are eyes which can discern the most refined particles of elementary existence. There are hands and fingers to whose refined touch all things are tangible.
>
> In the capacity of mortals, however, some of the elements are tangible, or visible, and others invisible. Those which are tangible to our senses, we call physical: those which are more subtle and refined, we call spiritual.[4]

In this view, spirit matter is literally "more fine" in the sense of being a more fundamental constituent. Spirit matter becomes a certain kind of particle that will assemble into higher and less "pure" states. Unfortunately, this relatively simple model does not flow coherently with the remainder of Pratt's claims. For example, he describes the spirit body as essentially a mirror to the physical body: "The spirit of man consists of an organization, or embodiment of the elements of spiritual matter, in the likeness and after the pattern of the fleshly tabernacle. It possesses, in fact, all the organs and parts exactly corresponding to the outward tabernacle."[5]

A body is an immensely complex structure with many higher-tiered structures at both a molecular and higher level. If spirit matter were simply a more fundamental constituent of physical matter, it would not be able to assemble to the higher structures without being essentially physical matter—that is, unless it were to assemble to higher structures along a divergent path. In that case, we might as well call this divergent path of structures spirit matter. Whether or not spirit matter is a fundamentally different kind of matter or if it is a divergent path of the assembly of some foundational constituents, the mirror model will take an agnostic view. In other respects, the mirror model closely resembles Pratt's model.

The mirror model, then, proposes that spirit matter and physical matter are similar but very different forms of matter. They are similar in that they probably have similar organizational abilities—can form molecules

---

4. Parley Parker Pratt, *Key to the Science of Theology* (Salt Lake City: Deseret News Steam Printing Establishment, 1874), 43–44.

5. Ibid., 125.

and such—but they are different in that they must use different forces. It is conceivable that physical matter and spirit matter are very different things, and it is true that there are probably some differences; but as a first approximation, the model will assume basically a 1:1 correspondence. A physical proton will electromagnetically attract a physical electron but not a "spirit electron." In particle physics parlance, spirit matter and physical matter will have different charges. (A possible exception would be gravity—the charge for gravity is mass.)

Separating the charges of spirit matter and physical matter into different forms means that the nature of light is different, too. Light for physical matter is the oscillation of electromagnetic fields. Light for spirit matter would be the oscillation of the spiritual analog of electromagnetic fields. In this way, spirit matter interacts only with spirit matter and physical matter interacts only with physical matter.

Spirits would inhabit a spirit planet that basically sits on top of our own planet. Spirit bodies would have to be bound to our physical bodies by a third constituent. (In Chapter 4, "Materialism, Free Will, and Mormonism," I argue the case for "intelligent matter.") How this third constituent is bound would have to be addressed; but by and large, all of the five elements are addressed by the mirror model. Still, a closer look reveals several problems.

Problems with the Mirror Model

The mirror model presents certain difficulties when it tries to adhere to strict co-locality. The concept of the spirit planet is illustrative.

First, spirits will occupy and walk the surface of a spirit earth. For them to be in the vicinity, as it were, the spirit earth must be the same size. Perhaps it was organized so. Second, to maintain its orbit, the spirit earth must have a gravitational source—a spirit sun. That sun, then, would have to be the exact same mass—or more accurately, the product of the spirit sun and spirit earth would have to be the same. Without this correspondence, the physical and spirit earth would soon become out of sync and no longer be co-local. And even if the spirit earth and sun were allowed the improbable situation of being organized with the same masses, the presence of the other planets in our physical solar system would de-synchronize the orbits—unless we were to again posit that the remainder of the planets and much of the interplanetary debris were similarly mirrored.

An alternative situation is to allow spirit matter and physical matter to interact gravitationally. In such a case, the orbits of the planets can be kept synchronized fairly easily. But this approach also fails to some degree because non-gravitational seismic calculations basically match the gravitationally predicted mass of the earth, leaving little room for additional mass from spirit matter.[6] It might be possible to arrange for some full strength physical-physical matter gravity interactions and full strength spirit-spirit matter gravity interactions and a greatly reduced spirit-physical gravity interaction, but other problems suggest that a different alternative would be more promising.

In the mirror model, much as the physical earth and the spirit earth are kept in sync through some mechanism, the physical bodies and the spirit bodies of individuals are kept in sync. The spirit world, however, is not a mere reflection of the physical earth. A building may be here but not on the other side. A mountain may be here, but not on the other side, and so on. But that which is living has its counterpart on the other side.

Spirit matter, in this model, interacts with other spirit matter. A spirit body can no more pass through the wall of a spirit building than a physical body can pass through the wall of a physical building. However, the physical body can pass through the wall of a spirit building and vice versa. This simple prescription leads to problems. Illustrative of this problem is this thought example: Imagine a man driving down a road. Ahead of the man is a building of spirit matter. His physical body and senses are completely unaware of it. Consequently, he passes right through it. What does his spirit body do? By all accounts of this model, the spirit body should interact with the physical body. Yet this does not appear to happen.

Another cause for concern with this model is more aesthetic. According to LDS doctrine, we existed as spirits long before coming to earth. The spirit body is a grown adult. What do our spirit bodies do while we inhabit the earth here? Do the limbs mimic the motions of our physical body or stand there passively? While intuition is not a sound argument, it does not seem to comport with the model.

In short, the mirror model suffers from too much of a separation between spirit matter and physical matter. The two worlds have to maintain a fair amount of synchronization and, simultaneously, a high amount of separation. The mirror model doesn't have the tools to satisfactorily maintain this balance. An alternative is to disconnect the physical and spirit matter separation. This kind of disconnect is achieved in a computational model.

---

6. Adam M. Dziewonski and Don L. Anderson, "Preliminary Reference Earth Model," *Physics of the Earth and Planetary Interiors* 25, no. 4 (1981): 297–356.

Computational Model

In the computational model, spirit matter is indeed a fundamental form of matter much as Parley P. Pratt had supposed. But instead of the spirit matter literally assembling itself into the forms of bodies, trees, mountains, and such, the spirit matter assembles into informational structures—a text, as it were, that describes how the structure would be manifest.

This kind of informational description seems implausible at first to our hard, engrained day-to-day experience of being in a physical body and interacting with things that are located in the space and time of the universe. But contemporary advances in computation give us an analogy to draw from. There are many games, simulated, or virtual realities that are available. Second Life is a common example, but there are several massively multiplayer games (MMOs) that allow creations to exist in a simulated or virtual reality. These realities can serve as a crude framework to understand the computational model of spirit matter.

In the model, spirit matter is still matter. The matter exists and is real and tangible, but the matter isn't a literal expression of the underlying reality. The matter organizes itself into information that is manifest as a reality elsewhere. For example, suppose spirit matter was really electrons or something similar. The electrons would be organized so that, when read and interpreted properly, it would describe a body. That body would be the "spirit body"—an "image," as it were, of the tangible electrons. The image does not exist by itself, in space and time, but the spirit matter that encodes the image does.

In the computational model, each individual has a spirit body. The fundamental existence is information. The specific particles that describe the information can change and move around, much the same way that a great many of the actual atoms in our physical bodies are replaced in the course of a lifetime. The body remains even though the particles making the body do not. The realization of that information is the identity of the individual.

But the spirit bodies need a way of interacting. Spirits talk, see each other, and interact in essentially every way that we are familiar with through our physical bodies. To enable such interactions require a spirit world. In addition to spirit bodies, there will be vast encodings of information that describe this spirit world. In addition to sentient spirits, the world will be inhabited with every manner of item, object, or structure that is associated with the spirit world.

The actual location of the spirit matter that encodes the information which is the spirit bodies and the spirit world is of little importance in the computational model. So long as the information has a way of communicating with itself, that is not a difficulty.

But, we are brought to where we must understand how the spirit body interacts with the physical body. In the computational model, the information that is the descriptor of the spirit individual must either reside directly in the physical body or maintain a constant communication with the physical body. When a person "dies," his or her identity ceases to process information acquired from the physical world through the physical body but switches to processing information from the spirit world.

The physical world and the spirit world do not directly interact at any point because the spirit world is not an actual place in the same sense that our physical world occupies space and time. The spirit matter that actually encodes the spirit individual and world can be accessed directly via the physical world but would not be directly translatable. For example, picking up and shaking a computer's hard drive is an "interaction" but not an interaction with the information.

Computational Model Problems

On the surface of it, the computational model solves all of the difficulties suffered by the physical model. The spirit world is manifestly disconnected in presentation from the physical universe. The spirit world and spirit bodies are interactions of information quite distinct from the actual mechanism of the information storage. Yet this scenario becomes problematic when its interface with the physical world is more closely examined, unless one is willing to assume that the physical world is a mere simulated reality (the disparaging term is "brain in the vat"). While philosophically intelligible, this situation tends to be intuitively repugnant to most.

The physical location of the spirit matter encoding an individual's spirit body has three basic choices. First, the spirit matter can be located physically with the spirit body. Second, the spirit matter can be at a remote location. Third, the spirit body can be some mixture of locations.

The first choice is dangerous, as the integrity of the information becomes suspect. It is generally assumed in Mormonism that an impairment of the physical body does not impair the spirit body. Indeed, Alma assures us that in the resurrection "not so much as a hair of [our] heads will be lost" (Alma 11:44). Much as rapidly shaking a computer's hard drive or breaking it into pieces damages the information stored on it, if the spirit matter that stores the spirit is encased in the physical body, the spirit becomes susceptible to damage quite easily.

Models of Spirit Matter

The alternative is to place the spirit matter that encodes the spirit body at a remote and safe location. In this situation, communication is necessary between the distant location and the physical body. The communication must occur, not just at death when the individual switches to processing input from the spirit body, but throughout life. Memory is stored of one's life[7] (Alma 5:18) and is independent of whether one suffers brain damage. How, then, could that communication occur?

If the remote storage and the physical body communicate, they must do via some form of medium. All currently known particles are limited by the speed of light.[8] Since the computational model limits itself to current particles and current physics, this requirement does not allow faster-than-light travel. Consequently, unless the remote storage is close, this demand will put quite a burden on the communication system's time frame. It can't be at a distant (nearby) star where light travel will take years. Near-death experience life reviews occur on the order of minutes during the interval of "death." Additionally, transmitting information must be directional and highly focused, or the signal's power would dissipate quite quickly. There is no known mechanism in the physical body for transmitting either very powerful or very directed signals of some form of radiation. Any remote storage location beyond the physical confines of the earth seems currently implausible, unless we posit that the physical body also contains a form of matter entirely foreign to known matter. The new matter would have to be compatible with superluminal communication to enable remote storage. But then the computational model loses one of its strong points—the lack of need for a foreign form of matter to explain spirit matter.

So, without invoking a different kind of matter, remote storage places the spirit matter that encodes the information within the boundaries of this earth. Unfortunately, I can think of no aspect of the earth that is compatible with the safe mass storage of billions of human beings.

The third option is to partition the information encoding the spirit body into various locations. Yet this solution ends up suffering all of the defects of both the local storage and remote storage approaches. Though a combined approach minimizes the flaws from either approach, it opens itself to the defects of both of the approaches with the result that the whole of the solution seems to fare no better than the originals.

Irrespective of what model the spirit body takes, the spirit world must utilize remote storage. There it conceivably has the communication abili-

---

7. Mauro, "Bright Lights, Big Mystery."
8. Particle Data Group, "The Particle Adventure," http://particleadventure.org/ (accessed January 2009).

ties to assemble and disseminate the information that allows all of the "users" (spirit bodies) to communicate and interact. Like spirit matter for individual spirit bodies, it can't be far from earth for the communication to be effective, since awakening after death is nearly instantaneous. But how detailed can the spirit world be?

The spirit world is very similar to our physical world. Scripturally it would technically be the opposite—with the physical world being patterned after the spirit world (Moses 3:7). But if the spirit world is information only, it is limited by the capacity of spirit matter to effectively store information. If we again assume that spirit matter is just a form of matter, the spirit world cannot have a full description of the world to the same degree as a description of the physical world without being nearly as large spatially. That is, the space and number of particles to describe the entirety of the information that is present in one atom is physically much more vast than the actual atom. If the spirit world were a complete description of its space to an atomic or subatomic level, the spirit matter would physically occupy a volume much larger than the space represented by the information. This statement seems somewhat contrary to our experiences. Engineers regularly model items and store the model in a small space. Those designs, however, are but a shell of the reality. Suppose an engineer is given a car. Reality gives place to every single atom—the type, its ionization, excitation levels, etc. No engineer in the world today can model a car to atomic detail. While I suppose it might be hypothetically possible, it would require storage space well beyond the size of the actual car. This requirement is the fundamental limitation of the information density available to currently known forms of matter.

As the spirit matter storing the spirit world cannot be distantly remote and the matter describing it must be at least somewhat discrete, then the spirit world must describe a world that is less detailed than the physical world. Whether this is a "problem" is up to the aesthetics of the individual interpreting the model.

Yet in the end, the computational model has several philosophical and engineering limitations. Currently known matter does not seem able to accommodate the storage and inter-communication of billions of human identities and the common spirit world. The physical body, at present, has no known capacity to communicate its vast stores of day-to-day information to the spirit matter storing the information of the spirit body.

Phase Model

The phase model attempts to redress some of the difficulties encountered by the mirror model. The phase model posits that spirit matter and physical matter can interact (or not) depending on their particular state or "phase." In particular, there would be at least four phases involving the two forms of matter:

- pure spirit matter phase
- coupled spirit matter phase
- hybrid matter phase
- pure physical matter phase

Spirit matter can exist in one of the two phases, pure spirit or coupled spirit matter. It can move from one phase to the other. When in the pure phase, spirit matter behaves and acts completely independent of physical matter, much as with the mirror model. In the coupled spirit matter phase, spirit matter "couples" with physical matter. The spirit matter intertwines with the physical matter and is basically subsumed by it during this phase, and the spirit matter ceases to interact with other spirit matter.

The coupled spirit matter phase is designed to address the issue of the spirit body and physical body. The spirit body of living, mortal humans does not seem to have an active presence in the spirit world. I am not aware of any account in which the spirit bodies of living humans are manifest in the spirit world. In addition to the absence of such accounts, a spirit body that is linked to a living human is problematic as exemplified in the discussion of the mirror matter model problems.

The pure physical matter phase is the phase of matter with which mortal humans are acquainted. In the hybrid matter phase, physical and spirit matter combine and become accessible to both physical and spirit matter. The hybrid phase would be invoked to solve the co-locality of the physical earth and the spirit world in orbit around the sun.

Another feature of the hybrid matter phase would be light. We presently conceptualize light as being a composite of oscillating electric and magnetic fields. In addition to those, in the phase model, light would have two additional oscillating components—the spirit matter analog of the electric and magnetic fields.

Light produced by hybrid matter would generate light with all components. When the light hits a pure spirit matter object, the spirit half of the light would be stopped while the physical half of the light would continue to propagate and vice versa. This kind of conceptualization is necessary because light cannot simply interact with both. If it did, the spirit world (or at least its shadow) would be immediately and utterly obvious to us.

Phase Model Problems

Though designed to solve some of the problems, the phase matter model has problems. Indeed, much of the problem comes from its feeling contrived and a bit ad hoc, even epicyclic. Yet despite this failing, the model can serve as a jumping-off point to a more correct understanding.

One of the problems with the hybrid model of the physical and the spirit earth is that the surface of the planets, at least, must still be distinct. Suppose, for example, a building constructed of spirit matter on a surface of hybrid matter ground. Completely unaware of that building, some individuals in the physical realm choose to dig a hole there. Does the hole destroy the building in the spirit world?

One possible solution would to be that some significant chunk of the earth is hybrid but that the earth has two surfaces—one of spirit matter and one of physical matter. But this proposal seems to suffer from the same "contrived" feeling as the entire model.

Another potential problem with the model is that it presently offers no mechanism for transition from one phase to another. When one "dies," the spirit matter decouples and reverts to a pure state. Moreover, this immediate decoupling upon death would be inconsistent with the accounts of near-death experiences in which the dead individual could see his or her physical matter body.[9]

Conclusion

Spirit matter continues to be an enigmatic but necessary component of Mormonism. I have discussed three models, but none is without problems. Nonetheless, these problems become challenges to furthering thought about models of spirit matter.

I discussed spirit matter in two contexts. In the first, spirit matter and physical matter are literal manifestations. These are the mirror matter and phase models. Two basic problems faced them. One of the problems was how the spirit body and the physical body can be co-local; but while we are alive, the spirit body does not seem to interact with the spirit world. The identity of the spirit body seems to be subsumed by the physical body. Yet the spirit body must be allowed to transcend the physical body in the

---

9. Mauro, "Bright Lights, Big Mystery."

Models of Spirit Matter

case of critical damage to the physical body and to retain the memory and identity of the individual.

The problem of the spirit world is an example of a different kind of behavior. The spirit world and the physical world must maintain co-locality. They must both orbit the sun precisely. This precision can be achieved only with a high degree of interaction between the two worlds. But at the same time, the two worlds must be distinct and separate as we do not appear to interact with the spirit world either consciously or unconsciously. The only known interaction is our unconscious interaction with our spirit body.

The second context for the discussion of spirit matter was the situation in which matter becomes a medium of information that is manifested only in the right conditions as spirit bodies and spirit worlds. One of the aims of this line of reasoning is to avoid a second kind of matter aside from the known forms, which was the case of the computational model. But the computational model suffered from two problems in a way similar to the dualist models. The first is the problem of the spirit body. Either the spirit body is co-local with the physical body to the degree that it is subject to the potential of catastrophic disruption when the physical body is damaged or it is remote—in which case, it must have communication capacity. But no such mechanism of communication is presently plausible in the context of known matter and our known physical bodies. The second problem relates to the spirit world. Because of the limitations of the speed of light, the spirit world must be close. Information density either severely limits the resolution of detail in the spirit world or makes the "server" for the spirit world implausibly large, given its proximity.

Despite these difficulties, I believe that a coherent model of spirit matter that is consistent with the known universe and our current limited understanding of spirit matter is possible. I hope that this discussion will facilitate that discovery.

2
A Standard Physics Model of Spirit

A. Scott Howe

Abstract

Electromagnetic energy or light (bosons) is the primary medium by which electrons (leptons) in atoms exchange energy with one another, form bonds, separate, or perform other chemical reactions that change the state of matter. According to Mormon doctrine, that light fills the immensity of space and is the law by which all things are governed. In LDS scripture, light is also said to be equivalent to spirit. Leptons or bosons—light or electromagnetic energy—could be fundamanetal spirit matter.

Introduction

It should be no surprise to us that spirit matter may have already been detected by our instruments. Many people have an image of spirit as being something supernatural and try hard to fit the interpretation to their image. But the scriptures do not support such an interpretation. In the scriptures, we read that Spirit is equivalent to truth and light: "For the word of the Lord is truth, and whatsoever is truth is light, and whatsoever is light is Spirit, even the Spirit of Jesus Christ" (D&C 84:45). We also read that intelligence is equivalent to light and truth. "The glory of God is intelligence, or, in other words, light and truth" (D&C 93:36). We learn that intelligence is eternal. "Man was also in the beginning with God. Intelligence, or the light of truth, was not created or made, neither indeed can be" (D&C 93:29). We also learn that truth somehow has agency that manifests itself as reality. "All truth is independent in that sphere in which God has placed it, to act for itself, as all intelligence also; otherwise there is no existence" (D&C 93:30). In this chapter, I will follow the logic that the electromagnetic energy that we experience every day may be exactly what the scriptures are talking about when describing light as spirit.

Personal Building Blocks

A simple, straightforward interpretation of scripture may be all that is needed to understand the nature of spirit matter. First let's look at intelligence, which is the equivalent of light in the scriptures. One characteristic of intelligence is that it can be added together:

> Whatever principle of intelligence we attain unto in this life, it will rise with us in the resurrection.
> And if a person gains more knowledge and intelligence in this life through his diligence and obedience than another, he will have so much the advantage in the world to come. (D&C 130:18–19)

Intelligence and light can be added upon until the individual has a fulness. "That which is of God is light; and he that receiveth light, and continueth in God, receiveth more light; and that light groweth brighter and brighter until the perfect day" (D&C 50:24). Intelligence can be taken away or lost, too: "For behold, thus saith the Lord God: I will give unto the children of men line upon line, precept upon precept, here a little and there a little; and blessed are those who hearken unto my precepts, and lend an ear unto my counsel, for they shall learn wisdom; for unto him that receiveth I will give more; and from them that shall say, We have enough, from them shall be taken away even that which they have" (2 Ne. 28:30).

Indeed, we are told that intelligence was organized into spirits before the foundations of the world, and some of those spirits became noble and great. "Now the Lord had shown unto me, Abraham, the intelligences that were organized before the world was; and among all these there were many of the noble and great ones" (Abr. 3:22). One interpretation is that "intelligence" in this context is a self-contained being with personality—these beings having been organized into families, communities, or some other administrative social structure. However, understanding that intelligence has the capacity to be added together begs the question of what part constitutes a fundamental self-contained personality and what part is added thereto. Are these personalities similar to a light wave that can have a variety of characteristics such as direction and frequency and still add to its energy without changing the fundamental personality?

While it is likely that the metrics for defining a human personality are not all apparent to us, yet the assumption that personalities are innate primitives of undividable, eternal entities introduces a complexity that may not be necessary. A more logical alternative is that "intelligences that were organized" refers to primitives of spirit matter that were assembled together into a personality. If we consider the entire extent of the Lord's domain, including animals, plants, minerals, and energy in the context of the LDS perspective that a loving Heavenly Father is raising His children to eventually be like Him as managers of creation, then why would not every member of the human race be considered leaders? "And God saw these souls that they were good, and he stood in the midst of them, and he said: These I will make my rulers; for he stood among those that were spirits, and he saw that they were good; and he said unto me: Abraham, thou art one of them; thou wast chosen before thou wast born" (Abr. 3:23). Could it be that the Lord is differentiating between the vast intelligences that make up the universe and inhabit every object, and the comparative few who would be His children—the entire human race—that had been organized into more complex spirits? The Abraham verses can clearly be interpreted either way, and indeed perhaps should be. More on this later.

Physical Action Preceded by Spiritual Transaction

Following the line of reasoning that intelligence and spirit are building blocks of a pure form of matter that can be added together, we can begin to shed misconceptions about the nature of spirit and take the scriptures at face value—spirit is light. We read that the light that is discussed in the scriptures is the same light that is defined by physics:

> And the light which shineth, which giveth you light, is through him who enlighteneth your eyes, which is the same light that quickeneth your understandings;
>
> Which light proceedeth forth from the presence of God to fill the immensity of space—
>
> The light which is in all things, which giveth life to all things, which is the law by which all things are governed, even the power of God who sitteth upon his throne, who is in the bosom of eternity, who is in the midst of all things. (D&C 88:11–13)

The implications of this statement are astounding. If intelligence, light, truth, and spirit are equivalent, then their effects are visible to us every minute of the day using our naked eyes. It also means that every interaction we have with the environment is a spiritual transaction before it is a physical transaction.

The Calculation of Truth

How can light be the same as truth? The scriptures define truth as "knowledge of things as they are, and as they were, and as they are to come" (D&C 93:24). We become aware of things by an excitation of our senses, by way of electromagnetic energy, or in other words, light. Although it may appear that the objects around us are static constructions of unchanging metal, stone, and other materials, in actuality there is a lot of activity constantly occurring at tiny scales. American author and inventor Ray Kurzweil explains that a one-kilogram rock contains approximately 10^{25} atoms that are "in continuous motion, sharing electrons back and forth, changing particle spins, and generating rapidly moving electromagnetic fields."[1] The activity occurring in the particles that make up the rock is identical to the computation that occurs in a computer, even if it is not meaningfully organized. Research has shown that "1,024 bits can be stored in the magnetic interactions of the protons of a single molecule containing nineteen hydrogen atoms," as Kurzweil points out.[2] Therefore, the state of the rock at any one moment represents at least 10^{27} bits of memory. Considering the electromagnetic interactions, there are at least 10^{15} changes in state per bit per second going on inside the rock, which represents about 10^{45} calculations per second. That is, according to Kurzweil, "about ten trillion times more powerful than all the human brains on Earth." By all accounts, in spite of the tremendous supercomputing capacity contained in the one-kilogram rock, all of it is random and not of much use to us—*or is it?* What could all that processing power be calculating that is so important?

The rock is calculating truth about itself. It is literally the Lord's electronics. All objects around us are calculating truth and broadcasting their current state to the rest of the universe. Objects in the universe are participating in the generation of reality.

Engineered Agency

How can light be the same as intelligence? The uncertainty in quantum particle behavior opens up the possibility of free will among individual particles. Physicists John Conway and Simon Kochen claim that experimental results for fundamental particles cannot be determined by prior

---

1. Ray Kurzweil, *The Singularity Is Near* (New York: Viking, 2005), 131.
2. R. Bennewitz, J. N. Crain, A. Kirakosian, J-L Lin, J. L. McChesney, D. Y. Petrovykh, and F. J. Himpsel, "Atomic Scale Memory at a Silicon Surface," *Nanotechnology* 13 (2002): 499–502, cited in ibid.

A Standard Physics Model of Spirit 21

conditions, implying that a deterministic prior cause may not connect to the results.[3] Conway and Kochen also prove that randomness is inadequate to explain the nondeterminism. Others have addressed a non-mechanistic view of particle interactions and suggest that it might be useful to think of fundamental particles as having primitive intelligence.[4] Primitive intelligence may be no more than the capacity to choose one quantum state or another when prompted by a participatory universe. Regarding agency, we read, "All truth is independent in that sphere in which God has placed it, to act for itself, as all intelligence also; otherwise there is no existence" (D&C 93:30). Also we read, "The Lord said unto Enoch: Behold these thy brethren; they are the workmanship of mine own hands, and I gave unto them their knowledge, in the day I created them; and in the Garden of Eden, gave I unto man his agency" (Moses 7:32). If we interpret these passages literally, then the capacity for gaining knowledge and the capacity for agency are attributes given by the Creator and not innate in the creature; perhaps they are engineered.

Is it possible to build genuine agency or free will out of a foundation of quantum uncertainty? It may be that free will, agency, and the capacity to gain and process knowledge depend on a function for extracting quantum states to inform macro structures. Tentatively, we may want to label this capacity as "intelligence," and any small degree of calculation occurring because of an exchange of light between particles may be defined as such. A close look at the "quantum foam" underlying reality reveals a chaotic world without dimension or time. An engineer's work is to take chaotic materials and organize them in some way toward a predefined purpose. Could it be that the laws of the universe are set up for the purpose of channeling the innate wild and unstructured behavior of fundamental free intelligences in such a way that ordered computation and a well-defined substrate is possible? Are natural laws optimized to make it attractive for these simple free agents to join in by their own free will, where the opportunities they crave to exchange light in a participatory universe are increased? At various levels of organization, greater complexity is achieved because of the order found in the underlying substrate. Wild fluctuations between energy and matter states bouncing back and forth in time,[5] give way to dimensional space and

---

3. John Conway and Simon Kochen, "The Strong Free Will Theorem," *Foundations of Physics* 36 (2006): 1441–73.

4. L. F Zaman, "Nature's Psychogenic Forces: Localized Quantum Consciousness," *The Journal of Mind and Behavior* 22, no. 4 (2002): 351–74.

5. Richard P. Feynman, "The Theory of Positrons," *Physical Review* 76 (September 15, 1949): 6.

an arrow of time with fundamental particles that can be assembled together into proteins, enzymes, and self-reproducing cellular factories to propagate order and to build complex organelles and organisms, finally resulting in a magnificent machine for seating intelligence capable of understanding it all.

From the LDS perspective, many have advocated the concept that all matter has some degree of intelligence. Bruce R. McConkie of the First Council of the Seventy, wrote, "Abraham used the name intelligences to apply to the spirit children of the Eternal Father. The intelligence or spirit element became intelligences after the spirits were born as individual entities" (Abr. 3:22–24). Use of this name designates both the primal element from which the spirit offspring were created and also their inherited capacity to grow in grace, knowledge, power, and intelligence itself, until such intelligences, gaining the fullness of all things, become like their Father, the Supreme Intelligence."[6] Apostle Spencer W. Kimball also discussed this concept when he wrote, "Our spirit matter was eternal and co-existent with God, but it was organized into spirit bodies by our Heavenly Father."[7] Apostle Marion G. Romney explained, "In origin, man is a son of God. The spirits of men 'are begotten sons and daughters unto God' (D&C 76:24). Through that birth process, self-existing intelligence was organized into individual spirit beings."[8] The exact meaning of Abraham's term "intelligence" is not known, and the idea that our spirits were constructed from primal intelligent matter is controversial in the Church. However, we do understand that light and intelligence are equivalent; and if visible and spiritual light is also equivalent, then we can reason about the existence of intelligent element as a building block for greater intelligence.

How can light be spirit? Understanding that light is equivalent to intelligence and functions as an informational medium for mechanical and energy transfers, we can finally make a discussion about what spirit matter may be. A spirit is defined as "the vital principle or animating force within living beings."[9] If we literally look at the physics of how living beings are animated, exchange of light between particles characterized by chemical reactions translate into cell stimulation and muscle movements. If we trace the signals from the muscles back to the brain, electromagnetic energy is

---

6. Bruce R. McConkie, *Mormon Doctrine*, 2d ed. (Salt Lake City: Bookcraft, 1966), 387.

7. Spencer W. Kimball, *The Miracle of Forgiveness* (Salt Lake City: Bookcraft, 1969), 5.

8. Marion G. Romney, "The Worth of Souls," *Ensign*, November 1978, 13–14.

9. *The American Heritage Dictionary of the English Language*, 4th ed., 2003, http://www.thefreedictionary.com/spirit, s.v. "spirit" (accessed February 22, 2009).

A Standard Physics Model of Spirit

involved every step of the way. Complex physical structures in the brain control the computation that naturally occurs in all matter (as I have discussed above), allowing the organism to monitor and react to its environment. Fundamentally, each atom may be an individual in possession of a spirit, where the electrons in the atom animate it and allow it to interact with others. Indeed, we read "there is a God, and he hath created all things, both the heavens and the earth, and all things that in them are, both things to act and things to be acted upon" (2 Ne 2:14).

Spirit and Physical Bodies

If we consider light to be equivalent to intelligence, then the energy transfers that occur within and between atoms are also spiritual in nature, and perhaps bring joy to the intelligence involved. Spirit and element temporarily connected receive a certain degree of joy, and "spirit and element, inseparably connected, receive a fulness of joy" (D&C 93:33). In this model, the spirit and intelligence of atoms may consist of the electrons belonging to it that obey the law of light (D&C 88:13) and form bonds or break bonds according to the commands received through the light. In a participatory universe, unorganized particles may receive and give light irregularly, or just enough to keep the particle from slipping back into dimensionless chaotic quantum foam. But organized particles are able to give and receive light from regular bonds and command structures. Light, intelligence, and energy cannot form such regular structures on their own, but must be associated with element. In this way, we can perhaps find a motivation for intelligence to stay organized—the greater the organization the more access to light and the greater joy it will experience. From this perspective, a creative act can be viewed as a work of charity, and the satisfaction we get from creating things may partly be because our actions are charitable toward the materials we have brought together and assembled.

However, we understand that it is not possible to construct a form out of electromagnetic energy that will remain coherent without being dispersed. Light is always traveling, and electrons cannot form bonds among themselves but, indeed, repel each other. Light can store up memory by impressing itself into the states of a physical substrate but cannot store truth in itself. Likewise, electrons use massive particles to stay anchored in space—otherwise they would be swept about by every electromagnetic field. All spirits, including our own, are subject to the same limitations: Spirits are incapable of growing, gaining intelligence, or indeed staying coherent without a physical medium.

When the premortal Jesus Christ appeared to the brother of Jared he explained, "Behold, this body, which ye now behold, is the body of my spirit; and man have I created after the body of my spirit; and even as I appear unto thee to be in the spirit will I appear unto my people in the flesh" (Ether 3:16). Also Doctrine and Covenants 77:2 describes "that which is spiritual [is] in the likeness of that which is temporal; and that which is temporal in the likeness of that which is spiritual; the spirit of man [is] in the likeness of his person." We interpret this to mean that our spirits and physical bodies have the same form as our spirits, and it is commonly understood in the LDS community that the spirit world resembles our own in many ways. Some have thought that the spirit is supernatural and therefore exists in a realm that may overlap with our own world, but which is invisible to our natural eyes. However, through Joseph Smith, we learn: "There is no such thing as immaterial matter. All spirit is matter, but it is more fine or pure, and can only be discerned by purer eyes" (D&C 131:7). This means that the spirit world must also be subject to the laws of the universe, and therefore our spirits and the realm beyond would maintain their form in some way. If we hold that our spirits consist of pure light, then the model would require spirits and the spirit world to be contained within a physical substrate in order to exist.

The common LDS view is that our spirits are co-located with our physical bodies. "The elements are the tabernacle of God; yea, man is the tabernacle of God, even temples; and whatsoever temple is defiled, God shall destroy that temple" (D&C 93:35). This view could fit with our model, because the body would provide a physical medium for the spirit. However, several problems arise if we insist on a co-located spirit constructed of electromagnetic energy. If we assume charged electrons to be conveyors of spirit, extra leptons in our bodies have not been observed; and indeed, given the laws of physics, how can extra electrons stay coherent without massive particles to anchor them? Physics allows for only a fixed number of electrons in each atom; any others would drift away. Second, we may say that electromagnetic energy quickening the electrons already in the matter making up our bodies might be the spirit, but this would not work either; what happens if the body dies and all the particles making up the body are scattered? There must be a place for the spirit to dwell. "For we know that if our earthly house of this tabernacle were dissolved, we have a building of God, an house not made with hands, eternal in the heavens" (2 Cor. 5:1).

In this model, it is proposed that the spirit world may consist of an advanced simulation, computed within a physical substrate. Indeed, the invention of the computer and its ability to house more and more complex structures of data and light energy ought to be a testimony to us that this could be so. Where that physical medium exists, whether it be on or near the earth, we cannot tell. However, we can make some observations that will help us understand the spirit world better and realize why resurrection and the permanent joining of spirit and element is so important. If we consider a computer simulation in which various agents are allowed to interact with each other, we know that, if the sequence goes in a direction we do not approve of, the simulation can be stopped, a backup downloaded and restored, and the simulation can be restarted from the point in the sequence before it went off course, make corrections, and restart the simulation until we get it right. Though we don't know the true nature of the spirit world, it may be that the same rules of cause and effect are not applicable. Consequences may be infinitely more devastating in the physical universe where a backup is unavailable, and our spirits would need to understand that. The only way for us to understand the connection between action and consequence would be to physically experience the real universe first hand.

This model would allow for the spirit of a person to reside safe and sound in the spirit world simulation and to link back to and "dwell" within the physical body via "wireless" coupling. Indeed, through this interpretation, we should consider radio and wireless technology to be a testimony that prayer and communication with a distant unseen partner may be possible—an evidence that was not available to people living a few hundred years ago. Assuming that we must eventually grow to be capable engineers just like our Heavenly Father, then some of the advanced engineering techniques that we already employ may provide an illustration along these lines. If we design an advanced fighter jet that has sophisticated software for automated piloting and control, we would provide the necessary hardware to interface with the environment—sensors and actuators. Actuators would allow the sophisticated computer system access to the control surfaces of the aircraft so that it may influence the state of the machine and thus react to the environment. The sensors would read and observe the environment and monitor how well the actuators had performed. We would not install the only copy of the control software into the machine without a backup, nor would we cut off all communication with it. We would probably build in the capacity to remotely monitor or control the aircraft. NASA spacecraft could be considered the epitome of this technology, where hundreds of data feeds constantly monitor telemetry through launch, transit, and deployment, and only time-sensitive computation occurs on board—most data are analyzed later on earth. In the same way, scientists can look for such technologies in our own bodies.

In another example, there are already cases where exact virtual CAD models of products have been used as a pattern for manufacturing the physical counterpart. Once the physical product has been put into operation, the CAD model is used as an interface to remotely monitor and control the actual product through sensors and actuators via direct digital control.

But if the spirit were actually present in a simulation somewhere, wouldn't such "wireless" communication require that the transmitter and receiver be quite close anyway, due to speed of light constraints on the signals? And wouldn't such "wireless" communication be detectable via our modern instruments? The remote signaling would necessarily include monitoring all of the sensor data and access to controllers and manufacturing processes in every one of the trillions of cells in the machine. Some local computation can occur, but other calculations would have to be done by the intelligence back in the spirit world.

With this scenario and these assumptions in mind, I propose a possible starting point for discovering a method for remote control if such exists. Inside each cell, ribosomes are a form of enzyme that are highly interconnected with microtubules. They read RNA strands and manufacture proteins that are building blocks for various cell structures. Microtubules function as both scaffolding and as microprocessors for the cell.[10] From an engineer's perspective, the microtubules (controller) and ribosomes (factory) would be exactly the sorts of functions where we would want to have a capacity for remote control. Quantum tunneling has been studied in ribosome enzymes as catalysis achieves low energy states.[11] Microtubules are thought to facilitate tunneling to achieve a resonance between information processing states,[12] and the information processing capacity of microtubules has been proposed as one of the mechanisms available to the neural networks in the brain. Indeed, it has been proposed, though controversial,

---

10. J. Tuszynski, B. Trpisova, D. Sept, and M. Sataric, "The Enigma of Microtubules and Their Self-Organizing Behavior in the Cytoskeleton," *Biosystems* 42 (1997): 153–75.

11. "Quantum Tunnelling" (posted February 22, 2009), *Wikipedia: The Free Encyclopedia*, http://en.wikipedia.org/wiki/Quantum_tunnelling (accessed February 23, 2009); J. K. Hwang and A. Warshel, "How Important Are Quantum Mechanical Nuclear Motions in Enzyme Catalysis?" *Journal of American Chemical Society* 118, no. 47 (1996): 11745–51; "Enzyme Catalysis" (posted January 8, 2009), *Wikipedia: The Free Encyclopedia*, http://en.wikipedia.org/wiki/Enzyme_catalysis (accessed February 23, 2009).

12. Friedrich Beck and John Eccles, "Quantum Aspects of Brain Activity and the Role of Consciousness," *Proceedings of the National Academy of Sciences of the United States of America* 89 (December 1, 1992): 11357–61.

that microtubules may have the capacity to perform quantum computing and provide a mechanism for consciousness.[13]

At the quantum level, particle interactions seem to be unstructured by the same spatial and time dimensions that apply to macro structures. Entanglement and other effects can occur regardless of the distances involved. Regardless of whether quantum computing occurs in the brain, if quantum tunneling has been observed in these two structures which are critical for information processing and manufacturing in each cell, what can we speculate about the possibility of quantum effects to facilitate remote control by a spirit in a remote spirit world?

The turbulent fabric of space at tiny scales is called quantum foam, and every cubic centimeter is theorized to be full of quantum wormholes that are spontaneously created and destroyed.[14] Wormholes are tunnels between two regions of space, and it is possible that, at the Planck scale, they can remain stable for extended periods of time without negative or exotic energy.[15] Since the vital control, manufacturing, and computational mechanisms of the cells in the body have been observed to use quantum effects, it may not be too far-fetched to think that an advanced Celestial Engineer as described by LDS theology might have discovered a way to use entanglement and other quantum effects, passing information back and forth through quantum wormholes that lead between the physical body and the spirit safely residing in the spirit world experiencing a total immersive environment. In the strictest sense, it may be hard to say that a remotely located spirit "dwells in the tabernacle." But if the experience is totally immersive, the spirit would not be able to tell if it were actually co-located with the body or "wirelessly" communicating with it. When a person dies, the entire physical machinery maintaining microtubule communication ports in an open and operational condition begins to break down, reducing the access of the spirit to the sensor and actuator telemetry from the body, until all communication is lost.

---

13. S. Hagan, Stuart R. Hameroff, and J. A. Tuszynski, "Quantum Computation in Brain Microtubules? Decoherence and Biological Feasibility," arXiv:quant-ph/0005025v1; Stuart R. Hameroff and Roger Penrose, "Conscious Events as Orchestrated Spacetime Selections," *Journal of Consciousness Studies* 3, no. 1 (1996): 3653.

14. "Quantum Foam" (posted February 22, 2009), *Wikipedia: The Free Encyclopedia*, http://en.wikipedia.org/wiki/Quantum_foam (accessed February 23, 2009).

15. Y. G. Shen, and D. M. Chen, "Cosmological Wave Function and Wormhole Wave Function with a Conformal Complex Scalar Field," *International Journal of Theoretical Physics* 38, no 2 (1999): 713–24.

In this model, the spirit only borrows the body in mortality, like a pilot in a well-crafted machine. Once the person is resurrected and the body is no longer subject to death (or particle dispersion), then the spirit can permanently remain co-located in the body in order to receive a fulness of joy.

Conclusion

Many complex models of spirit have been proposed, insisting on undetectable material. In this chapter, I show how spirit matter could consist of elementary particles already observed in the standard physics model. "Purer eyes" and sensitive instruments may have already observed the nature of spirit matter, but it is simply called by a different name or described in a different language. From an engineering perspective, if spirit truly consists of electromagnetic energy, then the digital products we produce such as software, CAD models, and data files may be considered genuine spirit entities, albeit in a primitive form. Certainly, if we as children of God sincerely believe that we will eventually become like our Heavenly Father, what better way to instruct us than to inspire the technologies and provide the means for us to participate in the experimentation and creation of spirit worlds, spirit patterns, and spirit objects that could give us the experience we need to eventually have spirit children of our own? With an LDS perspective that allows only for lawful interpretations, finally we are able to consider a simple model that may be completely empirical—in complete agreement with both physical and spiritual observations—where many of the major components have already been proven. The proofs are gifts for our benefit and growth, and perhaps all we need to do is to shed our prejudices and look at things in a new light.

3
A Technical Interpretation of Mormon Physics and Physiology

Lincoln Cannon and A. Scott Howe

Abstract

The spiritual aspect of the universe and our bodies, as described in Mormon scripture, may be empirically accessible, and we should embrace this assumption for practical and moral reasons. Some consider the spiritual aspect to be supernatural or otherwise empirically inaccessible, thereby presupposing its exclusion from science and technology. However, we propose that Mormon scripture and authorities support the idea that we commonly observe the spiritual aspect and that spiritual transactions are the basis of all observation and action. Because our eternal progression depends in part on learning about, governing, and organizing both the physical and the spiritual aspects of our universe and our bodies, we should assume the possibility of and seek after a technical understanding of their natures.

Introduction

This chapter consists of three sections. In the first two sections, we provide brief examples of technical interpretations of Mormon physics and physiology. We do not suppose these interpretations to be the only possible technical interpretations but intend them to illustrate a class of many possible interpretations that are compatible with contemporary science and technological trends that could be included as a subset of truth. Finally, in the third section, we present several practical and moral reasons for which Mormons should seek after and embrace technical interpretations.

As we proceed, please keep in mind that Mormons, although valuing their sacred texts as a full expression of the gospel of Christ, do not deem the texts to be infallible and are not bound to strictly literal interpretations. Joseph Smith rejected the infallibility of the Bible in the Eighth Article of Faith, canonized in 1880, and the LDS Church does not strictly subscribe to biblical inerrancy, infallibility or literalism.[1] Brigham Young even claimed that the Book of Mormon, if rewritten, might materially differ from its present text.[2] Moreover, a fundamental tenet of Mormonism is the idea of perpetual revelation (Ninth Article of Faith). Such positions allow for flexibility in the Mormon approach to technical interpretation, now and in the future.

A Technical Interpretation of Mormon Physics

Mormon physics, as expounded in scripture and by prominent authorities, lends itself to interpretations compatible with the methods and axioms of science, such as objectivity, causality, uniformity, and consistency, as long as those interpretations approach truth and are not formed from inaccurate data. Although most scripture does not concern itself with such matters, a few texts delve into the origins, composition, mechanics, and destiny of the universe. Principal among them are variations of the creation story, several sections of the Doctrine and Covenants, and some well known extracanonical texts from Mormon authorities, such as Joseph Smith's April 1844 sermon preached to honor the recently deceased Latter-day Saint King Follett.

The LDS perspective understands faith to be an active motivator for accomplishing works. Gordon B. Hinckley once said, "Faith is not a theological platitude. It is a fact of life.... There is no more compelling motivation to worthwhile endeavor than the knowledge that we are children of God, the Creator of the universe, our all-wise Heavenly Father!"[3] Faith is a spiritual handle for interfacing with the physical universe. Faith is a motivation that bridges the gap from what the mind thinks should be possible, to what actually gets accomplished. Christ said that, with the faith equivalent to the size of a grain of mustard seed, we can move mountains,

---

1. "Reverence for the Bible," LDS Newsroom, http://www.newsroom.lds.org/ldsnewsroom/eng/commentary/reverence-for-the-bible (accessed February 9, 2009).

2. Brigham Young, July 13, 1862, *Journal of Discourses*, 26 vols. (London and Liverpool: LDS Booksellers Depot, 1855–86), 9:311.

3. Gordon B. Hinckley, "With All Thy Getting Get Understanding," *Ensign*, August 1988, 2–5.

and nothing will be impossible to us (Matt. 17:20). The listeners of His era were amazed that such a powerful tool could be within their reach. However, in the modern age, the words of the Savior have been proved before our eyes again and again. We understand that, if we have faith, the turn of a key will start the engine of a bulldozer; and if we have patience, we can scoop the earth from the mountain and redeposit it somewhere else until the entire mountain is moved.

With the LDS perspective, we can see that the amazing inventions and technologies of our time have all come about because of faith and through spiritual means, whether or not the inventor recognizes them. Brigham Young explained: "The revealed religion of heaven is a pure science, and all true science in the possession of men now is a part of the religion of heaven and has been revealed from that source. But it is hard to get the people to believe that God is a scientific character, that He lives by science or strict law, that by this He is, and by law He was made what He is; and will remain to all eternity because of His faithful adherence to law."[4] Indeed, the scientific method, upon which all modern progress depends, is identical to the principles of faith as described by Alma. In the scientific method, we begin with base assumptions from an established paradigm ("soil," Alma 32:39). In the next step, the scientist or engineer will make observations of a phenomenon or process ("seed," Alma 32:28). The investigator will then form a hypothesis (the "seed will grow," Alma 32:28) and null hypothesis ("seed will not grow," Alma 32:32) regarding how the phenomenon or process will occur under certain conditions. The investigator then creates an experiment to test the hypothesis ("experiment to see if it grows," Alma 32:27, 36). Once the experiment is complete, the scientist or engineer will analyze the data and use them to make predictions, theories, models, and value judgments ("because it grew it is good," Alma 32:33). The investigation finally creates knowledge ("knowledge is perfect," Alma 32:34).

Mormon physics posits objectivity through materialism and empiricism. Everything is matter. Coarse matter is element. Fine matter is spirit (D&C 131:7), primal intelligence (D&C 93:29), or the light of truth in and through all things (D&C 88:7–13). All matter is eternal (D&C 93:33), uncreated (D&C 93:29) and indestructible, but malleable.[5] God, a material being (D&C 130:22), either emerged from or was organized out of chaotic matter,[6] and then continued to organize this matter (Abr. 3:24), first spirit, then element, iteratively (D&C 29:31–33). All matter,

---

4. Brigham Young, November 13, 1870, *Journal of Discourses*, 13:300.
5. Joseph Smith, April 6, 1844, *Journal of Discourses*, 6:6.
6. Ibid., 7.

including spirit, is discernible (Alma 32:35). Experience leads to knowledge (Alma 32:33), and knowledge leads to truth (D&C 93:24), which is contextual and dynamic (D&C 93:30). If we will seek, nothing will be withheld (D&C 121:26–33).

Mormon physics posits consistency, causality, and uniformity. Innumerable systems exist in space and time (Moses 1:35), and all have laws (D&C 88:36). Laws may differ from one system to another (D&C 88:38), and some systems may govern others (Abr. 3:2–19). Recurrently without definite beginning, God instituted laws[7] within the context of previous laws (Alma 42:13) and according to knowledge of those laws (Prov. 8:22–31). Likewise, we will attain no greater heaven than that we make according to law.[8] Faith without knowledge (D&C 130:21) and works (James 2:15–22) will not save us. Blessings are predicated on law (D&C 130:21). Even miracles, although marvelous in our eyes (Mormon 9:16), do not contravene law.[9] If we will seek, we can understand all mysteries (D&C 76:7–10).

A Technical Interpretation of Mormon Physiology

Mormon physiology, as expounded in scripture and by prominent authorities, lends itself to interpretations compatible with technological trends projected into hypothetical futures. Certainly, not all hypothetical technology will prove feasible, but contemporary science provides a wondrously broad scope within which to speculate about and argue for possibilities. Numerous Mormon texts reference physiological matters, working together to present a vision of spirits and souls, transfiguration and resurrection, immortality and glories that we may interpret in terms of physiological components, processes, and configurations.

Spirits and Souls as Physiological Components

As we observe matter closely, the finer our instruments, the clearer the picture becomes. With the proper instruments, it becomes apparent that surfaces that seemed solid with our natural eyes are actually made of extremely small particles. These atoms and molecules perform as building blocks in a very logical way; the hierarchy and nesting of primitive particles into larger and larger systems organize reality into macro-constructs

---

7. Ibid.

8. Brigham Young, June 15, 1856, *Journal of Discourses*, 3:336.

9. James E. Talmage, *Jesus the Christ* (1915; rpt., Salt Lake City: Deseret Book, 1983 printing), 143.

that have meaning to us. In a Mormon understanding of physiology, we can observe that systems of matter can be described as kingdoms each having its own laws of behavior. "And there are many kingdoms; for there is no space in the which there is no kingdom; and there is no kingdom in which there is no space, either a greater or a lesser kingdom" (D&C 88:37). We understand that both element and spirit are matter and that these two forms can be organized into bodies. It is usually agreed that the physical element described in the scriptures corresponds with the physical element that has been revealed to us by science. However, as Adam Davis illustrates in Chapter 1, there are varying perspectives on what the spirit element might correspond to.

Many people assume that spirit matter is of a supernatural nature, and thus is not detectable by the instruments of science. However, modern scriptures describe the nature of spirit matter and show that such an interpretation is inaccurate. "There is no such thing as immaterial matter. All spirit is matter, but it is more fine or pure, and can only be discerned by purer eyes" (D&C 131:7). If, as we have discussed previously, all things will be revealed to those who seek, and we are confident that even spirit matter conforms to the laws, then it should be no mystery to us that spirit matter may have already been detected by our instruments. Nowhere is there any indication that spirit is unobservable. As Scott Howe discusses in Chapter 2, we may have been observing spirit matter all along and have not yet realized what we were looking at.

Transfiguration and Resurrection as Physiological Processes

Prophets have long spoken of a time to come when humans, both the living and the dead, will undergo change to immortality (1 Cor. 15:51–54). In Mormon scripture, we read of a day of transfiguration when living mortals become immortal (D&C 63:20–21; D&C 101:29–31), and a day of resurrection when the dead rise to immortal life (D&C 63:49–52). Early Mormon prophets associated these changes with ordinances that we would perform for each other. Joseph Smith taught that transfiguration is a power of the priesthood to be revealed in the last times, preparatory for greater change,[10] and Brigham Young taught that immortal persons would receive keys to administer the ordinance of resurrection.[11]

---

10. Joseph Smith Jr. et al., *History of the Church of Jesus Christ of Latter-day Saints*, edited by B. H. Roberts, 2d ed. rev. (6 vols., 1902–12, Vol. 7, 1932; rpt., Salt Lake City: Deseret Book, 1948 printing), 4:209–10.

11. Brigham Young, August 24, 1872, *Journal of Discourses*, 15:136–39.

Two thousand years ago, life expectancy for persons living in the Roman Empire was probably in the range of twenty to thirty years.[12] Two hundred years ago, life expectancy for persons living in Victorian England was probably between thirty and forty years.[13] Today, life expectancy in the United States is nearly eighty years.[14] Observing the contemporary trend of rapid advance in information technology and its convergence with biological science, it's not difficult to imagine additional increases in life expectancy and perhaps even radical life extension, if we learn how to repair aging or prevent it altogether. Although speculative, such ideas may prove feasible. Consider, for example, the life expectancy of an automobile. With regular maintenance and repairs, and new paint or parts from time to time, an automobile can remain in good working order indefinitely. Why should our bodies be any different, except in degree of complexity? Could we maintain and repair human bodies indefinitely? Scientists are investigating these questions with increasing rigor.[15]

Yet more speculative, but nonetheless intending to operate within the scientific framework, some scientists have proposed means for restoring long dead persons to life. Perhaps the best-known proponent of such ideas is Frank Tipler, a mathematical physicist at Tulane University. Tipler argues that future computing technology could enable perfect emulation of all persons who have ever lived and their respective environments, as well as indefinitely expanding variations of other possible persons and environments.[16] In addition, he argues that such computing power could provide continuously expanding experiential time to persons emulated by them, even within the context of an otherwise aging universe. Another example is how genealogy has become more and more DNA-based. In a technical interpretation, one of the ways we can foresee a technology for resurrection would be to find the DNA of our ancestors and recreate their bodies from their DNA code of instructions.

Without committing ourselves to any particulars, we can see, in the hypotheses and trends of contemporary science and technology, the ten-

---

12. Walter Scheidel, *Debating Roman Demography* (Boston, Mass.: Brill Academic Publishers, 2000), 15.

13. Robert Woods, *The Demography of Victorian England and Wales* (Cambridge, England: Cambridge University Press, 2000), 4.

14. "Deaths: Final Data for 2005," Centers for Disease Control and Prevention, http://www.cdc.gov/nchs/data/nvsr/nvsr56/nvsr56_10.pdf (accessed February 13, 2009).

15. Aubrey de Grey and Michael Rae, *Ending Aging* (New York: St. Martin's Press, 2007).

16. Frank Tipler, *The Physics of Christianity* (Garden City, N.Y.: Doubleday, 2008).

tative outlines of possible futures in which human beings engineer the processes of transfiguration and resurrection. Research into radical life extension may lead to the development of processes that qualify as transfiguration, changing our aging bodies to agelessness, in preparation for still greater change. Additional time and research into physics and computation may lead to the development of processes that qualify as resurrection, providing a more robust and indefinitely enduring environment for both the living and the dead. We may understand transfiguration and resurrection, like birth and death, to be processes that change the components of our physiology from one configuration to another.

Consideration should be given to whether and how an engineering approach to transfiguration or resurrection is compatible with Mormon teachings on the atonement of Christ, exemplified by these words from the Book of Mormon: "If Christ had not risen from the dead ... there could have been no resurrection" (Mosiah 16:7). While such passages of scripture clearly indicate that Christ is essential to the resurrection, they do not indicate that only Jesus will participate in the work. There is well-accepted precedent for such interpretations of the Atonement in other areas. For example, Mormons hold that "through the Atonement of Christ, all mankind may be saved, by obedience to the laws and ordinances of the Gospel" (Third Article of Faith), but we do not expect Jesus Himself to teach everyone those laws or perform for each person those ordinances. Rather, we advocate taking on the identity of Christ (Mosiah 5:9) and joining Jesus as saviors (D&C 103:9). As we act in the name of Christ when we teach the gospel and perform proxy ordinances for the dead, so perhaps we will act in that name if ever we become able to extend our ordinances to that of resurrection. What better way could there be for us to learn to become as God than to perform the same works? Perhaps God provides the means that we, together as the body of Christ, must use to fulfill the prophecy?

Immortality and Glories as Physiological Configurations

Joseph Smith expanded on traditional notions of heaven and hell by introducing a paradigm of nearly universal salvation in innumerable worlds, whose inhabitants vary in glory, or degree of knowledge and power, according to their desires (D&C 88:14–41). Joseph described three principal categories of glory: telestial, terrestrial, and celestial (D&C 76). According to temple ritual, our world is an example of telestial glory, in which beings differ in knowledge and power as one star differs from another (D&C 76:98). Beyond the telestial, terrestrial beings exceed them in glory as the light of the moon exceeds that of the stars from our perspective on earth

(D&C 76:81). Likewise, the knowledge and power of celestial beings exceeds that of terrestrial beings, as the light of the sun exceeds that of the moon (D&C 76:71, 78). Celestial beings attain the creative capacities of gods (D&C 76:58) and begin to learn of yet higher glories (D&C 130:10). Thus, as explained by Joseph, we "have got to learn how to be Gods ... the same as all Gods have done before ... by going from one small degree to another, and from a small capacity to a great one."[17]

We live in a day when human knowledge and power are expanding dramatically. We now navigate depths of the sea that sunlight does not reach and rocket through the sky at speeds greater than that of sound. Computing power that once filled entire warehouses now fits in the palms of our hands. We've used them to form the internet and map the human genome. We've visited the moon, our robots are scouting Mars, and private reusable spacecraft are preparing the way for space tourism. We've even demonstrated on small scales the feasibility of what Harry Potter might call "invisibility," "levitation," and "telepathy."

These advances have become increasingly intimate. Surgeries, drugs, and prosthetics repair and enhance our bodies. In many cases, we can restore proper bodily functions. In other cases, we replace or compensate for damaged or missing body parts. Many who would not have lived a few decades ago, now survive, and some even thrive. Surgically repaired eyes have seen more clearly than ever before. Drug-soothed minds have experienced previously unimaginable peace. Prosthetic legs have outrun the rest. Our electronic computers were once exclusively massive machines housed in large warehouses far away from us. We would either drive to the warehouses, or eventually connect via terminals from home, to leverage those computers. In time, those computers became smaller, and we brought them into our homes. Soon after, we put them in our pockets. Now, we embed them in our clothing and bodies. The trend toward an increasingly intimate relation with our technology has been going on for quite a while, and there seems to be no reason to suppose that it will change any time soon.

What does the future hold? How might we use technology to shape our bodies, expanding our knowledge and power? Perhaps the best answers arise from extrapolating present trends into the future, while tempering expectations with scientific assessments of feasibility. Engaged in such exercises, some futurists predict a complete merger of human biological and information systems.[18] In such a world, beyond even radical life extension, it seems that traditional notions of death would no longer apply. We would persist

---

17. Joseph Smith, April 6, 1844, *Journal of Discourses*, 6:4.
18. Ray Kurzweil, *The Singularity Is Near* (New York: Viking, 2005).

as information persists, enduring perpetually with proper maintenance, recovering from disasters via backup systems, and adjusting quickly to adapt to changing circumstances. Moreover, as such beings, with minds expanding in knowledge and power beyond that of the greatest computer networks, it seems that our very thoughts would constitute creative acts, the formation of worlds and works beyond our present ability to imagine. Perhaps then, when our anatomy is indistinguishable from our sublime creations, we would comprehend how God is in and through all things (D&C 88:6–19, 34–45).

Practical and Moral Drivers for Technical Interpretations

In this section, we present several practical and moral reasons for which Mormons should seek after and embrace interpretations of their religion that are compatible with science and technology. We define "technical interpretations" to be the rich soil in which we can plant seeds of faith that leads to knowledge (Alma 32) in a particular field—it requires our own action and efforts combined with incremental inspiration, sometimes taking years and decades to reach that "aha!" moment when finally all the pieces come together and real results are achieved. No manner of truth would be excluded, whether it be knowledge about the nature of God, or physical processes, methods, tools, and machinery for bringing about a resurrection. As mentioned previously, many different technical interpretations are possible. Ideas expressed in the preceding sections are only examples and will prove of varying value and feasibility as research and development progress. However, whether or not you embrace the particular interpretations we've shared, there are strong reasons to embrace technical interpretations generally:

- Technical interpretations are our best bet for a better world.
- Technical interpretations help us combine value from multiple sources.
- Technical interpretations reflect the full extent of our Christian faith.

Technical Interpretations Are Our Best Bet for a Better World

Can works save us? Christians debate whether good works are necessary for salvation, with responses ranging from the extremes of Calvinism (salvation does not depend whatsoever on our efforts) to the extremes of Pelagianism (salvation depends almost entirely on our efforts). Most Christians situate themselves somewhere between these two extremes, but where should we situate ourselves? Here's a wager: Bet on better works. In any choice between ideologies, choose the one that you think will influence you to do better works. To the extent that Calvinism is accurate, your choice won't matter either way. To the extent that Pelagianism is accurate, your better works will save you.

Again, bet on better works. Regardless of how you define "salvation" or "good works," the wager stands. One may define salvation as "happiness" and good works as "benevolent power." Another may define salvation as "utility" and good works as "ethical technology." Will more benevolent power make you happier? From a secular pseudo-Calvinist perspective, it doesn't matter because something beyond your benevolent power will determine your happiness. In other words, to the extent pseudo-Calvinism is accurate, it can't hurt to bet on benevolent power. Will more ethical technology increase your utility? From a secular pseudo-Pelagianist perspective, your utility depends on your ethical technology. So, to the extent pseudo-Pelagianism is accurate, ethical technology is a good bet.

There are three ways of looking at the causal relation of good works and salvation:

1. They don't have a causal relation.
2. They have a negative causal relation.
3. They have a positive causal relation.

Number 1 is of no practical consequence, by definition. Practice is limited to works, power, and technology. If good works, benevolent power, and ethical technology are no more likely to cause salvation, happiness, and utility than are evil works, malevolent power, and unethical technology, then it doesn't matter whether we reject Number 1, even if we're wrong. Common sense rejects Number 2 as it should, again based on definitions. We don't hear anyone argue seriously that good works cause damnation, that benevolent power causes misery, or that ethical technology causes inutility, because it's nonsensical.

That leaves us with Number 3. We should embrace the idea that good works cause salvation, that benevolent power leads to happiness, and that ethical technology results in utility. Bet on better works, benevolent power, and ethical technology. In any choice between ideologies, choose the one that you think will influence you toward better works, more benevolent power, and more ethical technology. If there's anything you can do to achieve salvation, happiness, or utility, you will have done it. As expressed by Dieter Uchtdorf, second counselor in the First Presidency of the LDS Church, "When our wagon gets stuck in the mud, God is much more likely to assist the man who gets out to push than the man who merely raises his voice in prayer—no matter how eloquent the oration."[19]

---

19. Dieter F. Uchtdorf, "Two Principles for Any Economy," October 2009, The Church of Jesus Christ of Latter-day Saints, http://lds.org/general-conference/2009/10/two-principles-for-any-economy (accessed August 23, 2011).

Technical Interpretations Help Us Combine Value from Multiple Sources

Software engineers sometimes integrate information systems by writing a program that knows how to talk with each of the systems and enables them to exchange information. Integrated systems can leverage each other's strengths and increase the overall value of owning both systems. Without an integration program, the systems must act independently, sometimes duplicating efforts, and often forcing administrators to waste time on unnecessary work. For example, suppose you have an information system that monitors the performance of computers on your network and alerts you when their performance degrades. Suppose also that you have another system that can remote-control any computer on the network. Before the integration, when the first system alerts you of a problem computer, you have to note the name of the computer, open a console for the second system, search for the computer, and finally remote-control to check for and remedy the problem. After the integration, you can click on a link in the alert from the first system and immediately remote-control the problem computer in the console of the second system without error-prone notes or time-consuming searches. The integration enables higher productivity and cost-savings over time.

Human ideologies are information systems. Like computer information systems, which help us act sensibly within an environment of networked computers, ideologies help us act sensibly in our complex world. Although far richer than computer information systems, ideologies are still systems of inter-related symbols, codes, laws, words, and so forth. Also like information systems, which rely on integration programs to share data between them, ideologies are often unable to exchange ideas without assistance from an integrating or syncretizing ideology.

In addition to its distinct strengths, Mormonism can serve as an integration between two powerful ideologies: Judeo-Christian religion and the Enlightenment philosophy that gave rise to modern science. A technical interpretation of Mormonism can readily map symbols from each of these ideologies into symbols in the other. For example, the God of Judeo-Christian religion may map into Enlightenment philosophy as an advanced powerful material being; and Enlightenment philosophy's expected future of dramatic increases in human knowledge and power may map into Judeo-Christian religion as the millennium.

Integrations can be complex and messy. Sometimes data in one symbol system don't map well into the other system. Sometimes integrators make poor decisions about how to implement an integration. Always, an integration can be improved as the integrators become increasingly familiar with the systems they're integrating. This is also true of technical interpretations of Mormonism, whose mappings between the Judeo-Christian religion and Enlightenment philosophy present various limitations and opportunities for improvement.

Yet, beyond limitations, the integrated ideologies enable us to leverage the strengths of each with less difficulty. Mormons who embrace technical interpretations of their religion will find it easier to embrace science while maintaining a fulfilling relationship with their spiritual education and religious community. Moreover, by embracing technical interpretations, we're doing a better job of living our religion, as expressed by Joseph Smith: "One of the grand fundamental principles of 'Mormonism' is to receive truth, let it come from whence it may."[20] Mormonism is, on principle, an integrating ideology.

Technical Interpretations Reflect the Full Extent of Our Christian Faith

Mormons almost universally acknowledge that we have a moral obligation and capacity to participate in the work of God, to bring about the immortality and eternal life of humanity. This acknowledgement focuses primarily on the advance of spiritual salvation, particularly through missionary and temple work. Such a focus is important; but it does not, in itself, satisfy the full extent of our obligation, which also includes the advance of physical salvation. Both the LDS Church and individual Mormons regularly demonstrate real concern and concerted effort to advance physical salvation, through means ranging from neighborhood service projects to large-scale welfare and humanitarian programs. Yet we can and should do more.

Each day, around 150,000 persons die.[21] Many of them die of painful and debilitating diseases. Most of them die from something that is not commonly considered a disease, although it is altogether as painful and debilitating. It emaciates our muscles and bones, makes our hair fall out, blurs our vision, and stifles our hearing. Finally, if it doesn't kill us by clogging our hearts or setting off runaway cellular growth, it steals our memories. We've become accustomed to this inexorable degradation of our bodies, which we call "aging."

In the Book of Mormon, we read of Jesus asking twelve Nephite disciples what they desire (3 Ne. 28:1). Nine tell him that they desire to teach

---

20. Joseph Smith, quoted in *History of the Church*, 5:499.
21. "World Vital Events," U. S. Census Bureau, http://www.census.gov/cgi-bin/ipc/pcwe (accessed February 5, 2009).

the gospel for the remainder of their lives and then "speedily come unto thee in thy kingdom" (3 Ne. 28:2). Jesus tells them that they are blessed for this desire. The remaining three are hesitant to express their desire, but Jesus discerns that they would like to go on teaching the gospel without ever dying. He then tells them that they are more blessed for this desire. Here, Jesus affirms that God is a God of life, and that death, with hell, is indeed an awful monster, as described by Nephi (2 Ne. 9:10). More blessed are those who would, if possible, live for Christ than those who would die for Christ.

The message of this Book of Mormon passage is particularly pertinent to our time, when we are learning, through modern science and technology, how to extend and enhance life. There are some who argue that it's not moral to extend human life indefinitely. There are others who see such power as an endowment from God and as a means of deliverance from Nephi's awful monster. Will we, like the Three Nephites, be more blessed by making use of the means provided to us? Or will we sit still, supposing that God will deliver us despite our apathy (Alma 60:11)? Perhaps desire for life, expressed in our actions, will bring for us the prophesied day of transfiguration when mortal lives will be as the age of a tree, there is no death, and we are changed in the twinkling of an eye (D&C 101:26–34).

Conclusion

Technical interpretations of Mormon physics and physiology are both possible and beneficial. We need not presuppose our religion to be at odds with science and technology. Neither need we suppose that authentic interpretations of our religion necessarily exclude the possibility of empirical access to the spiritual aspect of the universe and our bodies. To the contrary, Mormon physics, as expounded in scripture and by authorities, lends itself to interpretations compatible with the methods and axioms of science, such as objectivity, causality, uniformity, and consistency. Likewise, Mormon physiology lends itself to interpretations compatible with technological trends projected into hypothetical futures, when new processes change our physiological composition into new configurations.

Most importantly, we have strong practical and moral reasons to seek after and embrace technical interpretations of Mormon physics and physiology. Whether or not we can play a role in making a better world, we certainly will not unless we first act on the possibility, so technical interpretations are our best bet. Technical interpretations can also help individuals and communities recognize and embrace the valuable aspects of multiple influential ideologies that might otherwise appear incompatible, unrelated, or too cumbersome in combination. Finally, we are called to emulate

Jesus, take on the identity of Christ, and participate in the work and glory of God to bring about immortality and eternal life, which we cannot do fully without acting on knowledge—including a technical interpretation, of physics and physiology.

4
Materialism, Free Will, and Mormonism

Adam N. Davis

Abstract

Contemporary science is essentially materialist. Mormonism can also nominally be materialist but there is the problem of free will and materialism being compatible. The Mormon doctrine of intelligent matter hypothetically resolves this difficulty.

Introduction

As a scientist, I find a great deal of appeal in the philosophy of materialism. As a Latter-day Saint (Mormon) I find comfort in the concept of free will. Historically, free will and materialism have a troubled past and a great deal of thought has gone into them. I personally find strength in agnostic arguments against free will such as that by philosopher Galen Strawson, The Basic Argument.[1] Intelligent matter resolves many aspects of the problem of evil,[2] which is closely related to free will. But I do not believe that it fully counters the Basic Argument's attack on free will as exemplified by the problem of information, or what I call the black box problem. I discuss the nature of the tension between materialism and free will, what is known of

---

1. Galen Strawson, *Real Materialism and Other Essays* (New York: Oxford University Press, 2008); and Galen Strawson, "The Bounds of Freedom," in *The Oxford Handbook of Free Will*, edited by R. Kane (New York: Oxford University Press, 2002), 441–60.

2. David L. Paulsen, "Joseph Smith and the Problem of Evil," *BYU Studies* 39, no. 1 (2000): 53–66, http://speeches.byu.edu/reader/reader.php?id=1644 (accessed January 2009); Blake T. Ostler, "Evil: A Real Problem for Evangelicals," *Farms Review* 15, no. 1 (2003): 201–13.

intelligent matter, and present a hypothesis for intelligent matter that would allow materialism and free will to peaceably coexist.

Materialism

While this paper uses "materialism," *physicalism* is the more contemporary term that avoids some of the restrictive senses of "material."[3] Materialism and physicalism can be considered synonymous in this article. One way of defining materialism is that it is the assertion that all concrete phenomena in the universe are physical—that every event, interaction, thought, behavior, and emotion is and has a reality that exists in both space and time.[4] For some things—flowers, planets, rocks, etc.—the suggestion of materialism is self-evident, but for other things—mental phenomena such as thoughts, emotions, decisions, etc.—the suggestion of materialism is not self-evident. Indeed, it is these latter quantities that are the subject of an entire branch of philosophy, the philosophy of mind. It is not the purpose of this chapter to discuss the various merits of the different schools of thought but rather it will tacitly assume that materialism is a desirable philosophy and examine its compatibility or incompatibility with Mormonism. Even when one adopts a materialist philosophy, how materialism explains mental phenomena is by no means a closed subject[5] and is also beyond the scope of the chapter.

A first question that might be asked is whether anything in Mormonism lends itself to one assuming a materialist outlook. Following a lecture by a Methodist preacher, Joseph Smith made the following correction to something that the preacher had said about the eternal duration of matter,[6] a statement that was later canonized as LDS scripture: "There is no such thing as immaterial matter. All spirit is matter, but is more fine or pure, and can only be discerned by purer eyes. We cannot see it, but when our bodies are purified, we shall see that it is all matter" (D&C 131:7–8).

While the context of the comment isn't entirely clear, I believe it probable that the preacher was commenting that matter is temporal and fickle and that only the spirit is eternal. Smith's correction would have then been to assert that all is matter—including spirit—negating the temporality of

---

3. D. Stoljar, *Physicalism*, Fall 2008. http://plato.stanford.edu/archives/fall2008/entries/physicalism/ (accessed January 2009).

4. Strawson, *Real Materialism and Other Essays*.

5. Stoljar, *Physicalism*.

6. Joseph Smith Jr. et al., *History of the Church of Jesus Christ of Latter-day Saints*, edited by B. H. Roberts, 2d ed. rev. (6 vols., 1902–12, Vol. 7, 1932; rpt., Salt Lake City: Deseret Book, 1964 printing), 6:302–17.

matter that the preacher may have suggested. This correction would be consistent with the statement, "The elements are eternal" (D&C 93:33).

While the concept that all spirit is matter opens the door for materialism, it does not actually demand a materialist interpretation of the universe. The assertion that immaterial "matter" exists does not preclude the possibility of other substances as required by dualism. Dualism is a branch of philosophy that argues that mental phenomena must in some respect not be physical—that another non-physical "substance" is necessary. This chapter restricts itself to the situation of assuming both materialism and Mormonism.

The Basic Argument

Materialism and "free will" prove to be problematic philosophical partners. For a traditional materialist, the entirety of one's being is physical matter and governed by laws. The matter simply has no choice but to react as it is acted upon. Galen Strawson is a materialist philosopher who has written a great deal about free will and argues that it is ultimately incompatible with materialism. The crux of his claim lies in what he calls "The Basic Argument":

1. We do what we do, in a given situation, because we are what we are.
2. In order to be ultimately responsible for what we do, we have to be ultimately responsible for what we are—at least in certain crucial mental respects.
3. But we cannot, as the first point avers, be ultimately responsible for what we are, because, simply, we are what we are; we cannot be *causa sui* (Latin for "the cause of itself").[7]

The thought behind this reasoning can be seen in discussing something like an electrical lamp. Few would ascribe any sort of free will to a lamp. The lamp does what it does because of what it is. If it is connected to a source of electrical power and if an external force turns the lamp on, it lights up. The lamp does not have a choice in the matter and can only do as it is "told." For a materialist like Strawson, a human body is composed basically of the same stuff that a lamp is. Strawson argues that, while immensely more complex, like a lamp humans do what they do because of their makeup. But they cannot "cause" their makeup and thus have no free will.

In presenting the example of a lamp, I must disavow the idea that the question of free will is simple and easy. It is a difficult and ancient question. The context is simplified a bit when restricting oneself to a ma-

---

7. Strawson, *Real Materialism and Other Essays*; Strawson, "The Bounds of Freedom," 441–60.

terialist universe. And for a materialist like Strawson, free will is an illusion. However, it seems that most of humanity believe in free will. In an interview, Strawson confessed that his own denial of free will bothers him.

> *Sommers*: Biologists, cognitive scientists, neurologists—they all seem to have an easier time, at least considering the possibility that there's no free will. But philosophers defend the concept against all odds, at the risk of terrible inconsistency with the rest of their views about the world. If it's a fact that there's no free will, why do philosophers have such a hard time accepting it?
>
> *Strawson*: There's a Very Large Question here, as Winnie the Pooh would say. There's a question about the pathology of philosophy, or more generally about the weird psychological mechanisms that underwrite commitment to treasured beliefs—religious, theoretical or whatever—in the face of overwhelming contrary evidence. But to be honest, I can't really accept it myself, and not because I'm a philosopher. As a philosopher I think the impossibility of free will and ultimate moral responsibility can be proved with complete certainty. It's just that I can't really live with this fact from day to day. Can you, really? As for the scientists, they may accept it in their white coats, but I'm sure they're just like the rest of us when they're out in the world—convinced of the reality of radical free will.[8]

Like Strawson, I am a materialist, but I am unable to deny free will and do not think I should. I believe in free will—a belief that is guided by my belief in Mormonism. That theological base firmly asserts the existence of free will or moral agency[9]—that "men are free according to the flesh" (2 Ne. 2:27). So I am left in a position where I must reconcile my belief in a materialist universe and agency. I am not free, as Strawson and other hard incompatibilists are, to deny free will. The Basic Argument gives a framework of discussion.

Intelligent Matter

The Basic Argument in its simplified form presented in this paper has three basic points. The first point is: "We do what we do, in a given situation, because we are what we are." To this I offer no objection. Similarly, to the second point, "In order to be ultimately responsible for what we do, we have to be ultimately responsible for what we are—at least in certain

---

8. T. Sommers, "Galen Strawson," *The Believer: You Cannot Make Yourself the Way You Are,* March 2003, http://www.believermag.com/issues/200303/?read=interview_strawson (accessed January 2009).

9. C. Terry Warner, "Agency," *Encyclopedia of Mormonism*, 4 vols. (New York: Macmillan Publishing, 1992), 1:26–27.

crucial mental respects." Again, I offer no objection. However, on the third point—"But we cannot, as the first point avers, be ultimately responsible for what we are, because, simply, we are what we are; we cannot be *causa sui*"—Mormonism allows an out.

The escape from the Basic Argument comes in the form of a unique Mormon doctrine of intelligences.[10] The term "intelligences" is perhaps a little unfortunate because it causes some confusion. As this article is discussing things in the framework of a materialist cosmos, I will use the term "intelligent matter" to avoid confusion with common usage of the word "intelligence." Very little is known of intelligent matter but a few points may be made:

- Intelligent matter exists in space and time.
- Intelligent matter is uncreated. It has always existed.
- Intelligent matter is the core of human agency.
- Intelligent matter is irreducible and simple.

The first point comes from the condition of materialism. There is no concrete reality that is not an actual substance, and actual substances must exist in space and time.

The second point follows from another LDS teaching: "Man was also in the beginning with God. Intelligence, or the light of truth, was not created or made, neither indeed can be" (D&C 93:29). Joseph Smith also taught:

> The mind of man—the immortal spirit. Where did it come from? All learned men and doctors of divinity say that God created it in the beginning; but it is not so. . . . I am going to tell of things more noble.
> We say that God himself is a self-existent being. . . . [But] who told you that man did not exist in like manner upon the same principles? Man does exist upon the same principles. God made a tabernacle and put a spirit into it, and it became a living soul. . . . How does it read in the Hebrew? It does not say in the Hebrew that God created the spirit of man. It says, "God made man out of the earth and put into him Adam's spirit, and so [he] became a living body.
> The mind or the intelligence which man possesses is co-equal [co-eternal] with God himself.[11]

It is established LDS doctrine that our spirit bodies are begotten of Heavenly Father—that we are literally His spirit children. The creation of

---

10. P. N. Hyde, "Intelligences," *Encyclopedia of Mormonism*, 4 vols. (New York: Macmillan Publishing, 1992), 1:26.

11. Joseph Fielding Smith, comp. and ed., *Teachings of the Prophet Joseph Smith* (Salt Lake City: Deseret Book, 1976), 352–53.

a spirit body and the concept that our existence is eternal can be reconciled only when viewed from the perspective that the fundamental component of an individual's identity/being existed before the creation of that individual's spirit body.

That intelligent matter existed before being coupled with a spirit body is also used to address a part of the problem of evil. One aspect of the problem of evil is an argument very similar to the Basic Argument. If God made us in our entirety and if we cannot help doing and being as we are, then God must be culpable for our behavior. Or to put it in a more specific example: "Why did not God simply create Adam with a disposition such that he would have chosen to not partake of the fruit of the tree of life?"

This particular problem is persistent in traditional Christian theology because of the dogma of *creatio ex nihilo* (Latin, "creation from nothing" or the idea that the material universe simply came into existence at God's will). Mormonism's escape is the doctrine of intelligent matter. As David L. Paulsen, professor of philosophy at Brigham Young University, states:

> Joseph Smith's way out of the conceptual incoherency generated by the traditional theological premises is to not go in. His revelations circumvent the theoretical problem of evil by denying the trouble-making postulate of absolute creation—and, consequently, the classical definition of divine omnipotence. Contrary to classical Christian thought, Joseph explicitly affirmed that there are entities and structures which are co-eternal with God himself. On my reading of Joseph's discourse, these eternal entities include chaotic matter, intelligences (or what I will call primal persons), and lawlike structures or principles. According to Joseph Smith, God's creative activity consists of bringing order out of disorder, of organizing a cosmos out of chaos—not in the production of something out of nothing.[12]

Similar reasoning is asserted by Blake T. Ostler, an attorney and LDS theologian, in his rebuttal of a criticism of Mormon theodicy.[13]

The fourth point on intelligent matter is that it is irreducible and simple. Irreducibility follows from its uncreated aspect. If it has component parts, then it could have existed at some point in the past as its component parts and been assembled later. But this scenario would contradict the uncreated aspect of intelligent matter: "Intelligence . . . was not created or made, neither indeed can be" (D&C 93:29).

One could also make the argument that intelligent matter has component parts but has never existed in its component parts. In that case, the concept of component parts becomes moot, unless one is willing to

---

12. Paulsen, "Joseph Smith and the Problem of Evil."
13. Ostler, "Evil: A Real Problem for Evangelicals."

speculate that, while it has never existed in component parts, it can be disassembled in the future with the impossibility of reassembly. This latter possibility I dismiss as improbable and inconsistent with a strictly materialist universe.

Simplicity then follows from irreducibility and the materialist universe. By "simple," I mean that intelligent matter is not capable of complex multi-process activities. The ability of intelligent matter to respond to interaction will be simple in the same manner that ordinary matter is simple.

These properties, as outlined, do not yet solve the question of free will. They may absolve God of culpability for our actions, but they do not answer the ultimate question of how free will, as insisted by Mormonism, can co-exist with a materialist cosmos in light of the Basic Argument. The problem comes because of the question of randomness. And to understand how randomness is an issue requires some understanding of determinism. I discuss these two points, then address the question at hand: how Mormonism can answer the Basic Argument.

Determinism and Randomness

Determinism is the idea that all events flow from the past. The past state uniquely determines the current state, and the current state uniquely determines the future state. This sequence becomes a problem for free will because if my "choices" automatically follow from my current state and my current state automatically follows from the past, then I am essentially not making the choice. The nature of reality and its progression is. A deterministic universe denies free will. (Those who argue that free will can be compatible with determinism are called compatibilists.[14])

To recover free will, philosophers as early as Epicurus with his idea of "swerve" introduced the idea that the universe is not deterministic.[15] More recently, quantum mechanics introduced the same possibility that the universe is not deterministic. (There are deterministic interpretations of quantum mechanics that have not been ruled out empirically.[16]) Does

---

14. M. McKenna, "Compatibilism," posted 2008, T*he Stanford Encyclopedia of Philosophy*, http://plato.stanford.edu/archives/fall2008/entries/compatibilism/ (accessed January 2009).

15. D. Konstan, "Epicurus," first published January 10, 2005, *The Stanford Encyclopedia of Philosophy*, http://plato.stanford.edu/archives/fall2008/entries/epicurus/ (accessed January 2009).

16. "Interpretation of Quantum Mechanics." *Wikipedia: The Free Encyclopedia*, http://en.wikipedia.org/wiki/Interpretation_of_quantum_mechanics (accessed January 2009).

free will then easily follow? The answer for some philosophers is no. Free will philosopher Robert Kane wrote,

> If free will is not compatible with determinism, it does not seem to be compatible with indeterminism either.... An event that is undetermined might occur or not occur, given the inter past. Thus, whether or not it actually occurs, given its past, would seem to be a matter of chance. But chance events are not under the control of anything, hence not under the control of the agent. How then could they be free and responsible actions? Reflections such as these have led to charges that undetermined choice or actions would be "arbitrary," "capricious," "random," "irrational," "uncontrolled," "inexplicable," or merely "matters of luck or chance," not really free and responsible actions at all.[17]

A random event does not automatically lead to free will and moral accountability. Indeed, the attempts to reconcile randomness with free will require meeting fairly specific conditions, which Randolfe Clarke describes: "Incompatibilist accounts require, first, that determinism be false. But more than this, they require that there be indeterminism of a certain sort (e.g., with some events entirely uncaused, or nondeterministically caused, or caused by agents and not deterministically caused by events) and that this indeterminism be located in specific places (generally, in the occurrence of decisions and other actions). What is our evidence with regard to these requirements' being satisfied?" Clarke answers his own question: "We do not have good evidence that any incompatibilist account is true."[18] In other words, we simply do not presently know whether or not the universe is deterministic or indeterministic.

Even if the universe is indeterministic, the Basic Argument still applies. The argument is agnostic with respect to determinism. Suppose that some agent came into being that is controlled by some indeterministic element. Points 1 and 2 of the Basic Argument are still true. Moreover, Point 3 also holds. The agent did not cause itself—did not cause the random element. The agent must do as it must—random or not.

What then is the answer to the Basic Argument provided by Mormonism? Intelligent matter. Intelligent matter avoids the third point of the Basic Argument by positing an uncreated core to free will agents. It

---

17. Robert Kane, "The Contours of Contemporary Free Will," in *The Oxford Handbook of Free Will*, edited by Robert Kane (New York: Oxford University Press, 2002), 22–23.

18. Randolphe Clarke, "Incompatibilist (Nondeterministic) Theories of Free Will," posted 2008, *The Stanford Encyclopedia of Philosophy*, http://plato.stanford.edu/archives/fall2008/entries/incompatibilism-theories/ (accessed January 2009).

may be argued that an uncreated entity cannot be held responsible for its properties because it had no "choice" in the nature of its being; this line of reasoning is central to the Basic Argument. But if it cannot be held accountable for the nature of its uncreated existence, then nothing at all can be held accountable for anything. Moral accountability would lose all definition. But simply being uncreated, while a necessary component, is insufficient. It may answer the question of the Basic Argument; but if the agent's actions are determined randomly, then meaningful moral agency is suspect. The behavior of the agent must be motivated and intentional. The nature of this latter issue is exemplified by what I call the black box problem.

The Black Box Problem

The model of free will that I use involves two basic components—the body and the core. The core is an irreducible, nondeterministic substance that has no creator. The body is the structure that feeds inputs to the core and responds to whatever output is given by the core. Free will requires that the outputs are *not* random. The challenge, then, is how or what kind of substance will meet the requirements outlined here in a materialist cosmos.

Suppose we are given two agents and wish to determine if they are free willed. The bodies are identical, but the cores are not. One core is random, the other "intelligent." A "black box" is put around these cores so that we are unable to look at the actual way they process the inputs from the body. We can observe only the inputs and the outputs. Can the two be distinguished? Can the "intelligent" core be identified?

The simple answer is that one agent will "appear" to be random (a random agent that is in control of the body would likely result in what could well be "spasms" or other sporadic behaviors). But the simple answer is inadequate. How do we determine what is random and what is not? We must compare the inputs to the outputs, a factor that places strict requirements on the inputs to the core. For randomness to be avoided, the core must have access to information—specifically, present information ("perception") and past information ("memory").

Perceptual information is necessary; otherwise the core is acting in the dark—much as a random-event generator would. The behavior would be capricious and arbitrary, having no relation to the current state of the agent.

Memory is also necessary; otherwise the core can make no distinction about the effectiveness of its behaviors. Without memory, all choices lose causal connectivity and the core is just as blind as if it had no perception.

Additionally, the simplicity of the intelligent matter requires that the inputs of perception and memory be simultaneous. Simple, irreducible matter (intelligent or otherwise) is incapable of taking a bit of information from source A, then a bit of information from source B, then a bit of information of source C, and so on before processing it. Being simple and irreducible, it cannot act as the temporary store for multiple sources of information. Matter receives information and acts then and there. The output can be simple, but the input must be a simultaneous delivery of complex information.

At present, no such substance that meets the above requirements is known. Classically, no matter is able to do such a thing. Particle A "hits" particle B and particle B responds. The information carried by particle A is not complex enough for the response of B to be either deterministic or potentially random. Intelligent matter must be of a sort that is different from presently known matter. (For a quick primer on current understanding, see the website *The Particle Adventure*.[19])

A Possible Solution and Challenge

The black box problem is the idea that the simple, indeterministic, uncreated core of a free-willed agent must have access to significant and simultaneous information. Classically, the requirements of the black box problem cannot be met. A particle that can respond to a simple stimulus in a manner of its own "choosing" would be indistinguishable from random events—and simple stimuli are the only kind available in a mechanistic, materialist universe. Classical computation can be reduced and replicated by Turing Machines, since their inputs are very simple. Fortunately, the universe is more complex.

Quantum mechanics allows for the superposition of many bits of information into a single state. This single state with all of the bits of information is passed on simultaneously. It is conceivable that the intelligent matter core would be able to process this complex assembly of information and give its output to the body. In this scenario, the output would be simple; the complex superposition of information would collapse to a single bit of information once it is acted upon. This is essentially the process behind quantum computers.[20]

This posited solution hypothesizes two very specific proposals:

- The human body will assemble information into a superposition of quantum states.

---

19. Particle Data Group, *The Particle Adventure*, http://particleadventure.org/ (accessed January 2009).

20. E. Bernstein and U. Vazirani, "Quantum Complexity Theory," *Proceedings of Symposium on the Theory of Computing* (New York: ACM, 1993), 11–20.

- Matter exists that can interact with these large complex states of information in a nondeterministic and nonrandom way.

I suspect that the second point will be more difficult to observe until such time that the first point is observed. Assuming that the information is assembled in the physical human body (as opposed to the "spirit body"), it is conceivable that neurophysics would be able to identity such concentration of information.

Alternatives and Consequences

The hypothesis of intelligent matter and its consequential observables is limited to the scope of a materialist universe. There exist other models of the mind and free will, but they do not easily coexist with materialism. One of the exceptions is the concept of emergence—specifically, ontological emergence; any other form of emergence fails the Basic Argument trivially. Emergence is the claim that fundamental properties arise in structures that are irreducible to the laws characterizing the component parts of that structure.[21] That is, new laws arise which are in no way causally dependent on the laws governing the constituents.

An emergent model of intelligence and free will removes the necessity of an uncreated core and posits that a complex body can be assembled in which a free will "core" emerges and is *causa sui*. The core here is not a simple component but is a complex entity seated in but above and beyond the body.

I see two problems with emergent intelligence. First, it does not meet the definitive aspect of intelligence in Mormonism in being uncreated. It sets a condition that intelligence is conceptually uncreated—but such a redefinition makes intelligence as insubstantive as the idea of a perfect circle. Materialism requires that actual entities exist concretely in space and time.

The second problem is an objection to the very concept of ontological emergence. When properties are allowed to emerge that have no causal connection to the constituent parts, one is free to allow any property to emerge. The rules of nature are essentially tossed out the window unless rules connect the emergent properties to the fundamental laws of its constituent elements. Yet such a requirement would, by definition, cause the emergent properties to be merely epiphemeral and not emergent at all. In short, ontological emergence is tantamount to magic. Magic is not necessary in a materialist cosmos.

---

21. T. O'Connor and H. Y. Wong, "Emergent Properties," *The Stanford Encyclopedia of Philosophy*, http://plato.stanford.edu/archives/spr2009/entries/properties-emergent/ (accessed January 2009).

Another consequence of the line of reasoning presented in this paper is the hypothetical impossibility of artificial intelligence (AI)—an entity that is created and has free will. Artificial intelligence fails the Basic Argument solidly whether the universe is deterministic or indeterministic. AI entities that are not true moral agents are allowed, but their moral culpability resides squarely in the nature of their being, over which the AI has no control. Even when an AI can evolve, the nature of that evolution is governed by the nature of its initial creation. Even with randomness, the creator will still posses some responsibility. As an extreme example, imagine a robot that is created with a bomb inside of it that will be triggered by nuclear decay for some unknown, yet unavoidable reason. The creator will have no control whether or when the bomb would go off. Yet we would intuitively still ascribe some degree of accountability to the creator if the robot happened to be in a crowded school when the bomb exploded.

Emergence is sometimes used to avoid this issue; but as stated already, I contend that emergence is unintelligible in the framework of materialism.

Conclusion

Mormonism and materialism appear to be compatible philosophies. God, human beings, and everything are allowed to exist in a strictly material sense in both fields. Free will is required in Mormonism and is difficult to justify in materialism as evidenced by reasoning such as Strawson's Basic Argument. The two fields can be reconciled with the introduction of a specific interpretation of the uniquely Mormon doctrine of intelligent matter. Intelligent matter is a primordial substance which is uncreated and irreducible. But positing intelligent matter alone does not solve the issue of free will because of the problem of information—the black box problem. Quantum mechanics allows for the superposition of many bits of information into a single state that can be passed simultaneously. I hypothesize that human bodies assemble information in just such a way and that an intelligent matter core interacts with that information in a nondeterministic and nonrandom way. Hypothetically, these two behaviors would be observable.

Section 2
Parallels in Mormon Thought: Philosophy and Engineering

Though some would say we naturally tend to see the actions of others through the filter of our own experience, the Latter-day Saints believe literally that many aspects of the human condition reflect divine attributes. This is particularly applicable to engineering, where we as children of God participate in the process of creating our environment.

In Allen Leigh's "God, the Perfect Engineer," a case is made where God also follows a design cycle of iteration and optimization that characterizes human engineering projects. Leigh believes that God follows eternal, preexisting natural laws to organize worlds out of fundamental particles but departs from other authors featured in this volume by his belief that the Creator's physical body may consist of "celestial matter" and not that of a "mortal universe." Leigh also unfolds an interesting argument on whether it is possible for God as an engineer to fail in His creations. Though Leigh illustrates the engineering design cycle that can result in discarded, unworkable prototypes before the functioning version is perfected, he advocates a God that got it right the first time around. One might ask, as we observe the variety of planets and many creatures present and past, whether the cycle is still going, and whether the human body might not be the latest, most perfect, round of the cycle that has indeed resulted in failed prototypes. Whether the reader comes to these conclusions or not, the chapter has some interesting insights worth considering.

In a discussion and critique on transhumanism written as much for Transhumanist or atheist readers as it is for LDS readers—Brent Allsop, Christopher Bradford, Lincoln Cannon, Andrew West, Joseph West, and Carl Youngblood—explain parallels between the technical perspective of manufacturing our own ideal environment and the teachings of the Mormon faith. "Complementary Aspects of Mormonism and Transhumanism" argues that many of the events and changes that Latter-day Saints espouse will occur in connection with the millennium. They point out that resurrection, transfiguration, and the ushering in of a celestial order may not take place unless we put forth the effort to make it happen. Technology is a benefit of the dispensation of the fulness of times, in which inspired inventions and knowledge are critical for setting a foundation for our salvation. Though the transhumanist approach may be a perspective some LDS readers haven't considered before, the insights and concepts discussed are sure to be of interest to all.

In a discussion that could also have been placed under Section 1 on physics and engineering, Scott Howe explains in "Quantified Morality" that all order, sin, transgression, creative, and charitable acts can be measured by how much they increase or decrease entropy in the universe. He makes the argument that providing an ordered nest in the natural chaos of the universe is necessary for advanced intelligences, such as God, to exist and that developing the technology and critical complexity adequate for self-replication and self-reproduction is the only way to manage and spread that ordered state. Howe also explains the relationship between cause, effect, justice, and consequence, thus setting the foundation for a discussion about Christ's atonement as a way to reconcile increases of entropy in our social environment. He hints that the need for a Messiah from a physics perspective may come within our understanding.

In "Theological Implications of the New God Argument," Lincoln Cannon and Joseph West argue the logic that an advanced civilization more benevolent than our own probably created our world. From one perspective, the discussion acknowledges that there may be other sentient races out in the universe, but LDS readers will recognize a celestial civilization that is intimately connected to our own—advanced beings who are concerned about our well-being and happiness.

5
God, the Perfect Engineer

Allen W. Leigh

Abstract

The Bible declares that God created the earth, but it doesn't say how He did it. This paper presents reasons for believing that He followed a procedure that has a broad parallel to design cycles typically used by human engineers. Since human engineers do not always succeed with their creations, the possibility that God can fail is considered. Reasons are given that assure us that God will not fail in His role as the Perfect Engineer of the universe.

Introduction

To understand the claim that God is the Perfect Engineer, we must understand the design cycle typically used by human engineers, and we must have a general overview how God created this earth. This understanding will allow us to determine if parallels exist between God's process of creation and design cycles used by our engineers.

The Engineering Design Cycle

In designing a device, an engineer typically follows a procedure that has been used in the past, a procedure that is known to work if followed carefully. This procedure consists of several steps or phases. The engineer first decides the type of device he or she would like to design. The engineer then studies the principles upon which the design will be based and decides how those laws can be used to create a device with desired functionality. Next, the engineer designs the details of the device. A prototype of the device is constructed and tested for desired functionality. If the device doesn't perform correctly, the engineer studies the design to understand why the device isn't working properly and changes the design and/or the prototype appropriately. This cycle of design, construction, and testing is repeated until the device is working correctly.

God's Creation of the Universe

To understand how God created the universe, we must turn to the scriptures for information. This presents a problem, because the scriptures generally don't tell *how* God performs His work, only *why* He does. Fortunately, the LDS scriptures, which were given through latter-day revelation, give some information explaining how God accomplishes His creations, and we can piece those verses together to give a general overview of God's creation of the earth. We must be aware, however, that using the scriptures in this way is subjective and open to individual interpretations and that any conclusions reached are those of the persons involved and do not necessarily represent doctrine of the Church of Jesus Christ of Latter-day Saints.

The Doctrine and Covenants speaks about the creation of the earth. One scripture describes the elements of matter used in the creation: "For man is spirit. The elements are eternal, and spirit and element, inseparably connected, receive a fulness of joy" (D&C 93:33). This verse tells us that the elements are eternal, and we can therefore deduce that God did not create the elements. This conclusion is significant, because a common belief in Christianity is that God created the elements.

The second scripture describes spirit: "There is no such thing as immaterial matter. All spirit is matter, but it is more fine or pure, and can only be discerned by purer eyes" (D&C 131:7). In declaring this revelation, Joseph Smith differentiates the matter that constitutes spirit from the matter that makes up this earth. Joseph didn't explain how spirit matter is different from physical matter, only that it is "more fine or pure."

From Moses's experience talking with God, we understand that differences between physical matter and spirit matter are great. Moses said he would have died if he had seen God with his natural eyes: "But now mine own eyes have beheld God; but not my natural, but my spiritual eyes, for my natural eyes could not have beheld; for I should have withered and died in his presence; but his glory was upon me; and I beheld his face, for I was transfigured before him" (Moses 1:11). In talking with God, Moses was talking with Jehovah or Jesus Christ before He was born to Mary—hence, while He was a spirit. Moses saw the spirit matter that composed the body of Jehovah.

Concerning physical and spirit matter, we learn from the Book of Moses that God created all things spiritually in heaven before He created them physically on the earth: "And every plant of the field before it was in the earth, and every herb of the field before it grew. For I, the Lord God, created all things, of which I have spoken, spiritually, before they were naturally upon the face of the earth. For I, the Lord God, had not caused it to rain upon the face of the earth. And I, the Lord God, had created all the children of men; and not yet a man to till the ground; for in heaven created I them; and there was not yet flesh upon the earth, neither in the water, neither in the air" (Moses 3:5). Joseph Smith said that all spirit is matter. Thus, we know that the heavenly creation used spirit matter.

A final important statement describes what was involved in creating the earth—that it meant organizing the elements: "And then the Lord said: Let us go down. And they went down at the beginning, and they, that is the Gods, organized and formed the heavens and the earth" (Abr. 4:1).

God did not create the earth from nothing. He organized the earth from preexisting but unorganized matter.

God Follows Eternal Laws

When God used unorganized matter in creating the earth, in what way was the matter unorganized? The scriptures don't answer that question, leaving us to propose hypotheses. One possibility is that molecules of the elements were present, implying that, on the molecular/micro level, the matter was organized. On a macro level, though, the molecules were not organized into stars, planets, moons, mountains, etc. Another possibility is that individual molecules did not exist and that the unorganized matter was actually energy. In this case, God transformed energy into molecules of matter.

Whatever happened, the important question is: Did God create universal laws that would organize the matter, or did He use preexisting laws to organize the matter? Insight toward a possible answer is in a description of those who are exalted in the celestial kingdom: "They are they into whose hands the Father has given all things—They are they who are priests and kings, who have received of his fulness, and of his glory" (D&C 76:55–56). Those who are exalted will receive the fulness and glory of our Heavenly Father and to whom He will give all things. Latter-day Saints believe that "all things" includes the power of creation.

Let's assume for the sake of discussion that we become exalted and receive the power of creation from our Father in Heaven. In order to use that power, will we have to create laws of nature that will govern the unorganized matter that we use to organize a world? No, of course not. Those laws were in effect before we were born into mortality. As exalted beings, we will have to learn to evoke those laws and how to use them to fulfill our purposes. So it is with our Father in Heaven. When God organized preexisting matter, He was, I believe, obedient to the laws that govern that matter. His works, especially miracles, do not contravene natural laws. He may, though, evoke higher laws that override the laws that normally are in control of the matter. This belief is a significant departure from the orthodox Christian teaching that God created the earth from nothing and, by implication, also created the laws that govern the elements of the earth.

We have seen that in addition to the physical matter of the universe, spirit matter was used in heaven to create this earth before it was created physically. We have also seen that, when God created the physical universe, He followed the physical laws that govern the cosmos. From this, we can assume that, when He created the earth spiritually in heaven, He followed the laws that govern spirit matter.

In saying that God follows the laws that govern physical and spirit matter, I am not saying that God Himself is subject to those laws. We know through latter-day revelation that God has a glorified body of flesh and bone: "The Father has a body of flesh and bones as tangible as man's; the Son also; but the Holy Ghost has not a body of flesh and bones, but is a personage of Spirit. Were it not so, the Holy Ghost could not dwell in us" (D&C 130:22). Our Father in Heaven and His Son Jesus Christ are subject to the laws that govern glorified bodies. We do not know much about those laws, but we do have scriptural justification for believing that glorified bodies do not die, can pass through physical matter such as walls, can eat physical food, and can be suspended in the air. We also usually assume, although without scriptural justification, that they can travel at high speeds and are not limited to the speed of light.

Some Latter-day Saints believe that God lives somewhere in the physical cosmos[1] that is studied by scientists. However, this view seems to be in-

---

1. People who believe God lives somewhere in the physical cosmos usually cite Abraham 3:1–19 as the source for their belief. These verses describe the experience of Abraham using the Urim and Thummim to view the stars and planets in the cosmos. Because Abraham used the Urim and Thummim to view the cosmos, I believe this cosmos was a spiritual cosmos rather than our physical cosmos. To understand why God gave this vision to Abraham, we need to realize that the Urim and Thummim was not a telescope that God gave to Abraham to teach him about astronomy. It was a device that allowed Abraham to view the creations and glory of God, and God gave Abraham this vision to teach him that God was the greatest of all. This knowledge was important to Abraham, because he was on the verge of entering Egypt, a land where people worshiped a multitude of gods.

consistent with the view that God has a glorified body of flesh and bones. It seems to me to be more likely that God resides in a spiritual or celestial cosmos having worlds made from spirit matter. Where God lives is, of course, a matter of speculation since the scriptures do not say where He lives.

Jesus Christ Organized the Earth

Section 88 of the Doctrine and Covenants describes, from a spiritual viewpoint, the role Jesus played as the creator of the earth under the direction of the Father. Verse 6 says Jesus Christ is in and through all things. That verse refers to Christ as the light of truth, implying that He followed natural laws in forming the earth, for natural laws define truth as truth pertains to this mortal world. Verses 7–13 say that truth is the light of Christ and that Christ is in the sun, the moon, the stars, the earth, and all things, and, further, that the light of Christ governs all things and is the power of God. Those are significant verses. If truth is the light of Christ, then it follows that natural laws are the light of Christ, which is another way of saying that Christ follows natural laws in His creations.

Those verses could easily be misunderstood to say that Christ created the laws that govern mortal matter. To avoid this misunderstanding, let us

---

The vision given to Abraham consists of three phases. In the first phase, Abraham learned that the bodies seen by the Urim and Thummim have different "reckonings of time" and that the planet with the greatest reckoning of time was called Kolob because it is near the throne of God. After God taught Abraham that the objects in the sky led to Him, He showed Abraham all the things that He had created. God told Abraham, that just as there were countless objects in the spiritual cosmos and just as there were countless sands in the physical sea, so the descendants of Abraham would be countless. Finally, in verse 19 God used His spirit children as an example that God is the greatest of all the intelligences. "And the Lord said unto me: These two facts do exist, that there are two spirits, one being more intelligent than the other; there shall be another more intelligent than they; I am the Lord thy God, I am more intelligent than they all." That is, through the vision given to Abraham through the Urim and Thummim, God used the objects in the spiritual cosmos as a metaphor to teach that God was greater than all the gods Abraham would encounter in Egypt. He used the multitude of objects in the sky and of the sands of the sea to teach Abraham that God is greater than all of His children and that, if Abraham followed God, his posterity would be so numerous they couldn't be counted. God was not giving Abraham a lesson in astronomy. He used astronomy as a metaphor to prepare Abraham for his entrance into Egypt, a land of many pagan gods.

remember that those verses were not given as a scientific treatise. They were given as a spiritual message to teach us to love and worship Jesus Christ as the creator of the earth (the *why* of creation). We should avoid taking those verses as a literal description of the creation (the *how* of creation). Instead, we should interpret those verses as descriptions of the majesty of God in bringing organization to unorganized matter.

As an illustration, consider the construction of a new building. The building has been designed, and the materials have been delivered, but no construction has begun. Piles of lumber, stones, shingles, bricks, etc., are scattered around the construction site. Finally, construction begins; and months later, the building is finished. People admire the building and say how beautiful it is. They marvel at the architect's ability to take piles of building materials and turn them into a grand building. They say the architect is everywhere in the building, by which they mean that the architect's influence and personality are visible in design choices throughout the building. Those people are not describing in technical terms how the architect accomplished the design. They are describing in emotional terms the magnificence of the achievement. So it is with the creation of the universe. Jesus Christ didn't create the unorganized matter that was used to create the cosmos, and He didn't create the laws of nature that govern that matter. That matter and its laws are eternal. Jesus used that matter to build the cosmos with all of its beauty and grace.

God Followed a Plan

We have seen that God created the universe by obeying eternal laws. We thus see God as a user of eternal laws rather than as the creator of those laws. God followed natural laws to achieve a "device" that has desired characteristics: an earth that supports intelligent life. God's use of natural laws implies His use of a plan. This plan has a broad parallel with design cycles used by human engineers. For example, consider an engineer who designs an AM radio receiver. The receiver needs several components: a tuner to pick up radio-frequency (RF) signals, a detector to extract the audio signal from the RF signal, an amplifier to amplify the audio signal, and speaker(s) to create sound waves that we hear. When God created our world, He needed several components: a star to provide heat and gravitational attraction to keep our earth in orbit around the star, large outer planets to deflect asteroids and comets before they could enter the space for smaller inner planets, a habitable zone with correct temperatures and other conditions for intelligent life, and a planet in the habitable zone upon which we would live.

We thus realize that God's creation of the earth and, by implication, His creation of the cosmos satisfy the first characteristic of an engineering design cycle: the use of a plan. Now, we must look at the second characteristic of a design cycle, the refinement of the plan until the "device" works correctly.

Engineers May Fail in Their Designs

It is common knowledge that engineers may not create perfect devices. Devices are recalled for being dangerous under certain conditions. The manufacturing costs of devices are reduced so much that the devices have limited life-cycles. Engineers usually have to modify their designs until the devices perform in satisfactory ways.

Can God Fail?

This failure of human engineers leads to the question: If our engineers can fail, does this imply that God can fail? We want to say no; but in fact, LDS scriptures do say that God can fail if He violates certain laws. This is not an emotionally satisfying conclusion and probably not one accepted by most Latter-day Saints, much less Christians in general. Let us, therefore, look at the scriptures that say that God can fail to see if we can understand what those scriptures teach.

As recorded in the Book of Mormon, Alma taught his son Corianton that, because of our choices to sin, we are separated from God. Through Christ's atonement, he provides a way for us to become clean and thus able to return to God. Alma explained that our mortality is a probationary time, a time to repent and serve God. Alma taught that if we were to return to God without repentance, the law of justice would be violated and "God would cease to be God"—that is, the atonement must be applied only to those who have repented:

> Therefore, according to justice, the plan of redemption could not be brought about, only on conditions of repentance of men in this probationary state, yea, this preparatory state; for except it were for these conditions, mercy could not take effect except it should destroy the work of justice. Now the work of justice could not be destroyed; if so, God would cease to be God.
>
> But there is a law given, and a punishment affixed, and a repentance granted; which repentance, mercy claimeth; otherwise, justice claimeth the creature and executeth the law, and the law inflicteth the punishment; if not so, the works of justice would be destroyed, and God would cease to be God.

> What, do ye suppose that mercy can rob justice? I say unto you, Nay; not one whit. If so, God would cease to be God. (Alma 42:13, 22, 25)

Lehi taught his son Jacob that under certain conditions the wisdom of God could be destroyed:

> For it must needs be, that there is an opposition in all things. If not so, my first-born in the wilderness, righteousness could not be brought to pass, neither wickedness, neither holiness nor misery, neither good nor bad. Wherefore, all things must needs be a compound in one; wherefore, if it should be one body it must needs remain as dead, having no life neither death, nor corruption nor incorruption, happiness nor misery, neither sense nor insensibility.
>
> Wherefore, it must needs have been created for a thing of naught; wherefore there would have been no purpose in the end of its creation. Wherefore, this thing must needs destroy the wisdom of God and his eternal purposes, and also the power, and the mercy, and the justice of God. (2 Ne. 2:11–12)

Lehi said, in effect, that mortality must be a time of choice between opposites and that, if God were to institute a different plan for mortality, His power to be God would be destroyed.

One way that God's design can seem to fail is if His children choose to disobey His commandments. This condition is not a failure of God or of His design of a plan of salvation. This condition is due to the choices made by some of His children. God knew that not all of His children would choose to follow Him, and He allowed for that eventuality in His plan. He provided for both those who choose to follow Him and those who choose to follow Satan. The Doctrine and Covenants explains that all of God's children except those who become sons (and daughters) of perdition will be redeemed in one of the three degrees of glory. Those who choose to follow Satan, however, will not be redeemed and will live eternally with Satan:

> These are they who shall go away into the lake of fire and brimstone, with the devil and his angels—
>
> And the only ones on whom the second death shall have any power;
>
> Yea, verily, the only ones who shall not be redeemed in the due time of the Lord, after the sufferings of his wrath.
>
> For all the rest shall be brought forth by the resurrection of the dead, through the triumph and the glory of the Lamb, who was slain, who was in the bosom of the Father before the worlds were made. (D&C 76:36–39)

We Need Assurance That God Has Not Failed

Just as God used eternal elements in the creation, so He must abide by eternal laws that govern His work. We, then, need assurance that God has not failed, that He has obeyed eternal laws.

First, we have the knowledge that our earth is not the first of God's creations. He has created other worlds: "And worlds without number have I created; and I also created them for mine own purpose; and by the Son I created them, which is mine Only Begotten" (Moses 1:33). The fact that God has created other worlds implies that He has not failed; if He were to fail, He would not be able to create subsequent worlds.

Next, the scriptures give us assurance that we can trust God and can have faith that He will do as He has said. Alma explained to one of his sons: "And now, O my son Helaman, behold, thou art in thy youth, and therefore, I beseech of thee that thou wilt hear my words and learn of me; for I do know that whosoever shall put their trust in God shall be supported in their trials, and their troubles, and their afflictions, and shall be lifted up at the last day" (Alma 36:3).

Third, even though the scriptures do not give much information about the attributes of our Heavenly Father, we do have information about His Only Begotten Son, Jesus Christ. Jesus told Philip that those who have seen Him have seen the Father: "Jesus saith unto him, Have I been so long time with you, and yet hast thou not known me, Philip? he that hath seen me hath seen the Father; and how sayest thou then, Shew us the Father?" (John 14:9). Even though Jesus and the Father are separate beings, Jesus was so obedient to the Father that His life in mortality was a shadow of the life of our Heavenly Father. Jesus was the epitome of consistency and honesty, and our faith that He embodied these qualities helps us have faith that our Father in Heaven has not failed in His role as the creator of the universe.

Fourth, we have the knowledge that Jesus Christ did not fail in accomplishing His atonement. The completion of the atonement is in the past. That miraculous event has happened.

Finally, another evidence that God won't fail is His creations. Because of science, we know the cosmos is vast and that it contains billions of galaxies and stars. Scientists have discovered over 300 exoplanets,[2] planets not part of our solar system. The planets discovered so far cannot support

---

2. Adam Hadhazy, "Top 10 Exoplanets: Weird Worlds in a Galaxy Not So Far Away," *Scientific American*, August 11, 2008, http://www.sciam.com/article.cfm?id=top-10-exoplanets (accessed November 17, 2008).

intelligent life as we know it because they are large gas balls, are too close to their stars, are too hot, and are bombarded with too much radiation. That is, those planets were not created in conditions or zones that support the existence of living organisms as we know life. Some people say that the existence of such planets is evidence that God failed in creating planets that could support intelligent life. That is, of course, one possible viewpoint. Another viewpoint that has a better fit with both science and the scriptures is that the existence of planets that cannot support intelligent life is evidence that God does follow natural laws in His creations. Scientists believe that, after the Big Bang, matter collided with other matter and larger particles were created. Those particles collided and formed even larger particles, and so on. Eventually, stars, planets, and moons were formed. There is no reason to believe that all planets would have intelligent life. Only a relatively few planets would form in zones hospitable to life, and even fewer planets would be in zones hospitable to intelligent life.

God's Plan Is a Perfect Plan

God has a grand plan for this earth. In speaking to Moses, He declared that His purpose is the salvation and eternal life of His children: "For behold, this is my work and my glory—to bring to pass the immortality and eternal life of man" (Moses 1:39). So far God has gone through several phases of creation, and He still has one phase of creation to complete. He first created this earth out of spirit matter. Next, he created this earth out of physical matter as the temporary, mortal home of His children. Eventually He will create this earth out of celestial matter as the permanent home of those who inherit the celestial kingdom: "And again, verily I say unto you, the earth abideth the law of a celestial kingdom, for it filleth the measure of its creation, and transgresseth not the law" (D&C 88:25). His plan is not just to create worlds, as if they were decorations of the cosmos. In addition, God is not making these changes to the earth to correct mistakes. He is making these changes to transform the earth so it will further help the progress of His children toward eternal life.

We have seen that in each phase of creation, God followed the natural laws that govern the matter used in the creation. We have seen that God has not and will not fail in his role as creator of the universe. This means that God got it right the first time. He is the Perfect Engineer of the universe. God has created other earths and will continue to create earths, and His design cycle will continue for the eternities.

6
Complementary Aspects of Mormonism and Transhumanism

Brent Allsop, Christopher Bradford, Lincoln Cannon, Andrew West, A. Joseph West, and Carl Youngblood

Abstract

Mormon tradition teaches that, throughout history, God has inspired and endowed humanity with knowledge and power in various dispensations or epochal transitions in the relationship between divinity and humanity. In this, the dispensation of the fulness of times, Mormons believe that God has restored all the knowledge and power of past dispensations and will continue to reveal, at an accelerated pace, new knowledge and tools that will assist in bringing to pass the renewal of the earth and the immortality of humanity. Though the language employed differs, the advancements foretold by Mormon prophets bear striking resemblance to the trends predicted by Ray Kurzweil and other Transhumanists. This presentation summarizes the parallels and complements between Mormonism and Transhumanism, and encourages further discussion on how these concepts can apply to Mormon thought.

Introduction

We must assume our existence as broadly as we in any way can; everything, even the unheard-of, must be possible in it. This is at bottom the only courage that is demanded of us: to have courage for the most strange, the most singular and the most inexplicable that we may encounter.[1]

---

1. Rainier Marie Rilke. *Letters to a Young Poet*, http://www.mythosandlogos.com/Rilke.html (accessed February 2, 2007).

Mormon tradition teaches that, throughout time, God has inspired and endowed humanity with knowledge and power in various dispensations, or epochal transitions in the relationship between divinity and humanity. In ours, the dispensation of the fulness of times, God is restoring all the knowledge and power of past dispensations while continuing to inspire and endow us more rapidly than in the past, to prepare for a greater future.

Joseph Smith proclaimed that knowledge restored and gained in our dispensation would be broad, encompassing matters related to history, astronomy, geology, theology, and more:

> God shall give unto you knowledge by his Holy Spirit, yea, by the unspeakable gift of the Holy Ghost, that has not been revealed since the world was until now;
>
> Which our forefathers have awaited with anxious expectation to be revealed in the last times, which their minds were pointed to by the angels, as held in reserve for the fulness of their glory;
>
> A time to come in which nothing shall be withheld, whether there be one God or many gods, they shall be manifest. All thrones and dominions, principalities and powers, shall be revealed and set forth upon all who have endured valiantly for the gospel of Jesus Christ. And also, if there be bounds set to the heavens or to the seas, or to the dry land, or to the sun, moon, or stars—
>
> All the times of their revolutions, all the appointed days, months, and years, and all the days of their days, months, and years, and all their glories, laws, and set times, shall be revealed in the days of the dispensation of the fulness of times—
>
> According to that which was ordained in the midst of the Council of the Eternal God of all other gods before this world was, that should be reserved unto the finishing and the end thereof, when every man shall enter into his eternal presence and into his immortal rest. (D&C 121:26–32)

Smith taught further that the inspiration and endowments gained in our dispensation would provide a foundation for greater knowledge and power in future dispensations:

> We are the favored people that God has made choice of to bring about the Latter-day glory; it is left for us to see, participate in and help to roll forward the Latter-day glory, "the dispensation of the fulness of times, when God will gather together all things that are in heaven, and all things that are upon the earth," "even in one"...
>
> The blessings of the Most High will rest upon our tabernacles, and our name will be handed down to future ages; our children will rise up and call us blessed; and generations yet unborn will dwell with peculiar delight upon the scenes that we have passed through, the privations we have

overcome in laying the foundation of a work that brought about the glory and blessing which they will realize; a work that God and angels have contemplated with delight for generations past; that fired the souls of the ancient patriarchs and prophets; a work that is destined to bring about the destruction of the powers of darkness, the renovation of the earth, the glory of God, and the salvation of the human family.[2]

The Bible indicates that God's work will proceed more rapidly at the end of our dispensation: "For in those days shall be affliction, such as was not from the beginning of the creation which God created unto this time, neither shall be. And except that the Lord had shortened those days, no flesh should be saved: but for the elect's sake, whom he hath chosen, he hath shortened the days" (Mark 13:19–20). Apostle George Q. Cannon preached on the same theme: "The work of God is being carried on far beyond that which we can see with our natural eyes. The work of the preparation of the earth, and of its inhabitants, is pressing forward with a rapidity that we who are taking part in it do not realize.... He is operating among the nations of the earth. His spirit has gone forth; and it is accomplishing that which He said should be accomplished. And this great work of the last days will be cut short in righteousness."[3]

In addition to these teachings regarding the advancement of God's work in our dispensation, the scriptures and prophetic commentary are replete with references to a day of transfiguration, of humans becoming physically immortal, the resurrection of the dead, the renewal of this world, and the discovery and creation of worlds without end. Yet the prophecies do not describe in detail the causes of their fulfillment and only hint about the human acts that may be required.

Given this vagueness, some Latter-day Saints find it difficult to exercise faith in such ideas and teachings, except in abstract ways. Hence, some conclude that certain ideas are simply beyond our mortal capacity to understand, but such a conclusion raises the question: What is the practical value of a belief in something one cannot understand? How can one possibly have meaningful faith in such an idea? This criticism is especially challenging to Latter-day Saints, who emphasize the importance of faith manifest in works. How can one work toward a future that is understood only vaguely, if at all?

During conversations across several years, the authors of this article observed that, although our faith was active in relation to many tenets of

---

2. Joseph Fielding Smith, comp. and ed., *Teachings of the Prophet Joseph Smith* (Salt Lake City: Deseret News Press, 1938), 231–32.

3. George Q. Cannon, March 18, 1883, *Journal of Discourses* (London and Liverpool: Latter-day Saints Booksellers Depot, 1855–86), 24:56.

Mormonism, it was mostly passive in relation to the more concrete aspects of future salvation: transfiguration and resurrection to physical immortality, the paradisiacal glory of the millennial earth, the organization of new worlds, and so forth. We found our passivity toward these ideas troubling. What is the effect of faith that is not active? Is it even faith? If not, how can we change so that our faith is active in these ideas that we value? Beyond that, we wondered: *Might active faith in these ideas be essential to realizing them?*

As we discussed ways to promote active faith in a Mormon view of the future, we observed that, in the broadest sense, science and technology are among the most obvious manifestations of active faith in the future: fighting disease and illness, improving communications, cleaning and beautifying environments, finding faster and more efficient ways to process genealogical records, and extending life spans. This realization led us to ask how we could promote an emphasis of science and technology within a Mormon view of the future, to bring them into dialogue with the plan of salvation and, more specifically, Mormon ideas about the exaltation of humanity to godhood. We have been encouraged to seek after "anything virtuous, lovely, or of good report" (13th Article of Faith) and to "seek ye out of the best books words of wisdom" (D&C 88:111; D&C 109:7), and we wondered whether there were others both inside and outside the faith that might have been inspired on the subject. Questions like this eventually led us to become acquainted with Transhumanism. In hindsight, this discovery seems to have been inevitable. The parallels and complements between Mormon and Transhumanist views of the future are remarkable, and we felt that many of the ideas and concepts advocated by Transhumanists may fall within the realm of "words of wisdom" that might be worth further discussion.

What Is Transhumanism?

Transhumanism is a young and dynamic ideology that is drawing persons of widely varying perspectives into careful consideration of the future and, in particular, the future evolution of humanity. Their common expectation is that technological advancement will enable humans to transform themselves gradually into persons whose capacities so radically exceed contemporary capacities that the term "human" may no longer adequately describe them. Transhumanists call these future persons "neohumans" or "posthumans" and refer to those in process of becoming them as "Transhumans."

Transhumanists generally trace their origins to humanism. Pre-Socratic Greek philosophers looked beyond traditional gods for scientific explanations of the world. Seventeenth-century astronomer Galileo

Galilei deferred to human observation when conflicting with ecclesiastical authority. The eighteenth-century scientist, the Marquis de Condorcet, claimed that medical science could be used to extend human life.

Although contemporary self-identifying Transhumanists are predominantly secular, religious humanism has made substantial contributions to the emergence of Transhumanism in the broadest sense. Early Christians taught of identifying with Christ and becoming gods. Thirteenth-century Scholastic theologians continued the recurring synthesis of Christianity with popular science. Nineteenth-century theologian Nikolai Fyodorov proclaimed that the common task of humanity should be the resuscitative resurrection of our ancestors. Likewise, as we will present more fully, the Prophet Joseph Smith and subsequent LDS leaders could be counted among religious humanists whose ideas have informed the emergence of Transhumanism.

An identifiable Transhumanist movement began in the last few decades of the twentieth century. In the 1960s, futurist Fereidoun M. Esfandiary, who later changed his name to "FM-2030" (in reference to his hope that he would live to celebrate his 100th birthday which would have come in 2030), began identifying as "Transhumans" persons who behave in a manner conducive to a posthuman future.[4] In the late 1980s, philosopher Max More formalized a Transhumanist doctrine, advocating the "Principles of Extropy" for continuously improving the human condition.[5]

In 1998, a group of influential Transhumanists authored the "Transhumanist Declaration" stating various ethical positions related to the use of and planning for technological advances.[6]

Of the Transhumanist organizations that have formed, the leading organization is Humanity+ (formerly the World Transhumanist Association), founded in 1998 by philosophers Nick Bostrom and David Pearce.[7] Humanity+ has a worldwide membership of approximately 6,000 persons from more than 100 countries. Other contemporary organizations

---

4. Of his name change, Esfandiary wrote: "2030 reflects my conviction that the years around 2030 will be a magical time. In 2030 we will be ageless and everyone will have an excellent chance to live forever. 2030 is a dream and a goal." "FM-2030," *Wikipedia: The Free Encyclopedia*, http://en.wikipedia.org/wiki/FM-2030 (accessed January 15, 2007).

5. For these principles, see Max More, "Prologue: What Is the Purpose of the Principles of Extropy?" 2003, http://www.extropy.org/principles.htm (accessed February 2, 2007).

6. Doug Bailey et al., "Transhumanist Declaration," 1998, *Humanity+*, http://humanityplus.org/learn/Transhumanist-declaration/ (accessed August 16, 2011).

7. Humanity+, http://humanityplus.org (accessed August 16, 2011).

with significant influence among Transhumanists include the Extropy Institute,[8] the Foresight Institute,[9] the Immortality Institute,[10] the Institute for Ethics and Emerging Technologies,[11] and the Singularity Institute for Artificial Intelligence.[12] In 2006, the World Transhumanist Association voted to affiliate with the Mormon Transhumanist Association;[13] and in 2010, Humanity+ renewed affiliation with the Mormon Transhumanist Association after a short discontinuation of all affiliations.

A Transhumanist View of the Future

This section presents a common Transhumanist view of the future, with a focus on accurately portraying the view rather than defending it. Although not all Transhumanists will agree with every aspect of this view, it reflects the ideas of persons who are generally recognized to have significantly influenced Transhumanism. Though we attempt to give an overall sense of major Transhumanist themes, we highlight the aspects that we believe closely parallel Mormon teaching and prophecy. In a later section, we will explicitly identify the parallels.

Transhumanists view human nature as a work-in-progress, a half-baked beginning that we can learn to remold in desirable ways. Current humanity need not be the endpoint of evolution. Transhumanists hope that by responsible use of science, technology, and other rational means, we shall eventually manage to become posthuman, beings with vastly greater capacities than present human beings have.[14]

The Fourth Epoch

The Transhumanist view states that our universe has evolved through epochal paradigms, each building on those that preceded it to produce increasingly complex systems at an accelerating rate. The First Epoch produced

---

8. See Extropy Institute, http://www.extropy.org (accessed February 2, 2007).

9. Foresight Institute, http://www.foresight.org (accessed February 2, 2007).

10. Immortality Institute, http://www.imminst.org (accessed February 2, 2007).

11. Institute for Ethics and Emerging Technologies, http://www.ieet.org (accessed February 2, 2007).

12. Singularity Institute for Artificial Intelligence, http://www.singinst.org (accessed February 2, 2007).

13. The Mormon Transhumanist Association, http://transfigurism.org (accessed August 16, 2011).

14. Nick Bostrom, "Transhumanist Values," http://www.nickbostrom.com/ethics/values.html (accessed August 16, 2011).

simple nonliving systems, such as atoms and stars, through principles we now classify into physics and chemistry. The Second Epoch produced biological systems, as planets condensed, cells organized, and DNA began replicating. The Third Epoch produced intelligent systems, as anatomies adapted to their environment according to natural selection and brains increased in size. We are now in the Fourth Epoch, characterized by technological systems, which have accelerated the rate of evolution to such extent that we can now readily observe the rate of change, as illustrated by advances in computing. Futurist Ray Kurzweil notes: "Combining the endowment of rational and abstract thought with our opposable thumb, our species ushered in the fourth epoch and the next level of indirection: the evolution of human-created technology. . . . Most advanced mammals have added about one cubic inch of brain matter every hundred thousand years, whereas we are roughly doubling the computational capacity of computers every year."[15]

Gordon Moore, one of the founders of Intel Corporation, observed in the 1960s that the ratio of complexity to cost for computer components doubled approximately every two years. Today this observation is known among computer scientists as "Moore's Law." In its original formulation, Moore's Law reflected the rate of advance of the transistor-based computer architecture of the time. More recently, Kurzweil and others recognized that Moore's Law also accounts for the rate of advance of previous computer architectures (electromechanical, relay, and vacuum tube computing) and subsequent computer architectures (integrated circuit computing), and that the rate of advance has been increasing. Furthermore, Kurzweil observed that Moore's Law could be generalized to describe accurately the rate of technological advance broadly, well beyond the field of computing. He called this generalization the "Law of Accelerating Returns,"[16] which holds that technology as a whole is advancing, and will continue to advance, at an exponential rate.

An exponential view of technological change contrasts with the intuitive linear view. Judging from past experience, we commonly expect future advances to occur at a rate similar to that which we have already observed. Such an expectation may approximate actual experience over short periods of exponential advance. However, over long periods, such an expectation results in surprises.

---

15. Ray Kurzweil, *The Singularity Is Near: When Humans Transcend Biology* (New York: Viking, 2005), 16.

16. For an overview, see "Accelerating Change," *Wikipedia: The Free Encyclopedia*, http://en.wikipedia.org/wiki/Accelerating_change (accessed January 15, 2007).

The story of the king and the mathematician illustrates the contrast between an exponential view and the intuitive linear view.[17] As the story goes, a king wanted to reward a mathematician for service to the kingdom. The mathematician asked only for rice, the number of grains to be determined by placing a single grain on the first square of a chessboard and doubling the number of grains on each subsequent square. The king quickly decreed that the mathematician should receive the requested reward. As servants began to place grains on the chessboard, it appeared to the king that the mathematician had requested a small reward. Filling the first row took a mere 255 grains—not even enough to fill a bowl. However, the king's perspective changed dramatically when, before his servants had placed grains on even half the squares, the board could no longer contain the accumulated grains (16,777,215 grains on the first three rows). Soon, the king realized he would be unable to fulfill his decree (18,446,744,073,709,551,615 grains on the whole board), even if he were to give his entire kingdom to the mathematician. Like the king, most of us have difficulty anticipating the full implications of exponential growth.

The Technological Singularity

Based on an exponential view, Transhumanists anticipate that increasingly rapid technological evolution will culminate in changes so dramatic that, given current limitations, we could not predict or direct them. However, the exponential view also suggests that we may adapt, enhancing our minds and bodies, and even our world, to such degree that we maintain an ability to predict and direct technological change. Transhumanists call this future period "the Singularity." Kurzweil writes: "What, then, is the Singularity? It's a future period during which the pace of technological change will be so rapid, its impact so deep, that human life will be irreversibly transformed. Although neither utopian nor dystopian, this epoch will transform the concepts that we rely on to give meaning to our lives, from our business models to the cycle of human life, including death itself."[18]

Mathematician Vernor Vinge associates the Singularity with the advent of superhuman intelligence: computers capable of recursively producing yet more intelligent computers at ever faster rates, without human intervention. Writing in 1993, Vinge predicted that the Singularity will

---

17. The many variations of this story may have originated in Hindu mythology. For more information, see "Ambalappuzha Sri Krishna Temple," http://en.wikipedia.org/wiki/Ambalappuzha_Sri_Krishna_Temple (accessed February 2, 2007).

18. Kurzweil, *The Singularity Is Near*, 7.

occur between 2005 and 2030.[19] In contrast to Vinge, Kurzweil associates the Singularity with a prevalence of superhuman intelligence, which he predicts will occur around 2045, when, extrapolating from present trends, $1,000 will buy computing power equivalent to that of all living human brains combined.[20]

Transhumanists recognize that the advent of the Singularity is associated with serious, even existential, risks that should be earnestly reviewed and mitigated. Indeed, the need to increase awareness of and open a dialogue about these risks has been among the primary motivators for the formation of Transhumanist organizations. In particular, an interest in adding a spiritual dimension to this dialogue motivated the formation of the Mormon Transhumanist Association in 2006. The MTA Constitution contains the "Mormon Transhumanist Affirmation," which states: "We feel a duty to use science and technology according to wisdom and inspiration, to identify and prepare for risks and responsibilities associated with future advances, and to persuade others to do likewise."[21]

Transhumans

"Transhuman" is the name Transhumanists give to a person who is evolving from a human to a neohuman state. Although the Singularity will accelerate this evolution, it has already begun. We are already Transhumans to the extent that we have modified ourselves through technology. The extent to which we typically modify ourselves through technology is increasing at an exponential rate. However, as in the story of the king and the mathematician, most of us simply have not yet realized how profoundly, and eventually rapidly, technology will change us over time. Looking forward, Kurzweil identifies three areas in which overlapping revolutions are likely to occur as we approach the Singularity: genetics, nanotech, and robotics.[22]

The genetics revolution is likely to occur within the next decade. Exponential growth in computing power has made it possible to sequence DNA strands rapidly and facilitate the decoding of complex protein-fold-

---

19. Vernor Vinge, "What Is the Singularity?" 1993, http://mindstalk.net/vinge/vinge-sing.html (accessed August 16, 2011).

20. Ray Kurzweil, "Law of Accelerating Returns," 2001, *KurzweilAI*, http://www.kurzweilai.net/the-law-of-accelerating-returns (accessed August 16, 2011). For an overview, see "Technological Singularity," *Wikipedia: The Free Encyclopedia*, http://en.wikipedia.org/wiki/Technological_singularity (accessed January 15, 2007).

21. Lincoln Cannon et al., "Mormon Transhumanist Affirmation," 2006, *Mormon Transhumanist Association*, http://transfigurism.org/pages/about/mormon-Transhumanist-affirmation/ (accessed August 16, 2011).

22. Kurzweil, "Law of Accelerating Returns."

ing sequences. A recent monumental achievement, and another example of the surprising nature of exponential growth, is the Human Genome Project. When the project began in 1990, critics pointed out that it would take thousands of years to finish, given the speed at which it began; but only fifteen years later, it was completed. The genetics revolution would enable us to treat defects in and make enhancements to our biological state, with treatments in the form of new drugs or gene therapies.

Following closely on the heels of the genetics revolution, the nanotech revolution is likely to begin in the 2020s. Nanotechnology will extend human abilities through miniaturization, enabling us to manipulate materials at an atomic scale. In his book, *Engines of Creation*, Eric Drexler, a specialist in molecular nanotechnology, outlined in some detail a universal molecular assembler that may be realized during this time.[23] Drexler envisions an atomic-scale builder directed by a computer that can create molecular structures, including copies of itself to assist in constructing complex structures in short periods of time. Although still theoretical, the essential physical properties of a molecular assembler, such as being able to manipulate individual atoms, have been demonstrated in the laboratory; and contemporary engineers are working, with increasing success, on implementing various components of the assembler as proofs-of-concept.[24] Such advances in miniaturization may shift genetic defect and enhancement treatments from drug to nanotech solutions.

The third revolution, in robotics, is likely to occur in the 2030s. By this time, nonbiological computing power should readily exceed the computing power of non-enhanced human brains. As understanding of and control over biology increases, humans would also learn to integrate biological and information technology. Robotics would take on increasingly sophisticated forms that may be visually and tactilely indistinguishable from biological bodies. Robotic interfaces would make it possible for humans to transfer their experiences and knowledge to one another or to nonbiological substrates to enable indefinite extension of life. The emergence of strong artificial intelligence in nonbiological or enhanced biological form would lead to the advent of the Singularity.

Even today, in advance of the revolutions outlined above, humans are beginning to enhance their bodies in ways that were previously impossible. For example, LASIK eye surgery is now commonplace and can improve patients' eyesight beyond native abilities. Pacemakers are widely used to extend human lives in ways that biology alone cannot. Prosthetics and

---

23. Eric Drexler, *Engines of Creation: The Coming Era of Nanotechnology* (New York: Bantam/Doubleday. 1986).

24. Kurzweil, *The Singularity Is Near*, 239.

cosmetic surgery are other examples of enhancements and reconstructions that, although formerly beyond our capabilities, have become conventional.

Worlds within Worlds

Although, by definition, the Singularity will change our nature and that of our world in currently unpredictable ways, we can speculate regarding possible post-Singularity futures, assisted to some extent by the application of logic to extrapolations from current trends.

For example, a common task to which computers are applied today is that of simulation. Flight and automobile simulators have been available both to the military and for entertainment for many years. Financial simulators have become important for investors, as medical simulators have improved our ability to train surgeons. Many persons enjoy playing games such as SimCity that simulate urban planning. Entire worlds are simulated, for both scientific and entertainment purposes, such as the popular virtual world named Second Life, in which persons buy and sell real estate, hold meetings, even dance, and generally engage in a virtual life through the proxy of their avatars—virtual representations of themselves.

Over time, the quality of simulations has greatly improved. Users of early flight simulators saw only bumpy black and white outlines of abstract geometric features representing terrain above an equally coarse rendition of a cockpit. Today, full-color, three-dimensional geographies and other aircraft can be wrapped around a user inside a machine that moves to provide for realistic physical sensations.

As the computing power available to us continues to advance exponentially, Transhumanists tell us that it seems reasonable to suppose that one of the things we might do is to run increasingly detailed simulations of our world or worlds like it. As the level of detail increases and the user interface improves, it would become ever more difficult to discern any difference between our world and the simulated worlds, to the point that, for all practical purposes, "simulation" or "virtual" would no longer accurately describe those worlds or the apparently conscious persons in them.

In his paper entitled "Are You Living in a Computer Simulation?," philosopher Nick Bostrom identifies and expounds on some interesting logical ramifications associated with the possibility of running simulations detailed enough to include persons like us. To paraphrase, he argues that at least one of the following is true:

1. Our civilization will never achieve the computing power required to run detailed world simulations;
2. Civilizations that achieve such computing power never run a significant number of detailed world simulations; or

3. We almost certainly live in a detailed world simulation ourselves.[25]

In other words, if ever we manage to run a world simulation that is detailed enough to be indistinguishable from our own, we should assume it is extremely unlikely that ours is the only or the first civilization to do so. It would then follow that there is a high probability that both (1) we are living in such a world ourselves, and (2) the world running our world is itself run by another, and so forth in indefinite regression. This is called the Simulation Argument.

For some, the first thing that comes to mind when they read of the Simulation Argument is *The Matrix*, a popular film that portrays a world in which humans are imprisoned in a simulation and used as an energy source for the machines running the simulation. However, this dystopian portrayal is not necessary. To the contrary, it seems that a more balanced portrayal would better account for the ramifications of worlds within worlds, as described by Bostrom:

> For example, if nobody can be sure that they are at the basement-level, then everybody would have to consider the possibility that their actions will be rewarded or punished, based perhaps on moral criteria, by their simulators. An afterlife would be a real possibility. Because of this fundamental uncertainty, even the basement civilization may have a reason to behave ethically. The fact that it has such a reason for moral behavior would of course add to everybody else's reason for behaving morally, and so on, in truly virtuous circle. One might get a kind of universal ethical imperative, which it would be in everybody's self-interest to obey, as it were "from nowhere."[26]

Neohumans

Transhumanists use the term "neohuman" or "posthuman" to refer to a person who has advanced to the point that, according to present standards, one may no longer consider or recognize the person to be human. Although descriptions of this state differ and accommodate a wide variety of perspectives, most Transhumanists see some form of radically enhanced personhood as their ultimate objective.[27]

---

25. Nick Bostrom, "Are You Living in a Computer Simulation?" 2002, http://www.simulation-argument.com/simulation.html (accessed January 15, 2007).
26. Ibid.
27. Max More et al., "Transhumanist FAQ: What Is a Posthuman?", *Extropy Institute*, http://www.extropy.org/faq.htm (accessed August 16, 2011).

This should not imply that becoming neohuman is a final destination. Neohumans would continue to evolve. The term is used simply to distinguish between humanity's current state and its future possibilities, as well as they can be envisioned at present. It is also inevitable that visions of a neohuman future will evolve as time goes on. As imagined now, possible neohuman traits, all involving technological enhancements to current human capacities, include:

Highly advanced intellectual capabilities, greater than ours in magnitude as ours are greater than those of other animals

- Physical bodies that are immune to disease and aging
- The ability to communicate complex thoughts and emotions instantaneously without visual aids or speech
- Expanded sensory inputs that enable higher awareness of even distant environs
- Superhuman strength and agility
- Perfect control of individual desires, moods, or mental states
- Increased capacity to experience joy, love, pleasure, and other emotions.

Not all perspectives associate posthumans with conventional bodies, biological or otherwise. Some Transhumanists desire to abandon bodies and "upload" their identities into some type of network or computer system where they would be free from the perceived demands and constraints of bodily form.

Neohumans, in whatever form, may interact, directly or indirectly, with humans as neohuman "gods."[28] Their interactions may include restoring dead humans to life, as speculated by mathematician Frank Tipler, or simulating human worlds.[29] Nick Bostrom writes:

> Although all the elements of such a system can be naturalistic, even physical, it is possible to draw some loose analogies with religious conceptions of the world. In some ways, the posthumans running a simulation are like gods in relation to the people inhabiting the simulation: the posthumans created the world we see; they are of superior intelligence; they are "omnipotent" in the sense that they can interfere in the workings of our world even in ways that violate its physical laws; and they are "omniscient" in the sense that they can monitor everything that happens.[30]

---

28. For an overview, see "Posthuman God," *Wikipedia: The Free Encyclopedia*, http://en.wikipedia.org/wiki/Posthuman_God (accessed February 2, 2007).

29. Frank Tipler, *Physics of Immortality: Modern Cosmology, God, and the Resurrection of the Dead* (New York: Doubleday, 1994), 219.

30. Bostrom, "Are You Living in a Computer Simulation?"

A Mormon View of the Future

In this section, we provide a brief overview of some significant Mormon notions about future events, especially those that touch on human flourishing and our potential godhood. As with the previous section, our goal is to describe rather than defend these teachings, and we will focus primarily on those for which we sense there are strong Transhumanist parallels. In the final section, we'll explicitly identify the parallels.

The Dispensation of the Fulness of Times

As described at the beginning of this article, the time in which we now live is the dispensation of the fulness of times, when God is bringing together "a whole and complete and perfect union" in which a "welding together of dispensations, and keys, and powers, and glories should take place," and in which "those things which never have been revealed from the foundation of the world . . . shall be revealed unto babes and sucklings" (D&C 128:18). According to Joseph Smith, this dispensation will see "a work that is destined to bring about the destruction of the powers of darkness, the renovation of the earth, the glory of God, and the salvation of the human family."[31] The dispensation of the fulness of times is also characterized by the speed at which God's work progresses. As George Q. Cannon stated, "The work of the preparation of the earth, and of its inhabitants, is pressing forward with a rapidity that we who are taking part in it do not realize. . . . [T]his great work of the last days will be cut short in righteousness."[32]

Transfiguration, the Millennium, and Immortality

Mormon tradition teaches of an imminent "day of transfiguration," expanding across a millennial period of time, when mortals are transfigured and resurrected to immortality (D&C 63:20–21). The Millennium is an imminent and widely unexpected future period, during which a progressive transfiguration and resurrection to immortality will occur as our knowledge and power continue to increase. The advent of the Millennium is associated with disruptive changes in world conditions, culminating in the return of Christ. Despite its imminence, many will not expect the Millennium to occur when it does, but a few will recognize the signs of its coming.

The Doctrine and Covenants describes conditions during the Millennium, including some aspects of transfiguration, as follows:

---

31. Joseph Fielding Smith, *Teachings of the Prophet Joseph Smith*, 232.
32. George Q. Cannon, March 18, 1883, *Journal of Discourses*, 24:61.

And in that day the enmity of man, and the enmity of beasts, yea, the enmity of all flesh, shall cease from before my face.

And in that day whatsoever any man shall ask, it shall be given unto him.

And in that day Satan shall not have power to tempt any man.

And there shall be no sorrow because there is no death.

In that day an infant shall not die until he is old; and his life shall be as the age of a tree;

And when he dies he shall not sleep, that is to say in the earth, but shall be changed in the twinkling of an eye, and shall be caught up, and his rest shall be glorious.

Yea, verily I say unto you, in that day when the Lord shall come, he shall reveal all things—

Things which have passed, and hidden things which no man knew, things of the earth, by which it was made, and the purpose and the end thereof—

Things most precious, things that are above, and things that are beneath, things that are in the earth, and upon the earth, and in heaven. (D&C 101:26–34)

Joseph Smith frequently expressed the imminence of the Millennium and encouraged the Saints to prepare for it: "When I contemplate the rapidity with which the great and glorious day of the coming of the Son of Man advances, when He shall come to receive His Saints unto Himself, where they shall dwell in His presence, and be crowned with glory and immortality . . . I cry out in my heart, What manner of persons ought we to be in all holy conversation and godliness!"[33]

Brigham Young suggested that many of us may not even know when the Millennium has already begun: "Will the Saints arise from the dead? Yes. Who will know it? But a few. When the resurrection commences, I say but few will know it. . . . Will the Saints rise from the dead before the world is converted? Yes. . . . When the Millennium is ushered in, no man or woman will know anything about it, only by the power of God. He will rule and reign, and His glory shall be in Zion, and the wicked will not know it is the hand of our God."[34]

Prophets have envisioned that, during the Millennium, we and other forms of life will be immortal. While immortality might be defined as achieving a perfect physical state, it is an ideal with diverse manifestations. Joseph Smith taught that being raised to an immortal state may involve moving from lesser to greater manifestations of immortality and that such

---

33. Joseph Fielding Smith, *Teachings of the Prophet Joseph Smith*, 29.

34. Elden J. Watson, ed. *Brigham Young Addresses*, 6 vols. (Salt Lake City: Elden J. Watson, 1979–84), 2:127.

progressions may involve ceremonial ordinances: "Now the doctrine of translation is a power which belongs to this Priesthood. There are many things which belong to the powers of the Priesthood and the keys thereof, that have been kept hid from before the foundation of the world; they are hid from the wise and prudent to be revealed in the last times."[35]

Brigham Young speculated: "I have friends on the earth, for God would raise them up for me to do my work. That is not all; by and by the Lord will say to the sleeping dust, awake and come forth out of your graves. I am on hand; the Lord wakes me up or sends somebody to do it that possesses the keys of the resurrection. My dust is waked up; my spirit is re-united to it, and it is made a celestial body filled with immortality and eternal life."[36]

Worlds without End

Mormon tradition teaches that the eternities consist of innumerable heavens of types and degrees toward which our world may advance. These heavens are inhabited by a plurality of gods whom we may join as we emulate and become as God. Prophets proclaim that innumerable worlds of diverse types and varying degrees have been and will be created. Further, they envision that these worlds advance through processes such as transfiguration and resurrection, becoming heavens according to the desire and work of their inhabitants and preparing their inhabitants for yet greater heavens. Brigham Young taught: "You may now be inclined to say, 'We wish to hear the mysteries of the kingdoms of the Gods who have existed from eternity, and of all the kingdoms in which they will dwell; we desire to have these things portrayed to our understandings.' Allow me to inform you that you are in the midst of it all now, that you are in just as good a kingdom as you will ever attain to, from now to all eternity, unless you make it yourselves by the grace of God, by the will of God, which is a code of laws perfectly calculated to govern and control eternal matter."[37]

The work of creating innumerable worlds and heavens may have neither beginning nor end. This idea is expressed in the Mormon hymn, "If You Could Hie to Kolob."[38] Moreover, there may be no end to the advance of heavens, as one heavenly degree prepares its inhabitants for yet another that is greater. A revelation given through Joseph Smith used our world

---

35. Joseph Fielding Smith, Teachings of the Prophet Joseph Smith, 170.
36. Watson, *Brigham Young Addresses*, 2:100.
37. Brigham Young, June 15, 1856, *Journal of Discourses*, 3:336.
38. W. W. Phelps, "If You Could Hie to Kolob," *Hymns of the Church of Jesus Christ of Latter-day Saints* (Salt Lake City: Church of Jesus Christ of Latter-day Saints, 1985), no. 284.

as an example, indicating that, even as it serves as a celestial heaven, its inhabitants would continue to learn of yet greater heavens:

> This earth, in its sanctified and immortal state, will be made like unto crystal and will be a Urim and Thummim to the inhabitants who dwell thereon, whereby all things pertaining to an inferior kingdom, or all kingdoms of a lower order, will be manifest to those who dwell on it; and this earth will be Christ's.
>
> Then the white stone mentioned in Revelation 2:17, will become a Urim and Thummim to each individual who receives one, whereby things pertaining to a higher order of kingdoms will be made known;
>
> And a white stone is given to each of those who come into the celestial kingdom. (D&C 130:9–11)

Gods

Latter-day prophets have proclaimed that there is a plurality of gods, each of which became so by emulating God, and that becoming gods ourselves is the ultimate destiny of humanity as children of God. These prophets envision that humans will join in the creation of worlds and heavens and the development of other gods, expanding our influence throughout eternity and engaging in yet greater works. Joseph Smith stated: "Here, then, is eternal life—to know the only wise and true God; and you have got to learn how to be Gods yourselves, and to be kings and priests to God, the same as all Gods have done before you—namely, by going from one small degree to another, and from a small capacity to a great one—from grace to grace, from exaltation to exaltation, until you attain to the resurrection of the dead, and are able to dwell in everlasting burnings and to sit in glory, as do those who sit enthroned in everlasting power."[39]

As Gods, we would join in the creation of worlds and heavens:

> We believe there are many, very many, who have entered into power, glory, might, and dominion, and are gathering around them thrones, and have power to organize elements, and make worlds, and bring into existence intelligent beings in all their variety, who, if they are faithful and obedient to their calling and creation, will in their turn be exalted in [the] eternal kingdoms of the Gods.[40]
>
> These children . . . through their faithfulness to the gospel, will progress and develop in knowledge, intelligence and power, in future eternities,

---

39. Joseph Fielding Smith, *Teachings of the Prophet Joseph Smith*, 346–47.

40. Brigham Young, Unpublished general conference address, October 8, 1854, http://www.xmission.com/~country/by/ 100854_2.htm (accessed February 28, 2007).

until they shall be able to go out into space where there is unorganized matter and call together the necessary elements, and through their knowledge of and control over the laws and powers of nature, to organize matter into worlds on which their posterity may dwell, and over which they shall rule as gods.[41]

Transhumanist Parallels with the Mormon View

In this final section, we identify some of the parallels between Transhumanist and Mormon views. We first note parallels—places where we see the sensibilities of the two groups matching very closely. We then present complements—spots within the two frameworks where we see that one might benefit from the insights of the other.

The Transhumanist and Mormon views parallel each other generally as follows:

- The present is a time of rapid progress in knowledge.
- A fundamental change in our nature and that of our world is imminent.
- We and our world can and will dramatically transcend our current limitations.

More specific parallels can be seen in the following areas:

- The LDS notion of the dispensation of the fulness of times parallels the Transhumanist idea of the "Fourth Epoch."
- LDS teachings about transfiguration, the Millennium, and immortality parallel Transhumanist notions of the Singularity and Transhumans.
- LDS teachings about worlds and heavens without end and the human potential for godhood parallel Transhumanist understandings of simulations and posthumans.

The Dispensation of the Fulness of Times and the Fourth Epoch

LDS teachings about the dispensation of the fulness of times parallel Transhumanist ideas regarding the Fourth Epoch in at least the following ways:

---

41. Lorenzo Snow, quoted in Leroi Snow, "Devotion to Divine Inspiration," *Improvement Era*, June 1919, 658–59.

1. Present knowledge and power are the culmination of multiple past periods. In the dispensation of the fulness of times, we benefit from the restoration of the knowledge and power of previous dispensations. Likewise, in the Fourth Epoch, the increasingly complex systems that evolved during previous epochs enable present technological evolution.
2. Acquisition of knowledge and power is accelerating. In the dispensation of the fulness of times, God is shortening the days and increasing the rapidity of the work. Similarly, in the Fourth Epoch, technological advances are recursively leveraging previous advances to progress exponentially.
3. Future progress depends on knowledge and power acquired today. In the dispensation of the fulness of times, we are establishing the foundation for yet greater dispensations to come. Analogously, in the Fourth Epoch, we are developing technologies on which evolutionary change in future epochs will build.

Transfiguration, the Millennium, Immortality, and the Singularity and Transhumans

Mormon teachings about transfiguration, the Millennium, and immortality parallel Transhumanist ideas regarding the Singularity and Transhumans in at least the following ways:

1. A period of dramatic and unexpected change is imminent. Mormon theology teaches that, though some ridicule and few have recognized its signs, the Millennium approaches, and we should prepare ourselves for the day of transfiguration and its attending changes. Likewise, although critics scoff and despite the intuitive linear view of change, Transhumanists believe the Singularity is near and that we should review and mitigate the associated risks.
2. Minds and bodies may be changed in diverse ways. Mormon doctrine speaks of how in the twinkling of an eye, we may be transfigured or resurrected to bodies of varying types and degrees of glory (D&C 88:27–32). Similarly, Transhumanists recognize that continued advancement in information technologies may enable genetics, nanotechnology, and robotics to enhance our minds and bodies.
3. Anatomical changes may extend lives indefinitely. Mormons teach that from one transfiguration to another, exchanging blood for spirit, we may renew our bodies and attain immortality (D&C 84:33). Analogously, as Transhumans, we may extend or exchange

our biological substrate with a different substrate to ensure the persistence of our identity.
4. Our work may contribute to these changes. Mormon authorities have suggested that transfiguration and resurrection may be ordinances for us to perform for each other. Comparatively, Transhumanists believe our science may provide technology that enables us to enhance ourselves and attain indefinite longevity.

Worlds without End and Worlds within Worlds

Mormon teachings related to worlds and heavens without end and the human potential for Godhood parallel Transhumanist ideas related to simulations and posthumans who act as Gods in at least the following ways:

1. Our world may be among infinite and diverse worlds. According to LDS teachings, there may be telestial, terrestrial, and celestial worlds without end, and heavens of yet higher orders, each reflecting the work and desire of its inhabitants. Likewise, there exists a Transhumanist notion that, in addition to the worlds of our space and time, there may be an indefinite regression of simulations, each with inhabitants adapted to varying physical laws.
2. We may one day utterly transcend our current knowledge and power. According to Joseph Smith and other prophets, as the children of God, we may learn to become like God, as we emulate and join in the plurality of gods. Similarly, Transhumanists believe we may one day be able to merge with our technology to become neohuman, with minds and bodies enhanced in ways far beyond what is currently imaginable.
3. Others may have produced us, and we may yet produce others. According to Mormon theology, God created our world and its inhabitants, and we may one day join in the creation of yet other worlds. Analogously, in Transhumanist speculation, neohumans in another world may very well be simulating our world, and we may eventually simulate yet other worlds. We are developing technologies on which evolutionary change in future epochs will build.
4. There may be no end to progress. The Mormon doctrine of eternal progression declares that God may progress forever, creating worlds without end, exalting others to immortality and eternal life, and expanding throughout eternity. Comparatively, Transhumanists posit

that neohumans may advance forever, sending their intelligence through time and space.

Transhumanist Complements to the Mormon View

The Transhumanist view may complement Mormon faith in at least three areas:

1. It provides a rational basis for certain LDS beliefs.
2. It promotes Latter-day Saints' exercising a more active faith in Mormon concepts about the future.
3. It encourages Latter-day Saints to have more optimistic expectations for the near future.

Superstitious versus Reasonable Hope

One of the criticisms of religion in today's postmodern world is that religious belief is superstitious. Critics often claim that faith in ideas such as immortality and theosis (human potential for godhood) have no basis in reality. Transhumanist ideology has the potential to answer these criticisms by providing believing Mormons with a relatively reasoned and detailed vision of possible future events. For Mormons willing to engage in discussion regarding Transhumanism topics, the future events toward which they look are based not only in esoteric teachings and prophecies but also in the predictions of rational and scientifically committed persons looking at the future. Many of the Transhumanist concepts can complement the Mormon view by adding rational grounds for belief.

Some Mormons may feel uncomfortable with the idea that our present knowledge is incomplete and that valuable extensions of our knowledge may come from secular sources, but such feelings seem to run contrary to established doctrine. For example, although Mormon scriptures proclaim the full gospel of Christ, they do not claim to contain all truth. One of the fundamental tenets of Mormonism, as expressed in the Ninth Article of Faith, is that God "will yet reveal many great and important things pertaining to the kingdom of heaven." Moreover, God does not exclude non-Mormons from inspiration. Hugh B. Brown, a member of the First Presidency, has described science as among the means of revelation: "We should all be interested in academic research. We must go out on the research front and continue to explore the vast unknown. We should be in the forefront of learning in all fields, for revelation does not come only through the prophet of God nor only directly from heaven in visions or dreams. Revelation may come in the laboratory, out of the test tube, out of the thinking mind and the inquiring soul, out of search and research and prayer and inspiration."[42]

We know that "there is a law, irrevocably decreed in heaven before the foundations of this world, upon which all blessings are predicated—and when we obtain any blessing from God, it is by obedience to that law upon which it is predicated" (D&C 130:20–21). Nowhere does this promise say that the blessing can come only to members of the Church; rather, the blessing is available to anyone who obeys the law. Joseph Fielding Smith explained, "The inspiration of the Lord has gone out and takes hold of the minds of men, though they know it not, and they are directed by the Lord. In this manner he brings them into his service that his purposes and his righteousness, in due time, may be supreme on the earth."[43]

Idle versus Working Faith

As discussed in the introduction, Mormonism contains many teachings about the future that are so vague that they are difficult to exercise faith in, except in very abstract ways. Critics rightly ask about the value of believing in something we cannot begin to understand. And given Mormonism's pragmatic view of the world and emphasis on the manifestation of faith through works, this criticism is especially challenging for Latter-day Saints.

Mormons engaging with the Spirit can take Transhumanist notions seriously as "words of wisdom" and can appeal to more than unexplainable or incomprehensible mysteries. They may appeal to rationality and science. Their arguments then become more understandable, meaningful, and practically applicable.

Many Transhumanism concepts can provide Mormons with something tangible toward which to work. In addition to wondering about the means by which God will bring about the resurrection, Mormons can work faithfully toward the promotion of related scientific research. In addition to speculating about scriptural mysteries, Mormons can apply the scriptures to their lives in more pragmatic ways by investing some of their time and resources in the ethical advancement of technology. In addition to wondering how God will provide a way for us to overcome physical ail-

---

42. Hugh B. Brown, quoted in Edwin B. Brown, ed., *The Memoirs of Hugh B Brown: An Abundant Life* (New York: Signature Books, 1988), 138.

43. Joseph Fielding Smith, *Conference Report*, October 1926, 117, as quoted in Boyd K. Packer and Russell M. Nelson, "Computerized Scriptures Now Available," *Ensign*, April 1988, 73.

ments and limitations, Mormons can promote the rights of individuals to cure and enhance themselves as the technology becomes available.

A More Optimistic View of the Immediate Future

Some Latter-day Saints believe that additional wars and disasters must occur before the return of Christ and the advent of the Millennium. Critics argue that faith in such interpretations of biblical prophecy could be self-fulfilling and result in needless suffering and death. Influenced by a Transhumanist perspective, Mormons may open themselves to more optimistic views of the near future. Given cause to believe that the prophetic promises of the Millennium could be realized without further war and destruction, Mormons are more likely to seek to bring about such prophecies through constructive efforts and are more likely to choose to view prophecies of destruction as warnings rather than inevitabilities. Hence, the Transhumanist view complements the Mormon view by encouraging an optimistic expectation for the near future of humanity.

Mormon Complements to the Transhumanist View

Mormonism may complement Transhumanism in at least three ways:

1. Mormon teachings about the human potential for godhood provide resources for adding love and a moral coloring to Transhumanist views of what it means to be neohuman.
2. Mormonism, along with other religious traditions, can encourage Transhumanists to adopt a more respectful and accurate view of certain traditional values and the important role they play in human lives.
3. The Mormon doctrine of nearly universal salvation can provide an important reminder in the work and thinking done in Transhumanist circles that technologies and opportunities should be available to all.

Brazen versus Sanctified Desire

Some religious critics charge that Transhumanists are "playing God" and that the desire to change the human condition is blasphemous. These critics claim that, while technology improves efficiencies, it does not make us holier. Instead, it feeds our desire for power. According to these critics, this desire is evil; and it is immoral to aspire to the kinds of power attributed to neohumans. They ask: To what end do we pursue these improvements over past states of being? Mormonism answers: godhood. The desire to work together toward godhood is the highest and most righteous desire and the fullest manifestation of love. Hence, the Mormon view complements the Transhumanist view by providing a spiritual justification for the desire to better the human condition.

Disdainful versus Respectful Attitude

There are detrimental consequences to acting with a negative or dismissive attitude toward established cultures, religions, and values. When the advocates of social or philosophical movements do not respect the traditions of persons they are trying to persuade, those advocates see decreased success.

In common with advocates of other nascent movements, some Transhumanists are negative or dismissive toward tradition. This attitude was demonstrated early in the Transhumanist movement when FM-2030 advocated that Transhumanists reject religious belief and traditional family values.[44]

More recently, the World Transhumanist Association acknowledged interest in finding better ways to communicate with and understand religious persons.[45] To that end, Transhumanists should not ignore others' religious lives but rather should take a closer look at core values at the heart of the various world religions. Many of these religious values can benefit Transhumanists as they work on the cutting edge of technological innovation, just as Transhumanists might be able to teach others how to complement their religious lives in practically beneficial ways.

Mormonism, with its Judeo-Christian roots, has much in common with established cultures, despite differences in various beliefs. Mormonism emphasizes the traditional values of charity and unity, the avoidance of unnecessary contention, and the building up of all persons, regardless of their beliefs. These and many other gospel teachings belong at the Transhumanist discussion table to impact the way future technological advancement unfolds.

---

44. For an overview, see "Transhuman," *Wikipedia: The Free Encyclopedia*, http://en.wikipedia.org/wiki/Transhuman (accessed January 15, 2007).

45. "People of Faith," *World Transhumanist Association*, http://www.Transhumanism.org/index.php/WTA/communities/religious/ (accessed January 15, 2007).

Elitist versus Universal Access

Critics of Transhumanism argue that emerging technologies will be disproportionately available to those with greater financial resources.[46] An elite class of neohumans may arise to the exclusion of poorer individuals.

Central to Mormon ideology is the assertion that all persons are invited through the atonement of Christ to partake in salvation and that nearly all will, whether or not they are Mormon. Mormonism even goes so far as to advocate trust that all persons will find happiness in a universal resurrection to immortality in heavens that vary according to their desires—the exceptions being only those who desire no part in any form of salvation (D&C 88:27–33).

Over the years, this faith has inspired large-scale egalitarian projects. Examples include worldwide humanitarian and local service projects, perpetual emigrating and education funds, efficient work and welfare programs, inexpensive cost-equalizing missionary organizations, and gargantuan cross-cultural genealogical databases. Of course, there have been egalitarian shortcomings, too, such as failed implementations of the united order, controversial stances on race relations, and interpretations of doctrine that promote exclusion rather than inclusion. Mormons, too, can still benefit from internalizing and acting on our own teachings.

Hence, the Mormon view complements the Transhumanist view by explicitly incorporating a moral imperative to advocate for universal access to whatever understanding of salvation and human flourishing emerges in the future.

Conclusion

We recognize that the Transhumanist ideas presented in this article may sound farfetched to persons who do not closely monitor what is occurring in technological and scientific circles. Still, we believe that many recognize that we, as a species, have reached a critical moment in human history. Through technological advancement in recent centuries, humans now navigate depths of the sea that sunlight does not reach and rocket through the sky at speeds greater than that of sound. For more than a half century now, humans have had the technological power to destroy themselves and a significant portion of the planet. Within just the past quarter century, we've seen the emergence of the personal computer, which now provides more power in a handheld device than what once filled entire

---

46. For an overview of criticisms of Transhumanism, see "Transhumanism," *Wikipedia: The Free Encyclopedia,* http://en.wikipedia.org/wiki/Transhumanism (accessed August 16, 2011).

warehouses and has even become a critical tool in the Church's fourfold mission by enabling the management of unimaginably complex genealogical records. Humans have visited the moon, space tourists are currently orbiting the Earth, and robots are scouting Mars. The human genome has been entirely sequenced. Worldwide data, text, audio, and video communications via the internet are inexpensive and commonplace. We regularly read in the news of advances toward cures for cancer. This is today!

Whether tomorrow is wonderful or horrible may depend on the extent to which persons with good minds and loving hearts become actively involved in shaping the future. God does not prevent us from misusing the power with which we have been endowed. Although the scriptures teach of a universal resurrection, they do not teach that it will be completed without any work on our part. It may be that we can avoid the prophesied horrors of the last days just as Nineveh avoided the unqualified prophecy of its destruction (Jonah 3). It may be that the transfiguration and resurrection to immortality will happen no faster than we do the work, as with the preaching of the gospel to all persons. More generally, it may be that charitable and working faith, leveraging all the inspiration and endowments we have received, is essential to the realization of prophetic visions of the future.

With such risks and opportunities at hand, what shall we do? Where do wisdom and inspiration guide us? As Captain Moroni asked in the Book of Mormon: "Do ye suppose that the Lord will still deliver us, while we sit upon our thrones and do not make use of the means which the Lord has provided for us?" (Alma 60:21). In response to such questions, we appeal to the words of Brigham Young: "You are in just as good a kingdom as you will ever attain to, from now to all eternity, unless you make it yourselves by the grace of God, by the will of God, which is a code of laws perfectly calculated to govern and control eternal matter. If you and I do not by this means make that better kingdom which we anticipate, we shall never enjoy it. We can only enjoy the kingdom we have labored to make."[47]

We recommend a prayerful study and discussion of Transhumanist concepts, firmly believing that they will prove of interest to LDS readers. Many Transhumanist ideas are truly among the "words of wisdom" and "the best books" and can add a truly insightful dimension to our understanding of the gospel.

---

47. Brigham Young, June 15, 1856, *Journal of Discourses*, 3:336.

7
Quantified Morality

A. Scott Howe

Abstract

Morality is defined in quantitative terms as a discussion on human potential: Moral choices increase potential, and immoral choices limit it. A "potentiality test" is presented that allows value comparisons of moral choices to be made based on the depth of nodes in a decision tree, where a proliferation of future possibilities increases the freedom of the individual. In a more rigorous approach, morality is discussed from an engineering perspective, where transgression increases entropy in the environment, but wise choices build potential and order into the environment that allows an individual to thrive. Based on an understanding of entropy, a possible mathematical model for morality is discussed.

The ultimate product of a process that proliferates future possibilities is an individual who is in complete control of all circumstance in the environment or, in other words, an omnipotent being perfected by obedience to natural laws as described in Latter-day Saint theology.

Introduction

We observe that it is possible to have great power to create or destroy based on our understanding of physical laws and our possession of the physical means to do so. Our knowledge of the laws governing natural realms such as the atom or genetic code, and advanced technologies for manipulating them have led to tremendous benefits and blessings for humankind, while at the same time they have provided opportunities for horrific destruction on massive scales. The Church of Jesus Christ of Latter-day Saints (LDS) teaches that God is a physical being who likely gained His power and achieved perfection through obedience to laws. If this is the case, then the Lord's work, which is to create worlds upon which His children may dwell and to "bring to pass the immortality and eternal life of man" (Moses 1:39), also proceeds through lawful means. Further tenets of the LDS faith are that human beings are the literal spirit offspring of God and that we, too, may eventually grow to become like Him. Thus, no matter how risky or potentially destructive, our knowledge and capacity to understand the laws of physics, chemistry, and biology are not merely incidental to our life in mortality but are essential in our growth toward Godhood and our ability to eventually take on *all* the Lord's work, including the building of worlds, the colonization of planets, and the resurrection of souls.

The difference between a person who uses natural laws to create and one who uses the same laws for destruction lies in the righteous traits possessed by the individual. God has achieved the status of an exalted being because He embraced the virtues that would guide His choices in directions away from self-destruction. Every action that we take may have consequences that could either lead to our own destruction or build on our future potential. Destruction comes when we find ourselves unprepared to cope in an environment containing forces outside our control. Our potential is increased when we organize ourselves and prepare for survival by controlling or anticipating circumstance. Those who, through knowledge and experience, are able to anticipate and prepare for all circumstances they find themselves in will be less likely to be caught in a harmful situation. Morality is related to order: Moral consequences increase or decrease order, and expand or restrict opportunities and potential. Thus, as children of God, it is in our nature to create and organize the environment around us to make our situation more pleasant, and the ordered condition empowers us to expand our capabilities. Morality, if quantifiable, could be a measure of how choices lead to an increase of potential.

The Decision Tree

A common secular method for determining right or wrong is to ask whether an action will be harmful to others or not. However, this test does not go nearly far enough, because it is often assumed that freedom of the individual equals less restraint—that is, one is free to do anything as long as it doesn't hurt someone else. This logic falls under the guise of preventing further damage but does nothing to improve what is already there. From the LDS perspective, it tends to avoid sins of commission but does nothing to prevent sins of omission.

Potentiality Test

A better way to intuitively explore morality issues is to use a "potentiality test." The potentiality test helps expand the number of choices and opportunities available and eliminates all boundaries. Actions and consequences are placed on a scale by degree rather than being black and white, motivation is built into the test because it attempts to increase the number of choices available in the future. The participant becomes less and less a victim of circumstances and gains more and truer freedom. An outcome that results in a greater number of potentialities has a greater value.

The way the potentiality test works is that, when faced with a decision, a person would ask which choice most increases the number of opportunities that will be available in the future. For example, if a person walked to the edge of a precipice, at least three choices are available: (1) back off and walk somewhere else, (2) climb down the cliff, or (3) jump off the cliff. If (1) or (2) is chosen, the person will have preserved all three choices and is still free to choose any of them. However, if (3) is chosen, the choice is irrevocable—neither (1) nor (2) will be available any more, and indeed the list of choices available becomes quite slim (cry out for help, wave arms, etc). If (2) is chosen, even though all choices remain available, there is a risk involved that may eventually put the person in a position that leaves only (3) as the remaining choice. The reason for this is because the person who chooses (3) may have consciously entered into an environment where all the factors influencing the number of future choices are not in his or her control. Having the mindset that all choices should increase the number of future opportunities, a person would hesitate to enter into an environment where those choices could be decreased by external factors. Instead, a person choosing (2) would more likely prepare in advance and bring along rope and climbing equipment to increase the chances that future choices would not be taken away.

A further extension of this concept is anticipation of the future. We can imagine a future condition that is desirable and map out the decisions along the way that will make it happen. Marc Geddes wrote, "People are more likely to be moral when they understand they will have to face the consequences of their actions in the future. It follows that the further into the future one plans for, the more moral one's behavior should become."[1]

---

1. Mark Geddes, "An Introduction to Immortalist Mortality," in Bruce Klein, ed., *Immortality Institute: The Scientific Conquest of Death: Essays on Infinite Lifespans* (Buenos Aires: LibrosEnRed, 2004), 243.

Freedom Characterized by Restraint

Using the potentiality test one can gain more and more freedom. However, the freedom is characterized by restraint[2] rather than the lack of it. We choose to back away from danger today so we can live to face more challenges tomorrow. Indeed, without restraint there can be no freedom at all. For example, we are all continually faced with the decision every moment to either end our lives, or continue living. If we choose the former, we lose our freedom to do anything else in life. Therefore, just staying alive is a form of restraint, even though most of us don't consider it a difficult choice. And even the very function and health of our bodies is characterized by restraint, where all the organs and subsystems precisely control physical cause and effect for the passage of fluids, gasses, and electrical impulses, allowing the organism the freedom to thrive.

A person concerned about increasing future choices may have many choices available, but the person who acts on some of the choices may begin to lose freedoms, since the number of choices available may shrink down considerably due to consequences of previous choices. If we eliminate choices that are less likely to proliferate future opportunities, or select one promising opportunity at the exclusion of another, we voluntarily restrain ourselves. Being forced into one outcome or another due to consequence is not as free as being bound to a course of action by choice. The most difficult challenge will be for the chooser to understand that voluntarily restraining oneself early on may result in a greater number of choices later.

So far, we've described a decision tree (Figure 1), where each decision forms a node, and in which the various options resulting from that decision form branches. The decision tree is a simple way to quantify the value of moral choices. Some of the branches proliferate future opportunities, while others limit future potential; and the number of decisions available at each node can be a measure of how free the individual is at any point in time. The individual will constantly weigh the balance of freedom versus potential. In the long run, we've assigned a higher value to branches that increase future opportunities. If the choices result in higher potential, then the restrained freedom that comes from paring off unfruitful branches is worth the sacrifice.

---

2. Tad R. Callister, *The Infinite Atonement* (Salt Lake City: Deseret Book, 2000), 257.

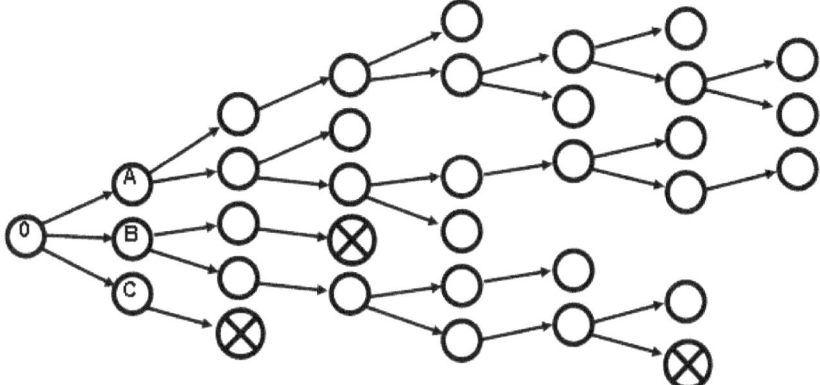

Figure 1. Decision Tree: The branches with deeper nodes generally quantify potential, and the number of branches at any node quantify freedom.

An Engineering Perspective on Morality

A more rigorous argument for an objective morality can define "sin" or "transgression" as an act that increases entropy (disorder) in the environment. Such a discussion might be difficult from a physics point of view, since entropy is neutral, and natural processes at an atomic or molecular level can increase entropy. But we may be able to discuss morality from an engineering point of view, since engineering *selects* between various entropic processes to *choose* where the energy will be used. A low-entropy environment is required for humans to survive. The human organism can thrive only in a highly ordered environment. An increase of entropy can be seen as harmful and may reduce the number of future opportunities available to the individual. Creative acts can artificially decrease entropy and build potential into the environment for expanding future opportunities.

Cause and Effect: Justice Must Be Satisfied

To more fully understand how entropy relates to morality, it will be important to have a discussion regarding "cause and effect." The "zeroeth law" of thermodynamics states that whenever two systems come into contact with each other there will be a net exchange of energy between them until they reach equilibrium.[3] This transfer of energy is the basis of all cause and

---

3. "Laws of Thermodynamics," posted December 27, 2008, in *Wikipedia: The Free Encyclopedia*, http://en.wikipedia.org/wiki/Laws_of_thermodynam-

effect, where the system with the higher energy influences the system with the lower energy, and a chain reaction continues from system to system. We understand that the energy transactions are relentless and that the only way to control the transfer is through isolation or by the careful configuration of systems in the path of energy flow. If the entire universe and all its parts were to be in equilibrium, all matter and energy would be fully mixed and homogenous, and there would be no more transfer of energy. Therefore, in order for organized structure to exist, there must be a difference of energy. Cause and effect are necessary for the creation and maintenance of organized structure.

Light and energy are the media by which we interact with our environment. From the LDS perspective, God uses the physical laws governing the exchange of light and energy to perpetuate structure in the universe and monitor its current state:

> And the light which shineth, which giveth you light, is through him who enlighteneth your eyes, which is the same light that quickeneth your understandings;
>
> Which light proceedeth forth from the presence of God to fill the immensity of space—
>
> The light which is in all things, which giveth life to all things, which is the law by which all things are governed, even the power of God who sitteth upon his throne, who is in the bosom of eternity, who is in the midst of all things. (D&C 88:1–13)

In a very real sense this is not a metaphor. The "justice" that is described in the scriptures is the same cause and effect found in physical systems, where an action must always lead to a consequence.[4] And for this reason, since God is bound to the physical laws for the purpose of perpetuating and monitoring the universe, *God is also bound to satisfy justice to preserve its structure.*

Entropy: A Quantifiable Measure of Order

We can measure disorder in a system by calculating its entropy, which is the "logarithm of the number of ways of arranging things in the system."[5] When considering the large numbers of possible ways gas particles can interact with each other, the measure of heat lost in the system can also mea-

---

ics (accessed January 2, 2009).

4. Callister, *The Infinite Atonement*, 68–69.

5. Daniel V. Schroeder, *Thermal Physics* (New York: Addison Wesley Longman, 2000), 75.

sure the randomness of a system.[6] Thermodynamic and configurational entropy have been shown to be related[7] and to measure order or disorder. The relationship between thermodynamic and configuration entropy is most apparent at the atomic and molecular level because the locations available for configurational bonding are usually identical to the possible paths that energy can take for exchange between the particles. The principles governing configurational entropy and the measure of order can be applied to any scale, including cells, organisms, humans, cities, planets, galaxies, etc.[8] The entropy of a system can be calculated and is quantifiable.

An increase of entropy is often characterized by decay, whereby particles in a system lose their coherence and begin to separate, as in rust and corrosion. As the particles separate, the unknown and unmanaged arrangements of the particles in relation to each other increase. On an atomic and molecular level, thermodynamic entropy is a statistical measure of the heat energy lost or unavailable in an irreversible process.[9] This is where the bounds of a system are sloppy, and contact with other systems allows the relentless cause and effect to leak out into the universe. Irreversible processes increase disorder and the entropy of the environment. Reversible processes transfer the entropy from one body to another, keeping the total entropy of the environment constant. Thus, the bounds of a system are configured in such a way that the cause and effect eventually loop back on themselves with minimal loss into the universe. Normally a positive value, considered over time, entropy can also be decreased and become negative relative to an arbitrary reference state in the immediate environment if conditions are right.[10]

How does the build-up of structure reduce entropy and increase order? The configurational entropy of a system containing two separated molecules would be dependent on the number of bonding locations on each molecule and on the orientations that would be possible between the two. However,

---

6 Raymond Chang, *Chemistry*, 10th ed. (New York: McGraw Hill, 2010), 803.

7 Hugh D. Young and Roger A. Freedman, *University Physics*, 12th ed. (San Francisco: Pearson Education, 2008), Microscopic Interpretation of Entropy, 697.

8. Richard L. Coren, "Empirical Evidence for a Law of Information Growth," *Entropy* 3 (2001): 259–72.

9. John D. Cutnell and Kenneth W. Johnson, *Physics*, 8th ed. (New York: John Wiley and Sons, 2009), 458.

10. Loet Leydesdorff, "Configurational Information as Potentially Negative Entropy: The Triple Helix Model," *Entropy* 12 (2008): 391–410.

once the molecules are actually connected, a structure is formed, and the entropy of the system is reduced. Order is increased because the number of uncertain connections is reduced to zero. If we take all the particles of a rock by themselves, the entropy value would be maximized, and the numbers of possible connections would be impossible to manage. However, when all the particles constituting a rock are managed as a single chunk, it is easy to pick up and throw; the particle count becomes one.

Order and Structure Expand Future Potential

Order and structure in the universe can exist only because of cause and effect, or the strict laws governing the exchange of light and energy between particles of matter. Everything that we can attribute to order in nature can be preserved and maintained only through this exchange. Order is a good thing; perhaps we can say that order and structure are ways to proliferate future opportunities in the individual particles comprising the physical universe. At the atomic and molecular level, order expands opportunities for particles to bond and participate in a controlled exchange of light, where individually such contact would be hit and miss in the participatory universe. At higher levels, order builds on the atomic and molecular substrate by allowing mechanical and electrical sensing and actuation to exist—a method for manipulating and responding to the environment.

If one can learn to manipulate the exchange of light and energy, or rechannel the natural paths of cause and effect, one would have the power to increase or decrease order and structure at will and to change the environment to proliferate future opportunities. One of the main purposes of our mortality is to learn how monitoring, channeling, and controlling cause and effect in the physical universe bring order at every level, from subatomic particles, to molecules, to cells, to organisms, to communities, and eventually to entire planets and galaxies. The first lessons we learn as newborn infants are sucking, crying, focusing our eyes—all of them with a certain measure of involuntary response; but within a few months, we are learning to control our limbs, crawl, walk, and focus on our environment. All of these activities are exercises in manipulating and understanding matter, thus proliferating our future opportunities. Every subsequent lesson we learn in mortality, from toddler to child to teenager and on through adult, extends this course of learning through tasks appropriate for the age and experience of the individual.

What is of greater interest for the topic of morality is the discussion of the survival of the individual in the environment, and how engineering and creative acts can increase the chances of survival (in other words, increase the number of future potential opportunities) through increased ordering. If all the atoms in a system combined to form a rock, the entropy would be reduced and complexity of the vast number of free particles would be encapsulated to the point that they could all be managed as one object. However the reduction of entropy would stop there because the object would be stable in itself. Instead, if we encapsulated processes as well, such that both the sum of the geometry and processes includes all the vast number of steps required for the object to reach out and capture free-floating chaotic parts from the environment and put them together to make copies of itself, the reduction of entropy would continue as long as the correct parts and energy are available in the environment. The presence of the correct types of parts in abundant numbers is critical for our self-copying object to abound. Therefore, the environment of our self-copying object must have a certain level of order for it to continue making copies.

We can consider the surface of the moon to be an ordered environment because at the molecular level energy transfer between particles is somewhat stabilized. However, at the level of higher-order molecules such as proteins and enzymes, the lunar surface environment is quite inhospitable. These particles require even greater order to survive. Single-celled organisms need higher order still, and we can take this discussion to the point where the human organism needs an extremely high degree of order to survive.

Simple self-replicating mechanisms take molecules from the soil and process them into higher-order parts which more complex mechanisms can use to replicate themselves. The waste products of one become the building blocks of another, or the building blocks of one become processed materials for another to use in its own self-reproduction process. The entire biosphere works in a symbiotic relationship to process chaotic raw atoms and molecules in fully reversible processes in an entropy-reducing cradle for intelligence. Regardless of how these self-reproducing mechanisms came about in the first place, it is evident that intelligence has harnessed this astounding power to bring order out of chaos for the purpose of making a more hospitable environment for itself through engineering. Engineering has extended our natural abilities to enable us to live comfortably in the harshest weather, the most extreme environments under the sea, in flight above the clouds, and even in outer space on distant planetary surfaces.

As an organism, the human system has the highest potential to reduce entropy in its local environment. The challenge will be how to calculate the entropic impact of various creative or destructive acts; but a more difficult task is estimating entropy for intangible transgressions or sins of omission.

Musings on a Mathematical Model for Morality

If consequences of moral choices can be phrased in a way that reduces or increases entropy, values can be calculated for objective comparison. It should be possible that the entropy in the environment and community caused by human activity (including moral choices) can also be objectively estimated. Though a truly rigorous mathematical model may be extremely complex, an approximated mental exercise of attaching entropy to various transgressions may still prove worthwhile.

The easiest calculations may be those that simply deal with creative or destructive acts. If we imagine all the particles in the universe atomized and unconnected, the universe would be at its maximal entropic value. All relationships and orientations of all particles to each other are unknown or unmanaged, and there is no transfer of energy. Any process that combines two or more particles would reduce the local entropy by the number of unknowns those connections eliminate. Conversely, any process that separates particles so as to increase the unknowns will increase entropy by that value. Simply forming dumb clumps of matter would be a minimal entropy-reducing action, while forming engineered artifacts or embedding potential into objects for directing future cause and effect would reduce entropy by the amount that any future use of the artifact would contribute.

The most difficult calculations will be for individual actions that are not physically creative or destructive. It will be helpful in looking at examples of these classifications to identify whether they have reversible or irreversible consequences. As discussed earlier, a reversible process transfers entropy from one body to another, leaving the system in the same state of order. In the case of morality, even if the consequences are reversible, actions with reversible consequences will still increase entropy unless the action is taken to reverse the damage. The entropy for irreversible consequences will continue to affect the environment and communities within which the individual resides.

Finally, we can consider a set of metrics that equate individuals in a community with particles in a physical system. As individuals abandon their selfish tendencies and foster the welfare of the group, allegiance of its members to specific unified purposes will allow the community to accomplish things that are out of the reach of the individual for the benefit of all. Entropy in the environment will be reduced, and increased order will allow communities and individuals to thrive. Morality then, as a code of conduct among individuals, can be objectively valued based upon entropy reduction or increase.

Discussion

Examples of how entropy could be calculated from the consequences of moral choices include the taking of a person's life, giving birth to a baby, vandalism, theft, and creative acts. More difficult examples include marriage, divorce, substance use and abuse, service to others, involuntary servitude, and idleness. Note that all the examples that follow are purely academic, and this paper is not advocating serious calculation in every case. The examples are for discussion purposes and may be incomplete.

Example 1: The Entropy of Taking a Person's Life

In the simplest of terms, the number of particles and non-decomposing elements that make up the body of a dead person by mass can be estimated, and the increase of entropy in the environment resulting from the free, unmanaged radicals can be calculated. Additional calculations would need to include rough estimates for how much creative work the deceased person may have engaged in had he or she remained alive, and whether the person was likely to reproduce. Beyond that, the entropy of a person in death may be difficult to calculate.

In the case of natural death, the entropy would not be increased by the act of anyone, and therefore the body would be subject to the reversible processes naturally occurring in the biosphere for decomposing and recycling the material making up the body. However, in the case of homicide or suicide, the guilty party could be held accountable for the value of the increased entropy which would equal the value of the creative work that the deceased individual is likely to have been engaged in had he or she survived. In the case of war, entropy increased due to actions encouraged by a government could be decreased by taking the life of an individual fighting for the cause of that government. At the individual level, the value of the potential creative acts of the deceased soldier would need to be weighed against the mass increase of entropy that the enemy government would encourage should they win their cause.

Example 2: The Entropy of Giving Birth to a Baby

Again, the simplest case would be that the entropy of the environment decreases by the number of particles that make up an adult body, plus estimations for creative acts an average person performs in his or her lifetime. Note that the calculation of whether the baby will eventually reproduce would be nearly impossible, because successful sequential generations of productive members of society could increase exponentially, at least in theory. The decrease of entropy would be credited to the parents for successfully bearing the child and rearing him or her to adulthood. Potentially, a person's existence continues to reduce entropy in all future generations. Choosing to have a child is a risk: Can the child be successfully raised to adulthood? The number would need to be adjusted if the parents lose the capacity to care for the child before he or she becomes a productive member of society. Refusing to have a child would increase entropy by a tremendous amount; an unborn child would not have the potential to become a productive member of society nor increase the parents' posterity.

Example 3: The Entropy of Theft

The entropy of theft can be calculated by the mass and complexity of the objects that were stolen (see "Creative Acts" below), unless they are returned. In the case of theft, the entropy adds to the environment by the amount of disorder caused by breaking up a collection or through a net loss experienced by the former owner who would have to perform more work to restore the stolen items. In addition, the energy expended to investigate and discover the thief, and the anguish of the owner over the missing items, may also have entropic values that would be added to the overall balance.

Example 4: The Entropy of Vandalism

The entropy of vandalism can be calculated directly by the mass and complexity of the property that was damaged, plus how much energy and effort it would take to reverse the destruction. (See "Creative Acts" below.) Particular care would need to go into the calculations for property that are difficult or impossible to replace, such as one-of-a-kind photographs burned in a fire.

Example 5: The Entropy of Creative Acts

The entropy of the creative process, including energy expended by all the machines and processes involved, would be balanced against the decrease of entropy that the finished product represents by the number of assembled particles and estimates of future decreases or increases of entropy the product may effect due to its purpose and use. In the manufacturing process, scraps and shavings would increase the entropy value, especially if they are thrown away and not recycled. Destruction of older versions (such as the demolition of a house in order to build a new one) would also follow the same rules of calculation; the old structure would increase entropy by the amount of all its constituent particles, especially if they are not reused. Digital manufacturing and production vastly decrease the entropy of fabrication processes, and completely self-contained reproduction (such as in natural cells and organisms that self-reproduce) is so efficient that entropy actually becomes negative (in other words, "negentropy" or "syntropy").

Example 6: The Entropy of Marriage

Similar to particles, higher-level structures also are subject to configurational entropy. If we consider the number of ways two macroscopic objects, such as two spheres can fit together, the actual number of points of contact and orientations are virtually unlimited.

However, if we manage them as single objects and not as collections of molecules, the rules for calculating the configurational entropy change. The distance between their centroids becomes the only unknown variable, and all the possible orientations become irrelevant. In the same way, each class of object has its own rules for configuration and bonding for reducing entropy and building up structure. In the case of organisms, the structures that are created are societies that co-manage resources and implement a division of labor for the betterment of each individual. A variety of structures has been proposed for human organisms, including families, companies, neighborhoods, etc. Each of these structures could be evaluated on its own merit for how much it increases or decreases entropy in the environment

Entropy is decreased through the pooling of resources and talents to allow each family member more advantage than could be obtained by separate individuals. For example, a human baby requires a highly ordered environment to survive infancy and childhood to become a productive member of society as a youth and an adult. The ordered environment includes the child's care, feeding, and education, from which the child's perspective appears to be automatic.

The entropy of marriage may be calculated on the increase of stability and productivity that comes out of happy, well-adjusted individuals who are members of the family. The creative works of each of the partners in the marriage, plus the number of productive additional members of society the marriage produces, can be used to calculate entropy in the marriage. Marriages that have greater entropy are less desirable than those that approach negative entropy due to reproduction and successful nurture.

Example 7: The Entropy of Divorce

In the same way that marriage decreases entropy by the increase of opportunities and exponential capacity for order, divorce becomes a division of all the forces of nurture and resource management that the individuals would normally rely on. Entropy would be increased by the lack of productivity and disorder resulting from emotional stress and the high cost of managing multiple family units. Many have discovered the extensive entropy that comes about through divorce—the mess can take an entire lifetime and perhaps beyond to clean up.

Example 8: The Entropy of Substance Use and Abuse

The mere consumption of minute amounts of some substances can kill cells and reduce the functional capacity of the body. Entropy of the cells lost, plus reduced productive capacity of the individual would be included in the calculation. Alcohol, tobacco, and drugs are obvious substances that have adverse effect on the body, but all other forms of food and drink could also be included. The entropy of substance use would be the loss balanced against the benefit, where side effects, overeating, weight gain, and other distractions would also be counted. On the other hand, wise use of substances including food and nourishment decrease entropy by encouraging the growth of healthy cells in the body.

Example 9: The Entropy of Service to Others

Service to others builds an atmosphere of cooperation with the result that larger and larger societal structures become possible. Where reimbursement for services becomes a model of fully reversible processes, resulting in virtually zero entropy, willing service without compensation may in some cases be considered to have a negative entropic value. Free acts of kindness generally encourage the benefactors to also act in kindness, and the originator will be able to reap the benefits of a more cooperative society. Reduction of entropy can be calculated based on the creativity of public works advanced by the community, not possible for any single individual.

Example 10: The Entropy of Involuntary Servitude

The forceful cooperative employment of others can have a vastly reduced entropic value at first, but such a system requires greater and greater hands-on management to ensure that the involuntary servants stay focused and productive, and do not rebel. In the end, the management will become unwieldy, and the maximum entropy will far exceed that of willingly cooperative service, because so much of the effort and efficiency will necessarily be wasted. Some elements of what we understand of Satan's plan could have depended on involuntary servitude, as will be discussed later.

Quantified Morality

Example 11: The Entropy of Idleness

At first glance, idleness seems to keep entropy levels constant; but in actuality, the gradual decay of the environment around us requires constant care and attention; idleness does not stop the decay nor improve the environment. Also, idleness harms the rest of the community because the person does not contribute efforts toward its betterment. Indeed, eventually greater effort is required by others in the environment to counteract the decay or disorder the idle person could have been working against.

Entropy for idleness can be calculated based on the actual number of items in the clutter surrounding the person, including the build-up of dust and other signs of disorder. Clearly, if we consider an ideal situation where relentless work and effort reduce entropy to near zero, or even highly efficient cooperation resulting in negative entropy, we all are guilty to some extent.

Other Points of Discussion

From the LDS perspective, the Lord's work is to accomplish engineering works of astounding scale, including the organization of worlds, solar systems, biospheres, and global colonization. Such works cannot be done by one person but require the cooperation of vast communities. The communities must "become one," and the complexities of the individuals must be encapsulated into a community that is of like mind. Through obedience, the individuals in such a community will enjoy levels of freedom that exceed our wildest imagination.[11]

Can the "potentiality test" justify Satan? From the LDS perspective, there can be two interpretations of Satan's motives and rebellion, both equally sinister in the long run. One interpretation is that Satan wished to force everyone to do good so that they would all return safely to Heavenly Father's presence. The other interpretation is that all would be allowed to do whatever they please; and in the end, the consequences of their actions would be eliminated and all would safely return to Heavenly Father's presence. Clearly we can see both interpretations being enacted in the world today—both forced servitude, and an attempt to eliminate consequences are Satan's powerful tools. It is possible that the spirit world does not have cause and effect as we know it and that consequences are handled differently. If so, Satan would not have understood that justice is relentless and unbreakable—that cause and effect emerge out of the immutable behavior of particles exchanging light and energy. This fact would make the second scenario impossible, even if that was Satan's intention. The very structure of the universe would unravel.

---

11. Callister, *The Infinite Atonement*, 258, 261.

In the first interpretation, individual freedom must be sacrificed similar to the personal restraint shown by producers in a community, but such restraint would be forced upon them. Such a system would not last because it is not sustainable. A system with forced labor and a lack of personal accountability would not be able to cradle and teach new intelligence with the goal of allowing it to go off independently on its own as a self-contained entropy-reducing agent.

Can a spirit separated from its body be considered free? Many philosophies and religions idealize a state in which the spirit is finally freed from the burdens of a physical body. Also, in our digital day and age, many spend more time in virtual worlds or online games, content to spend much of their time in a constructed idealized environment. Apostle David A. Bednar explained, "A young man or woman may waste countless hours, postpone or forfeit vocational or academic achievement, and ultimately sacrifice cherished human relationships because of mind- and spirit-numbing video and online games." Furthermore he wrote, "Video gaming and various types of computer-mediated communication can play a role in minimizing the importance of our physical bodies."[12] Movies and other entertainment media provide substitute experiences for real life. However, as has been discussed, we understand that, without the capacity for direct manipulation of matter around us, we have no recourse over the relentless entropy and decay that naturally occur in the environment around us. A retreat into an artificial environment simply ignores and postpones the work needed to maintain and counteract the natural decline around us. If we were somehow to develop a society that lives purely in a virtual or simulated environment, we would neglect the very physical machinery that maintains that imaginary world, and would eventually find that our universe is decaying around us—the virtual world would find its end. For this reason, it is likely that a spirit world cannot continue to exist on its own but would require a knowledge and understanding of physical element in order to keep it maintained. Thus "spirit and element, inseparably connected, receive a fullness of joy" (D&C 93:33).

We understand that, as spirits, no work can be performed (3 Ne. 27:33). It is a privilege of mortality that we are allowed to learn through difficult experience how to design, order, manage, and engineer our environment to make it more suitable for our survival and happiness. Any activity or state that does not eventually connect back to real work and the manipulation of physical matter would certainly have greater entropic value than an interactive state; and indeed, it may be the case that our very existence depends on our ability to stem the tide of entropy and decay.

---

12. David A. Bednar, "Things As They Really Are," *Ensign*, June 2010, 22–31.

Considering how entropy can be shown to increase from poor choices, it is interesting to note that one of the most effective ways to fight entropy is via self-replicating mechanisms that self-repair and self-reproduce. Self-replication appears to be an eternal principle to bring order out of chaos at all levels of scale. A simple moral choice of reproduction to bring a productive member into the community can be shown to exponentially decrease the entropy of the community. From an LDS perspective, the ultimate destiny is "exaltation," which is often characterized as "eternal lives." When we understand the relationship between order, chaos, and the struggle to counteract entropy or decay in the universe, it becomes interesting to note that "eternal lives" is a continuation of procreative powers forever, as an antithesis to decay (D&C 132:22).

An individual who strives to increase future opportunities and increase order in the environment may eventually be completely free and in control of all circumstance. No element would be outside of his or her control. The implications are that this individual has the knowledge and the means to employ all physical and spiritual laws in any creative project, and has the technical means of full situational awareness, possesses the tools to manipulate matter as needed, and can anticipate scenarios far into the future. The being would be, to all practical purposes, omnipotent and omniscient—an advanced engineer capable of bringing order out of a chaotic universe and conducting engineering projects on a planetary scale.[13] As we contemplate the eternal principle of self-replication as a way to combat entropy at all levels, we can speculate that self-replication also applies to planets—that the inhabitants of one world grow and progress until they eventually achieve the ability to replicate their biosphere on another world: "And as one earth shall pass away, and the heavens thereof even so shall another come; and there is no end to my works, neither to my words. For behold, this is my work and my glory—to bring to pass the immortality and eternal life of man" (Moses 1:38–39).

We can speculate that perhaps the ultimate purpose of God and His society of advanced engineers is to fight entropy and stave off the eventual fate of the universe. Choosing a configurationally closed system like the earth as a testing ground for mortality could be a protection against any entropic increase that may spread to other parts of the universe, resulting from our mistakes during the learning process. It will be interesting to consider

---

13. Joseph Smith, April 6, 1844, *Journal of Discourses*, 6:1, http://journalofdiscourses.org (accessed September 1, 2008). This address, called the King Follett Discourse, was reported by Willard Richards, Wilford Woodruff, Thomas Bullock, and William Clayton.

the role of the atonement of Jesus Christ from this perspective, and expand on the work of Elder Tad R. Callister, W. Cleon Skousen, and others.[14]

Conclusions

It's been shown how morality can be given a value based on how a decision will increase future opportunities. It has also been shown how sin and transgression increase entropy, resulting in a less-ordered environment. We have seen that an environment sufficiently ordered for its survival will allow an organism to thrive and how engineering and creative acts can increase the order and improve the ability to survive. Future choices and opportunities are increased when all potential disruptions in the environment can be mitigated and the individual becomes less and less a victim of circumstance.

The ultimate environment within which an individual can flourish is absolute freedom or control of every circumstance of his or her environment, with minimal entropy. In 1843 Joseph Smith explained, "Salvation is nothing more nor less than to triumph over all our enemies and put them under our feet. And when we have power to put all enemies under our feet in this world, and a knowledge to triumph over all evil spirits in the world to come, then we are saved, as in the case of Jesus, who was to reign until He had put all enemies under His feet, and the last enemy was death."[15]

Encapsulating unmanageable numbers of particles into a single entity reduces the number of unknowns of configurational possibilities, decreasing entropy and allowing all those particles to be manipulated as one unit. Engineering takes advantage of this ability to manage complexity and gives intelligent agents a handle by which to coax all those particles into cooperation for a higher purpose, which may be as simple as throwing a rock. We've also seen how communities can encapsulate the complexity of its member individuals, allowing that community to accomplish things far beyond the reach of the individual. Abandonment of selfishness, service to the community, and charity toward others temporarily seems to restrain an individual's freedom but actually results in a greater number of choices and opportunities later on. A possible basis for a mathematical model of morality was discussed, using the increase or decrease of entropy to assign values to various behavior and consequence.

---

14. Callister, *The Infinite Atonement*; W. Cleon Skousen, "A Personal Search for the Meaning of the Atonement," address given at a mission conference in Dallas, Texas, December 18, 1980, CD recording: Sounds of Zion, "Favorite Speech Series" (Salt Lake City: Ensign Productions, 2002).

15. Joseph Fielding Smith, comp. and ed., *Teachings of the Prophet Joseph Smith* (Salt Lake City: Deseret Book, 1938), 297.

8
Theological Implications of the New God Argument

Lincoln Cannon and A. Joseph West

Abstract

If humanity does not go extinct before becoming posthumans, then given assumptions consistent with contemporary science and technological trends, posthumans probably already exist who are more benevolent than we are and who created our world. If prehumans are probable, then posthumans probably already exist. If posthumans probably increased faster in destructive than defensive capacity, then posthumans probably are more benevolent than us. If posthumans probably create many worlds like those in their past, then posthumans probably created our world. The only alternative is that we probably will go extinct before becoming posthumans.

Introduction

We can use our rapidly advancing science and technology for constructive or destructive purposes. If we do not destroy ourselves, we will likely use the knowledge and power to enhance ourselves and our environment, radically extending our life span and abundantly expanding our resources. How far will we go? Assuming that limits continue to recede, we may reengineer our world such that present notions of poverty, warfare, and death would no longer be applicable. We may even engineer whole new worlds and attain presently unimaginable degrees of flourishing and creativity. In so doing, we would change. We would be different than we are now to at least the same degree as we are now different from our prehuman ancestors. We would be posthumans.

The New God Argument calls for faith in God, or trust in posthumans who may qualify as God in Mormon theology. The argument combines religious titles with secular content to emphasize parallels that are essential to its conclusion. The argument does not prove that God exists. Rather, it proves that, if we trust in our own posthuman potential, then we should trust that posthumans more benevolent than we created our world. Because such posthumans may qualify as God in Mormon theology, the argument suggests that faith in human potential should lead to faith in a particular kind of God. The New God Argument consists of four parts:

1. The Faith Position assumes that we will not go extinct before becoming posthumans.
2. The Angel Argument proves that, if prehumans are probable, then posthumans probably already exist.
3. The Benevolence Argument proves that, if posthumans probably increased faster in destructive than defensive capacity, then posthumans probably are more benevolent than we are.
4. The Creation Argument proves that, if posthumans probably create many worlds like those in their past, then posthumans probably created our world.

The Faith Position

The New God Argument begins with the Faith Position, which is trust that we will not go extinct before becoming posthumans. We'll assume that our human civilization will evolve, technologically and otherwise, into attributes and abilities that differ as much from ours as ours differ from those of prehuman species. The assumption does not require a narrow understanding of what we must be or do as posthumans or how long change may take. The only constraints are feasibility and assumptions we'll identify later.

Implicit in the Faith Position is Transhumanism: the observation that human evolution continues, and the proposition that humans can and should take control of their evolution into posthumans. Rather than devaluing humans, this assumption embraces a radical humanism: that human dignity arises in part from human overcoming. In other words, part of what it means to be human is to extend ourselves, as we've done for ages and to such an extent that early humans would perhaps already consider us posthumans. In context, then, the ethic of human dignity implies that of posthuman dignity.[1]

---

1. Nick Bostrom, "In Defense of Posthuman Dignity," 2005, http://www.nickbostrom.com/ethics/dignity.html (accessed March 21, 2010).

Theological Implications

Moreover, the morality of the posthuman esthetic derives from human desire. Although too often trivial or oppressive, desire can and does extend to the altruistic and rise to the sublime. We overcome ourselves not simply through tighter shirts, deeper pockets, or darker glasses but rather profoundly by realizing compassion and creation before only imagined. Achieving nothing less than such a level is the full moral weight of a Transhumanist perspective.

The Faith Position also implies a form of Pragmatism: that truth, in addition to being discovered, depends to some extent on intentional creation. For example, if we desire a chair and do not find one, we may make that chair.[2] Likewise, we may not be as desired, but trust and work could make a difference. Some suggest that optimism is not realistic because experience often differs from desire. To the extent that we lack power, they're right; but to the extent that we have power, optimism certainly is realistic, as we use power to promote desired experience. Also, since we don't know the extent of our power, we should carefully test limits. For example, you may not be the man of her dreams, but chances are better if you ask her out.[3]

While trusting in desired experience, we should not ignore the possibility of undesired experience. Complacency may prove as dangerous as hopelessness, and we must avoid both to optimize our power. Consider, for example, the attitude we should take toward global catastrophic risks like nuclear weapons and large asteroids. While some ignore, despair, or hope passively, the Faith Position entails support of reasonable mitigation efforts, reflecting trust that we will not go extinct before becoming posthumans.

The Angel Argument

Biologists trace human origins back through billions of years of evolution. A broad confluence of observations indicates that our prehuman ancestors, from simple cells to hominids, generally increased in complexity at an accelerating rate, suggesting that the initial evolution of prehumans was less probable than the subsequent evolution of humans.

---

2. Ferdinand Canning Scott Schiller, *Studies in Humanism* (London: Macmillan and Co., 1907), 430, http://books.google.com/books?id=LxE1A AAAIAAJ&dq=editions%3AnvBadm_1zygC&pg=PA430#v=onepage&q&f =false (accessed August 15, 2011).

3. William James, *The Will to Believe and Other Essays in Popular Philosophy* (New York: Longmans Green and Co., 1908), 26, http://books.google.com/books?id=Cl9GAAAAYAAJ&dq=editions%3APEKurFAL7OUC&pg=PA2 6#v=onepage&q&f=false (accessed August 15, 2011).

Yet physicist Enrico Fermi observed that the stars present us with paradox. Our universe appears old and large enough to have produced many planets capable of supporting prehumans, but a great silence leaves no objective evidence for posthumans.[4] If there's plenty of time and space for prehumans, and if subsequent evolution of humans or equivalents is yet more probable, where are the posthumans?

One possibility is that posthumans are improbable because their prehuman ancestors are already highly improbable. Even in a universe of 70 sextillion visible stars, maybe our planet is the only one on which life began. Counterintuitively, this would be good news for us because it would explain an absence of posthumans with a reason in our past rather than our future.[5] However, we're discovering life in increasingly hostile environments on earth, and we've also verified the presence of water on Mars. Such observations lead many to speculate that we'll soon discover life on other planets—away from the possibility that prehumans are improbable.

Another possibility is that posthumans are improbable because humans and equivalents almost always go extinct before becoming posthumans, perhaps destroying ourselves with super-weapons or environmental exploitation. This would be bad news because it puts the explanation for an absence of posthumans in our own future. Thus, as established by Dr. Robin Hanson, the great silence may imply a great filter.[6] In the vastness of time and space, along evolutionary paths to posthumans, something may be filtering innumerable possibilities to mere improbabilities. If prehumans are improbable. then the filter would be in our past. Otherwise, the filter is in our future, and we probably will go extinct before becoming posthumans.

The only alternative is that posthumans are actually probable, and we simply haven't yet found or recognized them. We don't have objective evidence for this possibility, but we know too little to reject it. As evidence for prehumans mounts and posthumans remain elusive, some may despair. Others will embrace the Angel Argument and trust that posthumans probably already exist because our future correlates with their probability. A lack of evidence is not evidence to the contrary, and this lack enables reasonable hope.

---

4. G. David Brin, "The Great Silence: The Controversy Concerning Extraterrestrial Intelligent Life," *Quarterly Journal of the Royal Astronomical Society* 24 (1983): 283–309.

5. Nick Bostrom, "Why I Hope the Search for Extraterrestrial Life Finds Nothing," *MIT Technology Review*, May/June 2008, 72–77.

6. Robin Hanson, "The Great Filter: Are We Almost Past It?" 1998, http://hanson.gmu.edu/greatfilter.html (accessed November 25, 2008).

The Benevolence Argument

Anthropologists observe that our destructive capacity is increasing at an exponential rate. We have evidence that our ancestors used spears 5 million years ago, but did not fire-harden the points until 500,000 years ago. Over 100,000 years later, we began making complex blades. Roughly 65,000 years after that, we began using the bow and arrow; 14,000 years after that, we began using gunpowder. Less than a thousand years later, we used a nuclear weapon in war.

Meanwhile, our defensive capacity increasingly lags. Clothing was not enough, shields were too small, armor was too slow, walls fell to gunpowder, and even oceans narrowed to intercontinental ballistic missiles. Today, the toughest personal armor is only bullet resistant, the most secure information systems depend on narrowing advantages, and we've persisted for decades with no practical defense against nuclear explosions.

Benevolence explains our survival and continuing evolution, given the growing gap between destructive and defensive capacities. Benevolence is not evenly distributed among us, and it's surely encouraged by self-interest. However, at least among the empowered and on the whole, our common interest has resulted in at least enough benevolence for us to get where we are. Although we haven't always paused before pulling the trigger, we've paused enough to enable the present. We haven't always chosen the right leaders or enacted the right laws, but we're still here. We've demonstrated at least that much benevolence.

Yet we need to set our expectations higher. Already the feasibility of greater destructive capacity haunts our imagination. We speculate about particle accelerators that open black holes, self-replicating nanobots that consume the biosphere, as well as the shrinking cost and proliferation of existing weapons of mass destruction. Do we collectively and severally have the good will to refrain? Judging from observations like suicide bombings and genocidal massacres, it appears we'll require greater benevolence to survive a greater gap between our destructive and defensive capacities.

Assuming we're not unique, posthumans probably have increased faster in destructive than defensive capacity; and according to the Benevolence Argument, posthumans probably are more benevolent than us. Otherwise, they probably wouldn't have survived long enough to become posthumans, and neither will we.

The Creation Argument

A common task to which we've applied computers is that of simulation. The earliest simulations provided basic numeric output. Later simulations interpreted their numbers into abstract visualizations. Today, simulations present whole worlds with three-dimensional geographies approaching photorealism and immersive interactivity for millions of users engaged in research, commerce, entertainment, and warfare by proxy of their avatars.

As computing power increases, we'll probably continue to run increasingly detailed world simulations. Unabated, increasing detail would eventually obfuscate differences between our world and computed worlds to the point that "simulation" and "virtual" would be poor descriptors. If posthumans attain such capacity and use it to compute many worlds like those in their past, then they probably are not the first or only people to do so. Rather, as established by philosopher Nick Bostrom in the Simulation Argument, as posthumans compute more worlds, it becomes more likely that they are themselves in a computed world, among the many actually computed rather than a theoretical non-computed world.[7] The same would be true for us.

We conferred with Dr. Bostrom to confirm that we can generalize his reasoning, which is valid for any creative process that is feasible and consistent with observation.[8] For example, either posthumans probably don't terraform or cosmoform many worlds like those in their past, or posthumans probably terraformed or cosmoformed our world. By extrapolation, either posthumans probably don't create many worlds like those in their past, or posthumans probably created our world. The only alternative is that we probably will go extinct before becoming posthumans.

Present trends are consistent with the possibility that posthumans actually would create many worlds like those in their past. The upper bounds of computing technology continue to rise, methodologies for space exploration continue to expand, and our understanding of the universe continues to grow. Moreover, the benefits from these efforts perpetuate our interest in forwarding them. At this point, it's easy to imagine that posthumans could and would realize potential that the human imagination has already grasped.

---

7. Nick Bostrom, "The Simulation Argument," 2003, http://www.simulation-argument.com/simulation.html (accessed November 25, 2008).

8. Bostrom updated his website to note agreement, on April 22, 2008, http://www.simulation-argument.com/faq.html (accessed June 28, 2010).

If ever we create many worlds like our own, we almost certainly would not be the first or only people to do so. Our perspective regarding our origin should account for our expectation regarding our creative potential. It would be remarkably inconsistent and improbable to assert that we will eventually create many worlds like our own without also acknowledging the Creation Argument, which is that posthumans probably created our world.

Analysis

Historically, and even presently, God arguments typically aim to justify traditional Christian perspectives. Those arguments have a particular context, and that context assumes particular values. From our perspective as Mormons, to limit ourselves to prior tradition when arguing for faith in God is to betray new revelation and admit failure before the task has begun. Some of the values assumed when we limit ourselves to prior tradition are the very dogmatisms from which new revelation would free us.

We identify with Paul, the apostle to the Gentiles, who argued that converts need not first become Jews before becoming Christians (Rom. 4:8–13). Similarly, we argue that we need not limit justification of our faith to the standards of the prior tradition from which ours emerged. With new revelation comes new context. It is with new context that we seek to justify our faith. Like Paul, we diverge from tradition. We aren't concerned with omnipotent *ex nihilo* creators or uncaused causes. In fact, some may say that we are atheistic in this regard. Our argument does not justify faith in the God of traditional Christian perspectives.

Rather, the New God Argument justifies faith in God as revealed in Mormon tradition. Joseph Smith proclaimed that God was once as we are now, became exalted, and instituted laws whereby others could learn how to be gods, the same as all gods have done before.[9] Brigham Young reasoned that we must prove ourselves as friends of God to earn the trust required to become Gods.[10] Wilford Woodruff taught that God is progressing in knowledge and power without end, and it is just so with us.[11] Lorenzo Snow prophesied that children now at play making mud worlds will progress in knowledge and power over nature to organize worlds as gods.[12]

---

9. Joseph Smith, April 6, 1844, *Journal of Discourses*, 26 vols. (London and Liverpool: LDS Booksellers Depot, 1855–86), 6:1.
10. Brigham Young, February 1, 1857, *Journal of Discourses*, 4:199–200.
11. Wilford Woodruff, December 6, 1857, *Journal of Discourses*, 6:120.
12. Lorenzo Snow, quoted in Leroi Snow, "Devotion to Divine Inspiration," *Improvement Era*, June 1919, 658–59.

So we formulated the New God Argument, in part, for a Mormon audience. According to Mormon philosopher Sterling M. McMurrin, "The primary task of theology is the reconciliation of the revelation to the culture, to make what is taken on faith as the word of God meaningful in the light of accepted science and philosophy."[13] The New God Argument does exactly that, reconciling faith in God as revealed in Mormon tradition with the logical implications of assumptions that are consistent with contemporary science and technological trends. This can inform practical decisions Mormons must make going forward as a religious people and facilitate Mormons' interaction with an increasingly secular world, perhaps even serving as a proselyting tool.

Another audience for whom we formulated the New God Argument is that of secularists who profess atheism, and particularly those with Transhumanist inclinations. Although the argument does not compel them to believe in God, assumptions widely shared among them logically imply they should trust in posthumans that may qualify as God, as illustrated by Mormon theology. Accordingly, the argument combines religious titles with secular content to emphasize the parallels and to exercise the value of theology as the application of symbol to substance and the creation of meaning. Yet the argument stands on its own, with or without consent to the theological implications.

Some will not be inclined to worship the God entailed by this argument. On the one hand, some will feel that this image is too cold, too distant, smelling too much of UFOs, and tasting too much of ET. On the other hand, some will challenge that nothing in this argument compels us to grovel in adoration. With both, we completely agree. An argument for faith in God cannot replace the esthetic of God, experienced in subjective communion. Moreover, no God worthy of worship commands groveling but rather earns and reciprocates our respect, emulation, and friendship. The New God Argument does not contend to provide a relationship with God. It only demonstrates that a common worldview, informed by contemporary science and technological trends, leads to and is wholly compatible with faith in a particular kind of God.

The New God Argument justifies faith in a natural material God that became God through natural material means, suggesting how we might do the same. As emphasized in the argument, benevolence and creation are among the means and essential to them. This is the God about whom we learned from our Mormon heritage, which so fully persuaded us of

---

13. Sterling M. McMurrin, *The Theological Foundations of the Mormon Religion* (Salt Lake City: University of Utah Press, 1965), 110.

the practical value of faith in such a God that we would posit this faith even if God didn't exist yet. However, the New God Argument proves the improbability of becoming like God unless God already exists, and so reinforces our obligation to faith.

Conclusion

We give our conclusion to perhaps the most unlikely and unwilling proponent of the New God Argument, the talented evolutionary biologist and leading voice of the New Atheist movement, Richard Dawkins, from his *The God Delusion*:

> Whether we ever get to know them or not, there are very probably alien civilizations that are superhuman, to the point of being god-like in ways that exceed anything a theologian could possibly imagine. Their technical achievements would seem as supernatural to us as ours would seem to a Dark Age peasant transported to the twenty-first century. Imagine his response to a laptop computer, a mobile telephone, a hydrogen bomb or a jumbo jet. As Arthur C. Clarke put it, in his Third Law: "Any sufficiently advanced technology is indistinguishable from magic." The miracles wrought by our technology would have seemed to the ancients no less remarkable than the tales of Moses parting the waters, or Jesus walking upon them. The aliens of our SETI signal would be to us like gods.... In what sense, then, would the most advanced SETI aliens not be gods? In what sense would they be superhuman but not supernatural? In a very important sense, which goes to the heart of this book, the crucial difference between gods and god-like extraterrestrials lies not in their properties but in their provenance. Entities that are complex enough to be intelligent are products of an evolutionary process. No matter how god-like they may seem when we encounter them, they didn't start that way. Science-fiction authors ... have even suggested (and I cannot think how to disprove it) that we live in a computer simulation, set up by some vastly superior civilization. But the simulators themselves would have to come from somewhere. The laws of probability forbid all notions of their spontaneously appearing without simpler antecedents. They probably owe their existence to a (perhaps unfamiliar) version of Darwinian evolution.[14]

"Eternal progression" is what Mormons call that perhaps unfamiliar version of Darwinian evolution. "God" is what Mormons call those god-like extraterrestrials that didn't start that way. Whether we ever get to

---

14. Richard Dawkins, *The God Delusion* (London: Bantam Books, 2006), 72–73.

know them or not, there are very probably gods. So says Richard Dawkins. So said Joseph Smith. So concludes the New God Argument.

The New God Argument

If we will not go extinct before becoming posthumans, then given assumptions consistent with contemporary science and technological trends, posthumans probably already exist that are more benevolent than we are and who created our world. If prehumans are probable, then posthumans probably already exist. If posthumans probably increased faster in destructive than defensive capacity, then posthumans probably are more benevolent than we are. If posthumans probably create many worlds like those in their past, then posthumans probably created our world. The only alternative is that we probably will go extinct before becoming posthumans.

The Faith Position

We will not go extinct before becoming posthumans.

F1) we will not go extinct before becoming posthumans [assumption]

The Angel Argument

If prehumans are probable, then posthumans probably already exist.

A1) EITHER prehumans are improbable OR we probably will go extinct before becoming posthumans OR posthumans probably already exist [great filter argument]
A2) prehumans are probable [assumption]
A3) EITHER we probably will go extinct before becoming posthumans OR posthumans probably already exist [from A1 and A2]
A4) posthumans probably already exist [from A3 and F1]

The Benevolence Argument

If posthumans probably have increased faster in destructive than defensive capacity, then posthumans probably are more benevolent than we are.

B1) EITHER posthumans probably have not increased faster in destructive than defensive capacity OR posthumans probably are more benevolent than us OR we probably will go extinct before becoming posthumans [assumption]
B2) posthumans probably have increased faster in destructive than defensive capacity [assumption]
B3) EITHER posthumans probably are more benevolent than us OR we probably will go extinct before becoming posthumans [from B1 and B2]

Theological Implications

B4) posthumans probably are more benevolent than us [from B3 and F1]

The Creation Argument

If posthumans probably create many worlds like those in their past, then posthumans probably created our world.

C1) EITHER we probably will go extinct before becoming posthumans OR posthumans probably do not create many worlds like those in their past OR posthumans probably created our world [simulation argument]
C2) EITHER we probably will go extinct before becoming posthumans OR posthumans probably do not create many worlds like those in their past OR posthumans probably created our world [generalization of C1]
C3) posthumans probably create many worlds like those in their past [assumption]
C4) EITHER we probably will go extinct before becoming posthumans OR posthumans probably created our world [from C2 and C3]
C5) posthumans probably created our world [from C4 and F1]

Assumptions

F1) we will not go extinct before becoming posthumans [faith position]
A1) EITHER prehumans are improbable OR we probably will go extinct before becoming posthumans OR posthumans probably already exist [great filter argument]
A2) prehumans are probable [assumption]
B1) EITHER posthumans probably have not increased faster in destructive than defensive capacity OR posthumans probably are more benevolent than we OR we probably will go extinct before becoming posthumans [assumption]
B2) posthumans probably have increased faster in destructive than defensive capacity [assumption]
C1) EITHER we probably will go extinct before becoming posthumans OR posthumans probably do not create many worlds like those in their past OR posthumans probably created our world [simulation argument]
C3) posthumans probably create many worlds like those in their past [assumption]

Conclusions

A4) posthumans probably already exist [angel argument]
B4) posthumans probably are more benevolent than we [benevolence argument]
C5) posthumans probably created our world [creation argument]

Section 3
Parallels in Mormon Thought: Practice and Engineering

Outside the realm of ideas and theory, the actual practice of engineering in these latter days may literally approach the lofty heights of the great Master Himself. In this era—the dispensation of the fulness of times—it is clear that the noble goals of learning how to manage the earth, understand the magnificence and complexity of the machine that is the human body, and even help the Lord place people on new worlds is gradually coming within our realm of responsibility.

In "Gaia, Mormonism, and Paradisiacal Earth," Roger Hansen argues that we not only strive toward perfection—an effort that will eventually result in our resurrection, immortality, and eternal life, but also argues that the earth also may gradually be gaining sentience through our efforts. He explains that an earth with a nervous system (the internet) and form of intelligence (computers) may be part of the plan, inspired through thousands of incremental inventions and improvements. Hansen uses remote monitoring and data collection of watersheds and rudimentary geo-engineering as examples of the real-world practice of engineers who are participating in the work of the Gods.

William Pickett, Scott Howe, and James W. Young describe their work in the space industry and provide a tender testimony of the pouring out of the Spirit they have witnessed among their colleagues. Since "when we obtain any blessing from God, it is by obedience to that law upon which it is predicated" (D&C 130:21), hard-working engineers, regardless of their standing in (or out of) the Church, have responded to the inspiration and are undertaking a divine mission: to colonize another world. In "Spiritual Underpinnings for a Space Program," Pickett, Howe, and Young argue that, throughout history, colonization has always characterized a new start among the Lord's people. Colonists such as the brother of Jared, Moses, Lehi, and Brigham Young are only a few examples in scriptural and modern LDS history.

In "Welcome to the Twenty-First Century: The Uncharted Future Ahead," David H. Bailey provides the most extensive coverage of modern advances in medicine, technology, robotics, nanotechnology, genetics, and many other topics, explaining that they are inspired in preparation for the ushering in of the Millennium. LDS readers will find these concepts exciting and inspiring.

9
Gaia, Mormonism, and Paradisiacal Earth

Roger D. Hansen

Abstract

Mormonism provides the seeds for an extraordinarily proactive attitude toward the earth as it evolves toward its paradisiacal glory. LDS theology teaches that, as humankind progresses toward our eternal reward, so does the earth. Brigham Young taught that we are co-creators of the evolving earth and that our participation in this terrestrial progression is part of our earthly sojourn and mortal test. I argue that the earth is a living organism—Gaia—which is rapidly progressing toward sentience and that we are agents of many aspects of this evolution. Such a belief requires LDS Church members to go past the role of stewardship to a more proactive stance. LDS Church members need a positive attitude toward the earth and its future.

Introduction

James Lovelock, after being inspired by images of the earth taken from space in the 1960s, proposed his "living" earth or Gaia hypothesis, which describes the earth's ecosystem as a self-regulating super-organism in which all of the geologic, hydrologic, and biologic cycles mutually self-regulate the conditions on the surface of the earth so as to perpetuate life.[1] But his idea is not totally original.

Many aboriginal societies, and even some modern religions, have gone further in expressing animist beliefs about the earth. Mormonism is among them. For example, John A. Widtsoe, an LDS scientist/theologian I greatly admire, stated: "Latter-day Saints look upon the earth as a living organism, one which is gloriously filling 'the measure of its creation.' They

---

1. James E. Lovelock, *A New Look at Life on Earth* (Oxford, England: Oxford University Press, 1979).

look upon the flood as a baptism of the earth, symbolizing a cleansing of the impurities of the past, and the beginning of a new life."[2] Similar ideas were preached by Brigham Young.[3] Regardless of one's beliefs about a universal flood (Widtsoe had his doubts), it is important that we take Widtsoe seriously and "look upon the earth as a living organism." But this is a concept that troubles Brigham Young University biology professor Duane E. Jeffrey:

> Many Latter-day Saints and students of our theology make us out to be animists who believe the earth to be a living thing and *therefore* in need of baptism. By this logic, then every living thing needs to be baptized. I'm not sure we'd want to take that on. If we choose to argue in some fashion that the earth needs baptism because it is a sentient entity with the capability of moral decision-making like that of humans, we run into further difficulty. Just for the sake of clarification, many animals have sentience far beyond anything we could likely adduce from the earth.... Admittedly, it is not clear what criteria one would use to evaluate sentience for a planet—but I personally find nothing remotely promising.[4]

Jeffrey is being too literal here. First, animism is not a bad word (which he seems to imply in his first sentence), particularly if it results in our looking at the earth and its environment through a more enlightened lens. Second, as I will show in this chapter, the earth, if it isn't already a living being, is evolving in that direction and, in the future, may become a sentient being.

Much is to be gained by regarding the earth as a living organism and treating it as such. For reasons I will discuss in this paper, LDS Church members need to admit that we are Gaians. According to historian Thomas G. Alexander: "In his prophetic utterances, Joseph Smith taught the sanctity and unity of all living things . . . from an outlook similar to that of many Native Americans and modern Gaians."[5]

---

2. John A. Widtsoe, *Evidences and Reconciliations: Aids to Faith in a Modern Day* (Salt Lake City: Bookcraft, 1943), 127–28.

3. "This earth, in its present condition and situation, is not a fit habitation for the sanctified; but it abides the law of its creation, has been baptized with water, will be baptized by fire and the Holy Ghost, and by-and-by will be prepared for the faithful to dwell upon." Brigham Young, June 12, 1860, *Journal of Discourses*, 27 vols. (Liverpool and London: LDS Booksellers Depot, 1855–86), 8:83, http://journalofdiscourses.org (accessed November 2, 2011).

4. Duane E. Jeffrey, "Noah's Flood: Modern Scholarship and Mormon Traditions," *Sunstone*, October 2004, 36–37.

5. Thomas G. Alexander, "Stewardship and Enterprise: The LDS Church and the Wasatch Oasis Environment, 1847–1930," *Western Historical Quarterly*,

While acceptable to many with an artistic or spiritual nature, the Gaia hypothesis developed many skeptics and critics beginning in the mid-1970s. However, it still survives more than forty years after the hypothesis was formally proposed; and with the recent concern over the earth's future, the Gaia hypothesis has gained new credence. Somewhat ironically, as the debate goes on, the earth is artificially evolving toward sentience.[6] For example, journalist Neil Gross argues that the earth is developing an electronic skin.[7] Given the exponential growth of the internet and linked computers, futurist Peter Russell rhetorically wonders if Gaia is not growing itself a central nervous system.[8]

Earth Sentience

Jesuit priest, paleontologist, and Widtsoe contemporary Pierre Teilhard de Chardin places the concept of the earth having a central nervous system and/or brain on a philosophical basis. In an effort to reconcile his Catholic belief structure with the truths of science, particularly evolution, he developed a particularly relevant theory, one that jettisoned the book of Genesis in favor of a more scientific explanation of the earth's development. In a posthumously published book, he suggested that the earth is evolving toward self-consciousness—that collectively we and our technology are that process.[9] For Teilhard, as humankind organizes itself into increasing complex social networks, the earth will increase in awareness until it reaches the Omega Point, which he saw as the apex of history. Teilhard saw Christianity as the driving force in this evolution.

Something similar to Teilhard's Omega Point is being suggested by transhumanists.[10] (See Chapter 6 in this volume.) Based on an exponential view of the growth of progress, transhumanists anticipate that increas-

---

August 1994, 341–64; .available at http://rsc.edu/print/book/export/html/1080 (accessed August 2, 2011); also rpt. in George B. Handley, Terry B. Ball, and Steven L. Peck, eds., *Stewardship and the Creation: LDS Perspectives on the Environment* (Provo, Utah: BYU Religious Studies Center, 2006), 15–32.

6. H. G. Wells, *World Brain* (London: Meuthuen & Co., 1938).

7. Neil Gross, "The Earth Will Don an Electric Skin," *Business Week*, August 1999, 30.

8. Peter Russell, *The Global Brain Awakens* (Palo Alto: Global Brain, 1995), 140.

9. Pierre Teilhard de Chardin, *The Phenomenon of Man*, 23rd ed., English translation by Bernard Wall (New York: Harper Perennial, 1975).

10. Mormon Transhumanist Association, "Transfiguration Parallels and Complements between Mormonism and Transhumanism," *Sunstone*, March 2007, 25–39.

ingly frequent technological advances will culminate in dramatic advances so rapid and astounding that, given current limitations, we cannot predict or direct them. However, the exponential view also suggests that we as humans may also adapt, enhancing our minds and bodies—even our world—to such a degree that we transcend these limitations and maintain an ability to predict and direct technological advances. Transhumanists call this future period the "Singularity."

River Basin Sentience

To see how Gaia is developing a central nervous system and brain, we need only look at what is occurring in river basins, natural subdivisions of the earth. From a biological perspective, river basins are an important symbol because they resemble the living circulatory system. From a theological perspective, water is an important religious symbol, with baptism an important Christian and LDS rite. Biblical tradition teaches us about the benefits of water, which is seen both literally and figuratively as a giver of life. A key phrase used is "living water," which in Hebrew scripture means water flowing free and pure (Jer. 2:13, 17:13; Song of Solomon 4:15; Zech. 14:8). In the Christian scriptures, Jesus appropriated the term "living water" to refer to himself as the source of genuine spiritual life (John 4:10–14, 7:37–38).

Widtsoe liked the symbolism of water and made frequent comparisons between the gospel and irrigation. Talking about the development of early poverty-stricken converts who had immigrated to Utah, he stated: "They have been fertilized by the Spirit of God from eternal truth, just as in irrigation the barren, dry soil is fertilized by the stream of water from the irrigation ditch onto the thirsty land."[11] Mormon history and that of the Intermountain West is closely tied to water resource development.

From a hydrologic perspective, a river basin is an important physical area. Environmental historian Donald Worster sees hydraulic societies at a crossroads and wonders if they will be able to resolve their water-related issues (over-allocation, salt and other pollutant loadings, drainage management, etc.).[12] He advocates a return to adventurer/bureaucrat John Wesley Powell's dream of management by river basin and watershed,[13] a concept recently endorsed by a wide range of organizations including the Western

---

11. John A. Widtsoe, "Symbolism in Irrigation," *Conference Report*, April 1952, 32–35.

12. Donald Worster, *Rivers of Empire: Water, Aridity, and the Growth of the American West* (New York: Pantheon Books, 1997).

13. John Wesley Powell, *Lands of the Arid Region of the United States* (1879; rpt., Boston, Mass.: Harvard Common Press, 1938).

Water Policy Review Advisory Commission: "We should organize water planning, programs, agencies, findings, and decision making around natural systems—the watershed and river basins."[14]

In Utah and the surrounding areas, systems of weather, hydrologic, and other environmental sensors are being distributed basinwide. And this trend will expand as motes[15] become more prevalent and nanotechnologies evolve. Data from ever more sophisticated environmental sensors combined with information from other sources (e.g., human, webcams, remote sensing) are linked by wireless and internet communications to data collections and analysis centers outfitted with data-fusion and decision-support tools (including increasingly realistic simulations). From this developing "central nervous center," signals are sent back to water control structures, thereby creating self-regulating river basins, something that will be critical for adapting to uncertain hydrologic variation created by global climate change. Regulated rivers will be susceptible to precise operations. For example, it will be possible to return diurnal fluctuation to stretches of a river. Real-time operating systems will also be the foundation for sustainable future development. They are also paving the way for sophisticated forms of geo-engineering. Can we improve on nature? Probably not, but we can help mitigate negative human impacts.

Geo-engineering, the application of technology to influence the conditions on a planet and generally thought to be a fringe discipline, has recently been rescued from kookdom by Nobel Prize-winner Paul Crutzen who suggested, rightly or wrongly, that it may be possible to regulate global temperatures by releasing vast amounts of sulfurous debris into the atmosphere.[16] And this concept is not that different from cloud seeding, which is currently being used to increase snowpack and rainfall. For example, in the high mountains of Utah, liquid propane is automatically released into the atmosphere when conditions are cloudy. This procedure is used to enhance the snowpack during dry years.

---

14. Western Water Policy Review Advisory Commission, *Water in the West: The Challenge for the Next Century* (1998), S-7; available from the Western Water Policy Review Office, P.O. Box 25007, D-5001, Denver, CO 80225-0007.

15. Mote: a shortened term for *remote*, also known as *smart dust*, which is a transmitter/receiver linked with a sensor to function as a remote sensor.

16. Paul J. Crutzen, "Albedo Enhancement by Stratospheric Sulfer Injections: A Contribution to Resolve a Policy Dilemma?" *Climatic Change* 77, nos. 3–4 (2006): 211–20.

As engineers and their ilk are developing the technical aspects of evolving toward Teilhard's Omega Point, the issue becomes: How will we use this technology? How will a river basin's "brain" operate in an ethical (value-centered) manner? How does it acquire its moral center? What is the role of the individual? Or more important to this book, what is the role of religion?

Issues like the following need to be discussed and, to some degree, resolved:

- During a drought, how should water be allocated or distributed?
- What is the role of water quality in determining how a river is operated?
- How much impact or interference in the natural environment is acceptable?
- How much fluctuation in a reservoir is acceptable? How do we deal with the tradeoffs?
- What role do recreation, aesthetics, and regional spiritual values play in the operation of a river?
- How will the river basin "brain" respect personal privacy?

Columbia River Basin

Continuing with the river basin example, there have been interesting developments in the Columbia River Basin of the United States and Canada. Here, Catholic bishops have interjected themselves into the process of river basin planning. In 2000, they issued an International Pastoral Letter titled: *The Columbia River Watershed: Caring for Creation and the Common Good*. Twenty-five percent of the river basin's total population are Catholics and make up the region's largest single church.

"The Columbia River, made by God and populated with His creatures of every sort, is holy and therefore polluting it, and treating it as a sewer, and stealing from it without regard to all creatures, human and otherwise, who depend upon it for sustenance is a grave offense to God and to the creatures created by God," the prelates boldly state. The letter denounced the political and economic division that so often characterizes debates over salmon recovery and dam management.

A key word in the pastoral letter is "stewardship." Humans "are created in the image and likeness of God and are commissioned as stewards of God's created and beautiful universe." Further amplifying this point: "Stewardship is the traditional expression of the role of people in relation to creation. Stewards, as caretakers for the things of God, are called to use wisely and distribute justly the goods of God's earth to meet the needs of God's children."[17]

I applaud the Catholic effort to get involved in river basin planning and operations. However, while it sets an interesting precedent, I am not sure it is a particularly useful model for the religious denominations to follow. I am somewhat skeptical about the potential of institutional religious involvement. Science and religion often have a strained relationship. A religion that is involved in this evolutionary planning process must respect science and alternate belief systems, and have faith in at least some of the developing technologies.

One environmental newspaper cynically stated: "Ideas are powerful, and as environmental problems become more obvious, the environmental movement has gained great influence over the last three decades, just as religion was seeing its influence wane. Billed as an effort to reclaim a river, the pastoral letter may also be an effort by the Catholic Church to reclaim its relevance."[18]

Co-Creators

While the succinct epigram "as man now is, God once was, as God now is, man may become," is most famously associated with Lorenzo Snow,[19] the concept began with Joseph Smith and was also taught by other prophets. Joseph Smith articulated the principle of eternal progression in the King Follett Discourse, the high point of Mormon theology for me. In that address, he states, "[God] once was a man like one of us and . . . God Himself, the Father of us all, once dwelled on an earth the same as Jesus Christ himself did in the flesh and like us."[20] Not only was God once a man, but human beings can progress to become gods.

---

17. Catholic Bishops of the Watershed Region, "The Columbia River Watershed: Caring for Creation and the Common Good," http://www.columbiariver.org (accessed February 8, 2009).

18. Jim Robbins, "Holy Water," *High Country News*, September 11, 2000.

19. Quoted in Eliza R. Snow Smith, *Biography and Family Record of Lorenzo Snow* (Salt Lake City: Deseret News Company, 1884), 46.

20. Joseph Smith Jr., April 6, 1844, *Journal of Discourses*, 6:3, "King Follett Discourse," reported by Willard Richards, Wilford Woodruff, Thomas Bullock, and William Clayton, http://journalofdiscourses.org (accessed September 1, 2008). For an evaluation of the discourse's doctrinal significance and implications, see Jacob T. Baker, "The Grandest Principle of the Gospel," *Dialogue: A Journal of Mormon Thought* 41, no. 3 (Fall 2008): 55–80.

The claim that God was once a man presupposes a process for God; otherwise, He would still be human. Not only did God once progress, but prophets have also stated that God still progresses. Consider this quotation from President Brigham Young: "The God I serve is progressing eternally, and so are his faithful."[21] This position was embraced and enhanced by such Mormon intellectuals as B. H. Roberts and John A. Widtsoe. Some scholars have noted that the doctrine of eternal progression has been more controversial in recent years.[22] However, whether the doctrine is in ascendency or decline at the moment, Mormonism at its heart can be said to hold the seeds of environmentalism and transhumanism—doctrines also found in process theology.

In process theology, God supplies the fundamental value patterns for creative synthesis.[23] Alfred North Whitehead, also a contemporary of Widtsoe, postulated: "The purpose of God is the attainment of value in the temporal world."[24] Whitehead declared that God is not Being, but Becoming. Becoming is not only the main characteristic of the world as we experience it but also the fundamental nature of the entire universe, including God. It should also be noted that, in process theology, we have absolute free will; God does not control the outcome of the creative process. Thus, Whitehead's universe is an open-ended, never-ending progression of creation.

According to Mormon doctrine and its contemporary—process theology—we are not just stewards of the earth but co-creators with God. According to Hugh Nibley, Brigham Young taught that the role God gives human beings is designed to test them, enabling them to show to themselves, to their fellow beings, and to God just how they would act if entrusted with God's power.[25] I would phrase it differently: We are here to work in conjunction with God on the continuing creation of the living earth. The creation is not a static event, but a dynamic one.

According Morris S. Petersen in the quasi-official *Encyclopedia of Mormonism*, the evolution of the earth is as follows (referencing D&C

---

21. Brigham Young, January 13, 1867, *Journal of Discourses*, 11:286, http://journalofdiscourses.org (accessed September 25, 2010).

22. David H. Bailey, "Mormonism and the Idea of Progress," draft, December 2001, 15, http://www.dhbailey.com/papers/dhb-progress.pdf (accessed November 2, 2011).

23. Rebecca Buchert, "Mormonism and the Creative Advance into Novelty," *Sunstone*, December 2008, 21–25.

24. Alfred North Whitehead, *Religion in the Making* (1926; rpt., New York: Fordham University Press, 1996), 100.

25. Hugh Nibley, "An Intellectual Autobiography," in *Nibley on the Timely and the Timeless* (Provo, Utah: BYU Religious Studies Center, 1978), 90.

88:18–19): "Because of the Fall . . . , it was transformed to a telestial state, or the present mortal earth. This interval will end with the return of the Savior, after which the earth will be changed to a terrestrial state and prepared during the Millennium for its final transformation into a celestial sphere."[26] If one assumes a dynamic process without large discrete discontinuities between states, one could make a strong case that Mormons have an ecclesiastical responsibility to stay engaged in the continuing evolution of the earth toward its paradisiacal glory. Or as Teilhard might describe it: Human science, led by the science of evolution, would converge in the human consciousness with the truth as embodied in Christianity; then humanity and the earth would experience the promised Second Coming.

It is imperative that, as the earth progresses from being just "a living organism" toward sentience, LDS Church members be actively involved. We must start looking at ourselves and the earth as a work in progress. After all, as co-creators we have a strong theological rationale for participation in the development of science and technology as it relates to the evolution of the earth. However, if we view the earth as a finished product, then our responsibility becomes that of steward, and not that of co-creator. I see the role of co-creator as intensely proactive; we become the progressive agents of the evolutionary change to our present and future world, both mortal and postmortal. So that I don't overstate my case, I also believe in the Wallace Stegner maxim: "Don't try to control the earth beyond the absolute minimum."[27] We need, however, to mitigate our human impacts. Also, as Latter-day Saints, we need to avoid the excuses we frequently use for ignoring the condition of the earth: "Well, it's the last days. The scriptures say things will get bad at the end. It's just a fulfillment of prophecy. There's nothing I can do about it." This type of logic does not stand up to prophetic injunctions about our responsibilities to the earth and are certainly contrary to a co-creator role. If we look at the more positive and proactive position suggested in this chapter, we will open ourselves to a more optimistic view of the near future.

Conclusion

For me, the earth is either a living being or very close to it. Furthermore, it is evolving toward sentience; it has its own plan of salvation but it needs

---

26. Morris S. Petersen, "Earth," *Encyclopedia of Mormonism*, http://eom.byu.edu/index.php/Earth (accessed November 2, 2011).

27. Wallace Stegner, quoted in Elia T. Ben-Ari, "Defender of the Voiceless: Wallace Stegner's Conservation Legacy," *BioScience* 50, no 3 (March 2000): 253–57.

our input. And that input is a good part of the reason we are here on earth. How that sentient being will evolve is subject to substantial human involvement. And the Mormonism of Joseph Smith, Brigham Young, and John A. Widtsoe provides a strong rationale for LDS Church members' participation in the process.

If our final goal in postmortality is to become creators, then it is paramount that we get experience here. And I would suggest that this is a critical part of our current religious journey. Modern revelation has told us that we are co-creators of the earth with God. This activity, at least for the moment, will have to be self-directed. To quote Thomas G. Alexander: "When faced with extraordinarily difficult problems, insightful and creative people within a cultural tradition may return to their roots to reappropriate or to reinterpret concepts and practices—religious or secular—forgotten in the contemporary society, which seem to apply to current problems. Joseph F. Smith and some of the early twentieth-century Latter-day Saints seem to have done that with the theology of environmental stewardship."[28]

As the earth progresses towards sentience and its paradisiacal glory, what will be the role of LDS Church members? Will we be neo-Luddites? Or will we participate with engineers, scientists, computer scientists, and others in the development of a not-so "Brave New World"? In a recent article in *Sunstone*, members of the Mormon Transhumanist Association warned: "Whether tomorrow is wonderful or horrible may depend on the extent to which persons with good minds and loving hearts become actively involved in shaping the future."[29] Instead of looking at our future—the earth's and our own—as careening toward an inevitable cataclysm, we need to look at it as an evolutionary continuum preparing the earth for the Second Coming.

---

28. Alexander, "Stewardship and Enterprise."
29. Mormon Transhumanist Association, "Transfiguration Parallels and Complements between Mormonism and Transhumanism," 38.

10
Spiritual Underpinnings for a Space Program

William R. Pickett, A. Scott Howe, and James W. Young

Abstract

This chapter presents a perspective that, in addition to benefits in science and education, a healthy space program may also have significance from a theological point of view and may in fact be the result of divine inspiration. The development of space technologies for science and exploration has been recognized as an engineering achievement while, at the same time, it is described as an expensive visionary venture that distracts us from more pressing human endeavors. However, a careful look at scriptural accounts, the teachings of prophets and other Church leaders, and our current knowledge about the solar system may suggest a different view: that the timing may not only be right for the development of this technology, but an argument can be made that it may even be instrumental to the salvation of ourselves and our posterity. The chapter suggests philosophical directions that may be worth further critical review.

Introduction

The development of space technologies for science and exploration has been recognized as an engineering achievement while, at the same time, it is described as an expensive visionary venture that distracts us from more pressing human endeavors. The Church of Jesus Christ of Latter-day Saints (LDS) holds as doctrine that God has established worlds without number where His children may dwell. It should be apparent that the peopling of other worlds will occur according to natural laws and that the recent outpouring of inspiration regarding space technology might be for the purpose of building a foundation of necessary technologies that will allow us to participate in this great work.

However, there are LDS members in good standing who do not understand the role technology can play in the building up of the Lord's kingdom. Some wonder if attention to any cause, no matter how worthy, might not be a distraction from more important things if that cause has not been specifically mentioned and condoned by the leadership of the Church—if it doesn't fall into the four-fold mission of the Church, to proclaim the gospel, redeem the dead, perfect the Saints, and care for the poor and needy. However, while the Church leadership concerns itself with the spiritual aspects of the building up of the Lord's kingdom, we often see that the Lord has a much wider perspective and inspires any who will be receptive to it. For example, during the 1930s when the electronic computer was just being developed, President George Albert Smith, his successor David O. McKay during the 1950–1970s, and later prophets did not encourage Church members to develop this technology or concentrate on improving it. Instead, the Lord inspired receptive individuals who responded and moved that work forward independent from the core spiritual efforts of the Church. Today, the computer is indispensible to at least one of the four-fold efforts, that of redeeming the dead, and the Church has embraced it for speeding up genealogical and temple work because of the tremendous power it possesses for shortening the time required to process the unimaginable numbers of names and information on our ancestors. Perhaps technology is the means by which the Lord will cut short His work in righteousness (D&C 52:11).

In spite of all the economic troubles and calamities we are experiencing today, we think that the world is on the brink of a wonderful era that few have dreamed about—one that could be characterized by space travel and the colonization of other worlds. This era may coincide with the ushering in of the Millennium. We have been told in spiritual terms some of the things that are in store for us in the Millennium, but are we prepared for what it could mean in terms of physical blessings and progress? We hope to show that the development of space technologies has at least the potential to have unimaginable impact on the perfection of the Saints and the care of the poor and the needy, perhaps as profoundly as the computer has had on genealogical research.

We will begin our discussion with several secular reasons for investing in space research and technology, then follow up with a discussion on the program's spiritual foundations and arguments, from an LDS point of view.

Perspective from Economics

Investment in focused technical research has a great potential for stimulating any economy. Challenging ourselves with a set of requirements and goals that set sights beyond current capability will stretch industry and bootstrap markets. This dynamic especially applies to investment in space technologies because they are aimed at concentrating and packaging infrastructures and resources in useful ways far away from their point of origin—precisely the sort of thing that benefits both the creators and the consumers of technology. And in contrast to defense spending, which also stimulates the economy, space technology is entirely devoted to the peaceful acquisition of knowledge, literally about who we are, where we came from, and where we are going. Amazingly, an entire government agency and industry have been built around answering these questions and have somehow been inspired to move forward in spite of all the distractions and competition for funds and resources.

Some skeptics say we should save the money we are spending on space development and use it "here on earth." These critics fail to notice the obvious: The money is never spent in space; it is all spent on earth. The materials for spacecraft are but a miniscule fraction of the space budget. Most of the funding for the space program goes to keeping the technical knowledge current and active through employing the experts who are keepers of the knowledge. If this funding source dries up, the knowledge will be lost, and high-tech jobs that help keep the United States in a leadership position will go away.

The technological spin-offs of the space program have improved the quality of life here on earth. *Nature* reported: "The economic benefits of NASA's programs are greater than generally realized. The main beneficiaries (the American public) may not even realize the source of their good fortune.[1]" The two big drivers of technological development are war and exploration. We can all agree that the space program is better than war as the source for technological development. We see some of these technological benefits ranging from medicine, transportation, public safety, and consumer products to environmental and agricultural resources, computer technology, and industrial productivity. These products are detailed in the yearly NASA publication called *Spinoff*.

---

1. Roger H. Bezdek and Robert M. Wendling, "Sharing Out NASA's Spoils," *Nature*, January 9, 1992, 105–6, doi:10.1038/355105a0, http://www.nature.com/nature/journal/v355/n6356/pdf/355105a0.pdf (accessed January 19, 2009).

Figure 1
NASA Yearly Budgets, 1958–2008

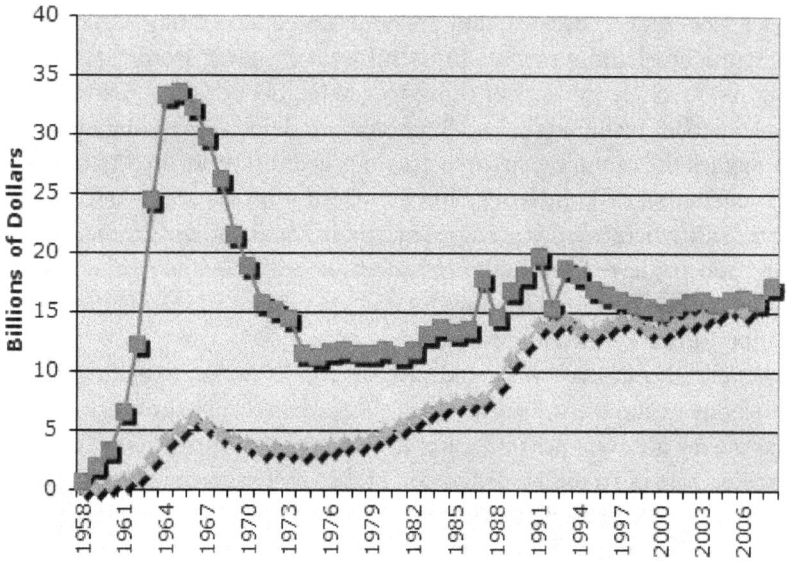

The $25 billion (in 1958 dollars) spent on civilian space R&D during the 1958–69 period returned $52 billion through 1971,[2] a 208% return on the investment. Since 1976, NASA has spent $361.5 billion (Figure 1), but spin-offs have resulted in more than 1,600 commercial products. NASA Tech Briefs (http://www.techbriefs.com) can be browsed online for descriptions of countless technologies in manufacturing and prototyping, machinery and automation, physical sciences, bio-medical, testing and measurement, electronics and computers, semiconductors and ICS, mechanics, information sciences, materials, and software, all produced as spin-off technology from NASA seed funding. Well-known examples include digital camera Charged-Coupled Device (CCD) chips, cell phone technologies, and the Global Positioning System (GPS).

The NASA budget for 2008 was $17.3 billion, or 0.6% (less than 1%) of the U.S. federal $2.9 trillion budget. Americans spent $116.2 billion on

---

2. NASA Budget, January 15, 2009, *Wikipedia: The Free Encyclopedia*, http://en.wikipedia.org/wiki/NASA_Budget (accessed January 19, 2009).

Spiritual Underpinnings

alcohol in 1999,[3] and the cosmetics industry averages $18 billion a year.[4] In 1997 Americans spent about $3.57 a week on tobacco products, $2.99 per week on jewelry, and $32.15 on recreation.[5] The current space budget amounts to a dollar a week for all Americans. That is a small price to pay to invest in the future. Less is spent each year than on cosmetics, tobacco, or alcohol: Which is the more worthy cause?

Some critics say that the billions being spent on space exploration would be better spent on feeding the poor, where one estimated figure for providing food for the needy is only $19 billion worldwide per year.[6] However, the efforts to combat poverty have been going on for hundreds of years, and poverty still exists. Therefore, we cannot say that we will start up the space program when all these other problems are solved on earth, because such a time may never come. Poverty and world hunger cannot be solved by giving money to the poor but by giving them opportunity. Space development provides inspiration to students and, if the projects are exciting enough, will motivate them to succeed. A probable benefit of their success is that they will motivate others to get involved. There are enough resources that we can feed the whole world. The Lord has promised, "For the earth is full, and there is enough and to spare; yea, I prepared all things, and have given unto the children of men to be agents unto themselves" (D&C 104:17). Our resources are start-up capital for the Lord's business of providing a place where His children may dwell. We should not be wasteful of these resources but use them wisely.

If there is any doubt that the earth has enough resources for all, there should be no doubt that the resources of the universe are practically unlimited. Some have pointed out that we have only a small window when we have the means to pursue space-based resources. After the earth-based resources are used up, they argue, we will no longer have the energy to go after the extraterrestrial resources. Like the computer industry, individuals are being inspired to develop space technology. An entire industry has grown up with employees that are trained for it, many of whom would likely lose interest and waste away if their purpose is taken away from

---

3. Ronald C. Hamdy and Melissa McManama Aukerman, "Alcohol on Trial: The Evidence: 1. Epidemiological Considerations of Alcohol Consumption," *Southern Medical Journal* 98, no. 1 (January 2005): 34–36.

4. Hillary Mayell. "As Consumerism Spreads, Earth Suffers, Study Says," *National Geographic News*, January 12, 2004 (accessed January 9, 2009).

5. Richard Braastad, "Putting NASA's Budget in Perspective," http://www.richardb.us/nasa.html (accessed February 1, 2009)

6. Mayell, "As Consumerism Spreads, Earth Suffers, Study Says."

them. Who is to say that, in the same way genealogical research has benefited from computer technology, the infinite resources available in near-earth space (moon, asteroids, etc.) might not be a means for blessing the poor and needy, but also for eliminating poverty altogether and providing an unimaginable economy of growth and prosperity?

Perspective from Energy, Environment, and Infrastructure

Many in the world today mistakenly believe that only limited resources are available to humankind. This idea trickles down into all sorts of philosophies that sometimes have moral implications, such as population control and politics. Many of today's wars are fought over slices of the pie. In actuality, there is no limit to resources. Instead, our challenge is keeping a balance with technology development and infrastructure growth. Most readers are familiar with the modern parable of the well pump and the thirsting soul. If he uses the cup of water to prime the pump, he can have unlimited water, but if he drinks the water in the cup, he cannot prime the pump, and he has only temporarily delayed his death by dehydration. Such may well be the case with us. The earth's resources may be all we need to build upon for obtaining the limitless resources of the universe, if only we wisely manage our technology and infrastructures.

A space-based infrastructure would consist of a transportation system for lifting materials out of the earth's gravity well and delivering goods from orbit back to earth again. Other infrastructures could include space-based mining equipment and orbital or lunar factories for processing the materials on location for in-situ resource utilization (ISRU).

One of the first space-based resources that can be leveraged is energy. We already have a market for solar power, which is technically a space-based resource. However, it will be possible to place solar panels in orbit where they have exposure twenty-four hours a day to sunlight and to beam the power down to earth where it is needed.[7] In 2008, John Mankins of Managed Energy Technologies successfully completed live power beaming via microwaves in Hawaii, proving that the technology was feasible from a remote location.[8]

---

7. Nobuyuki Kaya, Masashi Iwashita, and John C. Mankins, "Hawaii Project for Microwave Power Transmission, IAC-03-R.3.05," Paper presented at the 54th International Astronautical Congress of the International Astronautical Federation, September 20–October 3, 2003, Bremen, Germany.

8. Jeff Foust, "A Step Forward for Space Solar Power," *The Space Review: Essays and Commentary about the Final Frontier*, September 15, 2008, http://

Spiritual Underpinnings

A science fiction story by Robert Heinlein, "The Moon Is a Harsh Mistress," foresees a future where lunar colonies specialize in mining and hydroponic gardening, exporting the products back to earth via a catapult or mass driver. Many engineers have been inspired by similar stories and are currently working toward bringing the ideas to reality to help deal with resource issues on earth. On earth, common metals such as iron and aluminum are found in abundance, while other useful materials needed for electronics and manufacturing are considered rare. This situation exists because the heavier materials, such as gold, platinum, and palladium, sank to the core when the early planet was in its molten state.[9] The sources for rare materials that we have today are thought to have come from asteroids that impacted the earth at a late stage in its formation, adding a layer that contained rare materials. Though the moon is made of like elements as the earth, the bombardment of asteroids has given the lunar surface similar concentrations of useful metals and other materials. Metals, basalts, olivine, gases, and other volatiles and minerals are abundant on the moon, as determined from Apollo samples, and also on the asteroids through spectrographic analysis.[10] Business models for mining the moon's platinum-based metals[11] and lunar factories have been proposed.[12] Spectrographic analysis confirms that asteroids have large amounts of metals and minerals that would be available to us if we wisely plan ahead to create the right infrastructure.[12]

Because of their lower gravity, asteroids likely still have these materials on or near their surface. Asteroids and comet cores with orbits near or crossing that of earth are called near earth objects (NEOs). According to

---

www.thespacereview.com/article/1210/1 (accessed February 1, 2009).

9. James M. Brenan and William F. McDonough, "Core Formation and Metal–Silicate Fractionation of Osmium and Iridium from Gold," *Nature Geoscience*, 2 (October 18, 2009): 798–801.

10. Richard A. Freitas and William P. Gilbreath, *Advanced Automation for Space Missions*, Proceedings of the 1980 NASA/ASEE Summer Study: Conference Publication 2255 (Washington, D.C.: NASA Scientific and Technical Information Branch, 1980), 81–82.

11. Bill White, "Priming the Pump for Lunar PGM Mining," *The Space Review: Essays and Commentary about the Final Frontier*, October 24, 2005, http://www.thespacereview.com/article/479/1 (accessed February 1, 2009).

12. Richard P. Binzel, Andrew S. Rivkin, J. Scott Stuart, Alan W. Harris, Schelte J. Bus, and Thomas H, Burbine, "Observed Spectral Properties of Near Earth Objects: Results for Population Distribution, Source Regions, and Space Weathering Processes," *Icarus* 170 (2004): 259–94.

planetary scientist John Lewis[13] the smallest known NEO (in 1996) metallic asteroid is 3554 Amun, which is 2 kilometers in diameter, about the size of a typical open-pit mine on earth. In earth mining, you have to dig through all the worthless dirt and rock to follow the vein to the ore. But in space, these metallic asteroids are large concentrations and mostly pure. In 1996 market values, the 30 billion ton Amun Asteroid would yield $8,000 billion in iron and nickel, $6,000 billion in cobalt, and $6,000 billion in platinum-group metals, making a total of $20,000 billion in market value, which is about one-third of the entire world gross national product. That doesn't count all the rare earth elements on the asteroid that are so vital to the electronics industry that we currently import from a meteor impact site in China. All that material could be dropped back down into earth's gravity well easily enough, especially platinum-based metals and rare earth elements, with over $6,000 billion in returns, but most of the iron and such could be used right there in space to build up space infrastructure (habitats, rockets, vehicles, rovers, outposts, probes, etc.) and to put in place an earth protection system to deflect or mine other asteroids.

Astronomers Christina Thomas and Robert Binzel have begun to map asteroids back to their source regions, based on spectroscopic data and mineral content.[14] Once we gain a foothold on NEOs and the moon and establish an infrastructure for acquiring and processing materials in the low gravity wells of asteroids and comet cores, the resources available to us will be virtually unlimited. John Lewis estimates that just the resources on the one small NEO 3554 Amun would provide financing for a space program tens of thousands of times larger in scale than the current NASA budget, and would put the infrastructure in place to access the entire asteroid belt worth $35,000,000,000,000,000,000 in iron alone[15]—that's enough to take care of the world gross national product (in 2010 dollars) for 460,0000 years!

Education will be stimulated by space research and development, as young people realize that they, too, may go into space rather than just watch others do so on video. In this day and age where there is great concern for the environment, Patrick Collins and Adriano Autino proclaimed that "the earth is not sick, she is pregnant," about to give birth to a space-

---

13. John S. Lewis, *Mining the Sky: Untold Riches from the Asteroids, Comets, and Planets* (New York: Perseus, 1997), 112.

14. Christina A. Thomas and Richard P. Binzel, "Identifying Meteorite Source Regions through Near Earth Object Spectroscopy," *Icarus* 205 (2010): 419–29.

15. Lewis, *Mining the Sky*, 196.

Spiritual Underpinnings 143

faring society. They also pointed out that expansion into near-earth space is the only alternative to endless "resource wars."[16]

It will be important for nations who want to remain strategically viable to stay abreast of the new technologies for the utilization of space-based resources. The day will soon come where the nation that fails to move quickly will find itself an economic backwater.

Perspective from Planetary Protection

Another reason to develop space is for earth's protection. Many scientists say that, 65 million years ago, an asteroid several kilometers wide hit the earth around Chicxulub, Mexico, and caused an extinction-level event (ELE). An ELE is one in which environmental conditions become sharply inhospitable to some species, and they die off. The event in question is said to have been the one that wiped out the dinosaurs.[17] Though the scenario proposed by the Chicxulub asteroid event is controversial, the fact that asteroids and meteors regularly pass nearby and even impact the earth with surprising regularity is well known. An estimated 500 meteorites ranging in size from marbles to basketballs or larger reach the earth's surface each year,[18] and estimates for the mass of material that falls on the earth each year range from 37,000 to 78,000 tons. Most of this mass arrives as dust-sized particles.[19] Another study estimates that 0.010kg to 1kg interval—to between 2,900 and 7,300 kg/yr, or 18,000 to 84,000 meteorites bigger than 0.010kg—fall on the earth per year.[20] Here are some of the more publicized meteorites:

---

16. Patrick Collins and Adriano Autino, "What the Growth of a Space Tourism Industry Could Contribute to Employment, Economic Growth, Environmental Protection, Education, Culture and World Peace," Plenary Session of the *International Academy of Astronautics' First Symposium on Private Human Access to Space*, May 25–28, 2008, Arcachon, France.

17. "Chicxulub crater," in *Wikipedia: The Free Encyclopedia*, http://en.wikipedia.org/wiki/Chicxulub_crater (accessed October 22, 2011).

18. "Meteorite," posted September 25, 2009, in *Wikipedia: The Free Encyclopedia*, http://en.wikipedia.org/wiki/Meteorite (accessed September 25, 2009).

19. Cornell University, "How Many Meteorites Hit Earth Each Year?" (posted 2003), in *Curious about Astronomy? Ask An Astronomer*, http://curious.astro.cornell.edu/question.php?number=470 (accessed September 25, 2009).

20. P. A. Bland, T. B. Smith, A.J.T. Jull, F. J. Berry, A.W.R. Bevan, S. Cloudt, and C. T. Pillinger, "The Flux of Meteorites to the Earth over the Last 50,000

- On July 30, 1908, an object estimated to be about 80m in diameter exploded in the sky over Tunguska in Siberia, flattening trees and causing general destruction for miles around. The Tunguska event had enough power to destroy an entire city. Similar impacts are said to occur once every hundred years. No one is certain of the exact nature of this object, but a meteor or small comet has been suggested.[21]
- On August 10, 1972, a 1,000-ton object estimated at up to 80 meters in diameter, skimmed the edge of the earth's atmosphere about 60 km above Grand Teton National Park, then skipped back into space.[22]
- On January 19, 1993, a meteoroid exploded over Lugo, Italy, with a 14-kiloton blast.
- On October 7, 2008, an estimated 3–4m diameter "asteroid," designated as 2008 TC3, impacted in northern Sudan.

The possibility of an ELE is alarming but has been considered to be so rare that leaders in the field thought it not worth taking seriously. However, scientists and world leaders got a wakeup call on July 16–22, 1994, when Comet P/Shoemaker-Levy 9 (SL9) impacted Jupiter right under our cameras. The largest fragment, "G," which was up to 5km across, hit on July 18 and produced an explosion estimated to be equivalent to 6 million megatons of TNT (600 times the world's nuclear arsenal). The impact of SL9 inspired more diligent attention to the possibility that an asteroid could also cause an ELE on earth.[23] In July 2009 a scar approximately the size of the earth was observed on Jupiter, hinting that another major impact had happened on the same planet almost exactly fifteen years after the impact of SL9.[24] Had the same object hit our planet, it would have caused catastrophic damage to human civilization.[25] The Near Earth Asteroid Rendezvous (NEAR) project has been surveying near-earth ob-

---

Years," *Monthly Notices of the Royal Astronomical Society* 283 (1996): 551–65.

21. "Tunguska Event," in *Wikipedia: The Free Encyclopedia*, http://en.wikipedia.org/wiki/Tunguska_event (accessed October 22, 2011).

22. "Daylight Fireball of August 10, 1972," http://web.archive.org/web/20050120051405/www.maa.agleia.de/Comet/Other/1972.html (accessed January 16, 2011).

23. "Comet Shoemaker-Levy" in *Wikipedia: The Free Encyclopedia*, http://en.wikipedia.org/wiki/Comet_Shoemaker-Levy_9 (accessed October 22, 2011).

24. Lisa Grossman (posted 2009), "Jupiter Sports New 'Bruise' from Impact," *New Scientist*, online edition, http://www.newscientist.com/article/dn17491-jupiter-sports-new-bruise-from-impact.html (accessed August 1, 2009).

25. Alexis Madrigal (posted July 24, 2009), "Hubble Snaps the Sharpest Image Yet of Jupiter Impact," *Wired Science*, http://www.wired.com/wired-

Spiritual Underpinnings   145

jects and recommending to world leaders methods for deflecting or destroying dangerous earth-crossing asteroids.

Though no known impacts are imminent, several close calls and possible distant future impacts have been identified. We have chosen several examples that we use to illustrate the potential hazard of impact. However, it must be noted that all asteroid (minor planet) orbits are being refined on a daily basis, and our examples listed below may eventually prove to be more or less of a hazard than what is known at the time of this writing:

- On March 21, 2014, asteroid 2003 QQ47, which is estimated at 1.24km in diameter, will miss impacting the earth by about 12 million miles. An asteroid of that size would most assuredly cause an ELE and would produce an explosion equivalent to 350,000 megatons of TNT.[26] Even though 2003 QQ47 is a flyby, an unfortunate result of passing near the earth and/or other planets is that the asteroid's orbit may be influenced such that an impact could occur during a later flyby.
- In 2029 asteroid 99942 Apophis will make an earth flyby, followed by another flyby in 2036. If the asteroid's orbit is influenced by the earth's mass such that it hits a specific window during its 2029 pass, it could impact the earth on the later 2036 pass.[27]
- On March 16, 2880, asteroid 29075-1950 DA (more than 1km diameter) is predicted to have a high possibility of impacting the earth. It is well within the size that would cause an ELE.[28] Fortunately we have more than 800 years to figure out how to stop it or control it.
- Many other large asteroids are being tracked, such as 69230 Hermes, a binary asteroid, each component with an approximate diameter of 400m.[29] As with Apophis, asteroids that pass close to the earth and other planets may have their orbits altered in ways that will make them a future danger.

---

science/2009/07/hubble-snaps-sharpest-image-yet-of-jupiter-impact/ (accessed August 1, 2009).

26. "2003 QQ47," in *Wikipedia: The Free Encyclopedia*, http://en.wikipedia.org/wiki/2003_QQ47 (accessed October 22, 2011).

27. "99942 Apophis" in *Wikipedia: The Free Encyclopedia*, http://en.wikipedia.org/wiki/99942_Apophis (accessed October 22, 2011).

28. "29075-1950 DA," in *Wikipedia: The Free Encyclopedia*, http://en.wikipedia.org/wiki/29075)_1950_DA (accessed October 22, 2011).

29. Ibid.; National Aeronautics and Space Administration, (posted October 31, 2003); "The Curious Tale of Asteroid Hermes," http://science.nasa.gov/headlines/y2003/31oct_hermes.htm (accessed February 1, 2009).

It might be worthwhile at this juncture to give the reader a short primer on asteroid classifications. Those known as main-belt objects are located between the orbits of Mars and Jupiter and pose no threat to the earth. Those asteroids generally lie between 60 and 390 million miles from the earth at their closest approach. Objects that have orbits between 5 and 28 million miles of the earth are called near-earth objects (NEOs). And further, objects that approach the earth with orbits that bring them closer than 5 million miles are designated as potentially hazardous objects (PHOs). Since all of these objects are usually identified as either asteroids or comets (by their appearance), asteroids are specifically known as NEAs and PHAs and comprise the vast majority of these objects.

69230 Hermes, noted in the above listing, has an especially interesting history. 69230 Hermes was discovered on October 28, 1937, but was lost five days later. Measuring asteroid positions in 1937 was not the simple straightforward task it is with today's modern astronomy. When NASA funding programs for NEO discoveries became a priority in 1998, teams of observers at various astronomical related institutes and observatories began a vigorous discovery program. On October 15, 2003, Hermes was recovered by just such a team, with James W. Young, co-author of this chapter, assisting in the confirmation recovery from NASA's JPL Table Mountain Observatory.[30] With its orbit now well determined, 69230 Hermes (a PHA) had come closer to the earth than any other object known to the astronomical community as of 1937.[31] On October 23, 2011, 1,256 PHAs were listed on Space Weather.com, while the IAU/Minor Planet Center showed more than 1,120 in their February 12, 2010 listing. These numbers are in constant flux as new ones continue to be discovered.

It is estimated that there are around a thousand asteroids over 2km dia. Asteroids up to 0.100km diameter explode in the sky, like the Tunguska meteor, due to pressure differences at the top and bottom of the object. Anything larger than that will impact the earth and cause a crater. In the NEAR program, more than 80 percent of the asteroids 1km in diameter and greater have been surveyed,[32] but fewer than 15 percent of asteroids

---

30. Steven R. Chesley and Paul W. Chodas (posted October 16, 2003), "Orbit for Hermes Dynamically Linked from 1937 to 2003," *NASA NEO Program News*, Jet Propulsion Laboratory (accessed February 1, 2009).

31. "69230 Hermes" in *Wikipedia: The Free Encyclopedia*, http://en.wikipedia.org/wiki/69230_Hermes (accessed October 22, 2011).

32. Don Yeomans (posted January 21, 2009), "Chicken Little Was Right! The Sky Is Falling," Lecture given at NASA Jet Propulsion Laboratory, January 21, 2009. Notes in possession of A. Scott Howe.

in the smaller 0.100km–1km range have been found; these smaller objects probably cannot be spotted far in advance of impact. Unfortunately an asteroid the size of a small garage could destroy a city. This is quite alarming, meaning that 85 percent of the 0.100km–1km range asteroids, well within the definition for an ELE, could hit with little or no advance warning.

It will be immensely worth our effort to develop space technologies and find ways to safely live and work in space, not only via robotic tools but also via direct human presence. The Shoemaker-Levy 9 and July 2009 Jupiter impacts may be a warning we cannot afford to ignore.

Spiritual Insights

Having discussed the secular motivations for engaging in space research and development, we think the stronger argument for Latter-day Saints should be a spiritual perspective. In our experience of working for a national space agency, the three of us have witnessed engineers and scientists achieve what might normally have been considered impossible or miraculous. We daily sit in meetings and lectures and feel our hearts burn as we listen to the visionary solutions and enthusiasm as one or another of our colleagues proposes radically new concepts and technologies for the exploration and development of space. We think the reason for this reaction is simple: The purpose is to further our knowledge of the Lord's creations; and in everyone's minds, LDS or non-LDS, each is serving the entire human race, benefiting untold billions of Heavenly Father's children. Brigham Young once said, "The construction of the electric telegraph and the method of using it, enabling the people to send messages from one end of the earth to the other, is just as much a revelation from God as any ever given. The same is true with regard to making machinery, whether it be a steamboat, a carding machine, a sailing vessel, a rowing vessel, a plow, harrow, rake, sewing machine, threshing machine, or anything else, it makes no difference—these things have existed from all eternity and will continue to all eternity, and the Lord has revealed them to His children."[33] Elder Russell M. Nelson, a contemporary apostle, explained, "God is inspiring the minds of great people to create inventions that further the work of the Lord in ways this world has never known."[34]

---

33. Brigham Young, November 13, 1870, *Journal of Discourses*, 26 vols. (London and Liverpool: LDS Booksellers Depot, 1855–86), 13:305, http://journalofdiscourses.org (accessed August 1, 2008).

34. Boyd K. Packer and Russell M. Nelson, "Computerized Scriptures Now Available: A Conversation with Elder Boyd K. Packer and Elder Russell M. Nelson about the New Computerized Scriptures," *Ensign*, April 1988, 73.

Joseph Fielding Smith, apostle and Church president, said:

> I maintain that had there been no restoration of the gospel, and no organization of the Church of Jesus Christ of Latter-day Saints, there would have been no radio; there would have been no airplane, and there would not have been the wonderful discoveries in medicine, chemistry, electricity, and the many other things wherein the world has been benefited by such discoveries. Under such conditions these blessings would have been withheld, for they belong to the Dispensation of the Fulness of Times of which the restoration of the gospel and the organization of the Church constitute the central point, from which radiates the Spirit of the Lord throughout the world. The inspiration of the Lord has gone out and takes hold of the minds of men, though they know it not, and they are directed by the Lord. In this manner he brings them into his service that his purposes and his righteousness, in due time, may be supreme on the earth. . . . I do not believe for one moment that these discoveries have come by chance, or that they have come because of superior intelligence possessed by men today over those who lived in ages that are past. They have come and are coming because the time is ripe, because the Lord has willed it, and because he has poured out his Spirit on all flesh.[35]

We believe that the great outpouring of inspiration in regard to space technology and development is for an as-yet-unspecified role in building up the kingdom of God. "Where there is no vision the people perish" (Prov. 29:18). It is imagination that must motivate the research. Things that were once relegated to the realm of science fiction are now becoming reality. All three of us witness and are a part of the bringing forth of technologies that we read about as fiction in our youth. We can also find inspiration for advanced technologies in the scriptures. For instance, when we think of Joseph Smith's description of the arrival of Moroni in his bedroom in a tube of light, we can speculate that the Lord has available to him a mode of transportation between two distant points that allows almost instantaneous travel, as if the speed of light is no limitation (Joseph Smith—History 1:43). Science fiction uses similar contrivances such as wormholes and personnel transport systems. Can it be that some of those authors were inspired by fantastic concepts and that the Lord has poured out these concepts for the purpose of sparking ideas in later generations? Joseph's description gives one proof that such modes of transportation might be possible and may be worth pursuing as a technology. Already the concept of traversable wormholes, allowing for passage between two points

---

35. Joseph Fielding Smith, *Conference Report*, October 1926, 117, quoted in ibid., 73.

in the universe without violating the speed of light, is being discussed in a scholarly way. Kip Thorne and others have shown mathematically that traversable wormholes may be possible.[36] Given a thousand years, engineers may be able to solve the problem. The Holy Spirit sparks change in the way this knowledge is viewed in order to cause things to be invented and developed at the time when they are needed to further the work of the Lord. We believe that even if the use of such higher technologies is not available to mortals, it will still be our responsibility to learn and understand advanced technologies someday, as we progress toward godhood. Would the Lord trust us with the power if we did not first go from grace to grace and learn for ourselves the pitfalls and dangers of that power?

Scriptural Connections

When asked whether it is important to establish a space program or to develop space-faring technologies, many are confused, even among Latter-day Saints, and assume that such a program could not have any relation to the work of the Lord. Pointing out that our world is vulnerable to asteroid impact or other dangers beyond the fragile envelope of our atmosphere only brings the response: "If an asteroid were to endanger the earth, I'm sure the Lord would protect us." However, what they fail to understand is that, if the inspiration for these space-faring technologies are being revealed to us in these latter days as part of the dispensation of the fulness of times, then there must be a reason that the Lord would prepare us in this way. General Moroni said: "Behold, could ye suppose that ye could sit upon your thrones, and because of the exceeding goodness of God ye could do nothing and he would deliver you? Behold, if ye have supposed this ye have supposed in vain. . . . Or do ye suppose that the Lord will still deliver us, while we sit upon our thrones and do not make use of the means which the Lord has provided for us?" (Alma 60:11, 21) From the second sentence, we can infer that, if the earth is in danger from near-earth space objects, then we must do whatever we can to protect ourselves or those "flaming mountains" (Rev. 8:8) will surely do more damage than we can possibly imagine. Perhaps the Lord is protecting us by inspiring us to develop the means to protect ourselves.

---

36. Kip S. Thorne, "Closed Timelike Curves," Paper presented at the Thirteenth International Conference on General Relativity and Gravitation, 28 June—4 July 1992, Cordoba, Argentina; Hiroko Koyama, and Sean A. Hayward, "Construction and Enlargement of Traversable Wormholes from Schwarzschild Black Holes," *Physical Review* D 70 (June 2004): 084001.

Latter-day Saints believe that God was once a man who, through obedience to co-eternal laws, progressed from one degree to another until He was exalted and attained perfection. The Prophet Joseph Smith taught, "God himself was once as we are now, and is an exalted Man."[37] Lorenzo Snow taught, "As man now is, God once was; as God now is, man may be."[38] John Taylor, apostle and Church president, stated: "As the horse, the ox, the sheep, and every living creature, including man, propagates its own species and perpetuates its own kind, so does God perpetuate His."[39] And there are hints that God not only perpetuates His race like all living creatures, but also that the earth may also be able to perpetuate itself through us, as we will discuss later. Joseph Fielding Smith wrote: "The great universe of stars has multiplied beyond the comprehension of men. Evidently each of these great systems is governed by divine law; with divine presiding Gods, for it would be unreasonable to assume that each was not so governed."[40] This perspective suggests that God's skills for organizing and creating may have begun in an engineering environment similar to our own and that, should we persist in disciplining ourselves in the proper use of creative powers and organizing skills, we may also eventually achieve godhood. The implication is that God our Father is a representative of a race of celestial engineers who have the capacity to find or form planets and adapt them for life. Using engineered organisms, the race of advanced celestial engineers phase by phase enhance the complexity in the native environment until it is able to support their own offspring. This "terraforming" exercise is so important that it was described three times by two different prophets: by Moses in the books of Genesis and Moses, and by Abraham in the book of Abraham. Indeed, Abraham attributes the Creation to the "Gods," implying a community effort of the Godhead, and perhaps others as well.[41]

---

37. Joseph Smith, April 6, 1844, "King Follett Discourse," reported by Willard Richards, Wilford Woodruff, Thomas Bullock, and William Clayton, *Journal of Discourses* 6:3, http://journalofdiscourses.org (accessed September 1, 2008).

38. Lorenzo Snow, quoted in Eliza R. Snow Smith, *Biography and Family Record of Lorenzo Snow* (Salt Lake City: Deseret News Company, 1884), 46.

39. John Taylor, *The Mediation and Atonement* (Salt Lake City: Deseret News Printing, 1882), 150.

40. Joseph Fielding Smith, *Answers to Gospel Questions*, 5 vols. (Salt Lake City: Deseret Book, 1958): 2:144.

41. See the biblical account, attributed to Moses in Genesis chapter 1, and the Pearl of Great Price where scripture received by Joseph Smith gives the

Spiritual Underpinnings

As children of God, we are expected to shoulder the work of the Lord. We understand that the Lord's work is to "bring to pass the immortality and eternal life of man" (Moses 1:39). Unfortunately, many take this verse out of context. Preceding this verse are passages explaining that the Lord's work is to provide worlds upon which His children may dwell, so that they can achieve immortality and eternal life:

> And he beheld many lands; and each land was called earth, and there were inhabitants on the face thereof. (Moses 1:29)
>
> And worlds without number have I created; and I also created them for mine own purpose; and by the Son I created them, which is mine Only Begotten. (Moses 1:33)
>
> And as one earth shall pass away, and the heavens thereof even so shall another come, and there is no end to my work, neither to my words.
>
> For behold, this is my work and my glory—to bring to pass the immortality and eternal life of man. (Moses 1:38–39)

Other passages also suggest that the Lord as an engineer prepared the earth for His children to dwell upon:

> Behold the Lord hath created the earth that it should be inhabited; and he hath created his children that they should possess it. (1 Ne. 17:36)
>
> That by him, and through him, and of him, the worlds are and were created, and the inhabitants thereof are begotten sons and daughters unto God. (D&C 76:24)

It should be a logical conclusion that the process of peopling other worlds would be one of our responsibilities at some point, and perhaps the current outpouring of inspiration regarding space technology is in preparation for that time. Might it be that, through our means, the earth may reproduce and perpetuate its biosphere on another world, thus "giving birth" to another living planet? Again and again, our hearts burn as we participate in the effort to establish a permanent outpost on the moon or to provide a habitable vehicle for long-duration missions to asteroids, other near-earth objects, and even Mars in preparation for humanity to live and work in space and on other worlds. We sorrow when there is talk of abandoning or reducing the scope of space research by those who lack vision and inspiration.

In considering the process the Lord might take to place His children on other worlds, it is apparent that the Lord has followed similar processes while peopling other continents here on earth: "And behold I prepare you

---

creation account twice, in Moses chapter 2 and Abraham chapters 4–5. For Abraham's references to "the Gods," see, for example, Abraham 4:3, 4:7, and 5:4.

against these things," he explained to the Jaredites, "for ye cannot cross this great deep save I prepare you against the waves of the sea, and the winds which have gone forth, and the floods which shall come" (Ether 2:25).

How did the Lord prepare Jared and his brother against the waves of the sea? He prepared them by giving them inspiration about how to build water-tight barges or submarines that would be able to remain intact "as a whale in the midst of the sea" (Ether 2:24). Thus, the Lord commanded His servants to prepare in advance for survival in the extreme environments they would encounter.

Insights from LDS Church Authorities

Church authorities have had opinions about life on other planets and the colonization of the earth that should, at the least, cause us to reflect rather than dismiss the concept out of hand. Brigham Young taught that God "is our Father—the Father of our spirits, and was once a man in mortal flesh as we are, and is now an exalted Being. . . . [T]here never was a time when there were not Gods and worlds, and when men were not passing through the same ordeals that we are now passing through."[42] God created humankind to become gods. Brigham preached in another sermon: "The Lord has organized mankind for the express purpose of increasing that intelligence and truth, which is with God, until he is capable of creating worlds on worlds, and becoming Gods, even the sons of God."[43] Young also taught "Though we have it in history that our father Adam was made of the dust of this earth, and that he knew nothing about his God previous to being made here, yet it is not so; and when we learn the truth we shall see and understand that he helped to make this world, and was the chief manager in that operation. He was the person who brought the animals and the seeds from other planets to this world, and brought a wife with him and stayed here. . . . Adam was made from the dust of an earth, but not from the dust of this earth."[44] He repeated this point in another sermon: "Mankind are here because they are the offspring of parents who were first brought here from another planet,

---

42. Brigham Young, October 8, 1859, *Journal of Discourses*, 7:333, http://journalofdiscourses.org (accessed February 1, 2009).

43. Brigham Young, August 8, 1852, *Journal of Discourses*, 3:93, http://journalofdiscourses.org (accessed February 1, 2009).

44. Brigham Young, April 20, 1856, *Journal of Discourses*, 3:319, http://journalofdiscourses.org (accessed February 1, 2009).

and power was given them to propagate their species, and they were commanded to multiply and replenish the earth."[45]

Brigham's counselor in the First Presidency, Heber C. Kimball, similarly taught: "The religion of Jesus Christ, of angels, of Brigham, and of all good men is to take care of and improve and adorn the earth as Adam did. When he planted the garden, he planted it with seeds he brought with him; and he also brought the animals from the earth he lived upon, where his Father dwelt."[46]

Joseph Fielding Smith, a twentieth-century apostle and Church president, explained, "We are not the only people that the Lord has created. We have brothers and sisters on other earths. They look like us because they, too, are the children of God and were created in his image, for they are also his offspring."[47]

Even more recently, Spencer W. Kimball, another apostle who also became Church president, taught: "We learn both the spiritual things and the secular things so that we may one day create worlds, people and govern them."[48] Most recently, Apostle Neal A. Maxwell wrote, "We do not know how many inhabited worlds there are, or where they are. But certainly we are not alone."[49]

Discussion

It is the Lord's way to direct the work while His servants perform the work. Therefore it is logical to consider that the peopling of other worlds will occur according to natural laws and that the recent outpouring of inspiration regarding space technology is for the purpose of building a foundation of necessary technologies that will allow us to participate in this great work. We cannot be certain whether this will occur in our mortal phase or afterwards, but we can be clear that sooner or later we will be required to learn these technologies.

---

45. Brigham Young, October 9, 1859, *Journal of Discourses*, 7:282, http://journalofdiscourses.org (accessed August 1, 2008).

46. Heber C. Kimball, June 12, 1860, *Journal of Discourses*, 8:243–44, http://journalofdiscourses.org (accessed August 1, 2008).

47. Joseph Fielding Smith, *Doctrines of Salvation: Sermons and Writings of Joseph Fielding Smith*, edited by Bruce R. McConkie, 3 vols. (Salt Lake City: Bookcraft, 1954–56), 1:62.

48. Edward L. Kimball, comp. and ed., *The Teachings of Spencer W. Kimball* (Salt Lake City: Deseret Book, 1982), 386.

49. Neal A. Maxwell, *Wonderful Flood of Light* (Salt Lake City: Bookcraft, 1990), 25.

The Lord's people have always been colonizers brought from distant lands to the "land of promise." Remember Noah who prepared an ark that was protected from the flood, Abraham who was inspired to relocate to Canaan, Moses who led the children of Israel across the desert, the brother of Jared who led his people across the sea safely in watertight "barges," Mulek who settled Zerahemla, Lehi who left Jerusalem and crossed the ocean to the New World, and Brigham Young who led his people across the plains to the Rocky Mountains. Even today, in a spiritual sense, the Church is active in colonization; in the frontier of the Church, missionaries are frequently asked to leave established cities and open up new branches where Church members are few, if any.

And there are other interesting items to note by way of discussion. The Garden of Eden was watered by mist when the world outside was a wilderness (Gen. 2:6; Moses 3:6). Was the Garden of Eden the first earth incubator? Could the Garden of Eden have been a first outpost, established on the earth for the purposes of colonization, complete with automated environmental control and life support systems (a term used to describe life support systems on spacecraft)? Did the wilderness describe a harsh wasteland, similar to what we observe on Mars, not quite complete in its terraforming process?

Another interesting concept, also for the purposes of discussion, is that the geological record could be showing the results of evolution—or it could be showing the evidence of a long process of terraforming. The Creation story seems to describe what might be a terraforming process. Indeed evolution may be one of the tools that terraformers would use to optimize engineered organisms and gradually prepare the highly complex biosphere needed for human organisms to survive. Considering self-replicating cells to be programmable building blocks for all sorts of structures, an advanced race of celestial engineers could gradually introduce off-the-shelf solutions into their terraforming projects as the need arises or invent new ones on-the-fly. Adaptable engineering that responds to changes in the environment over multiple generations, selecting from pre-packaged programs taking their cues from external signals and being optimized through emergence would be a logical approach for the engineers to take. Perhaps the evidence shows a kinship of all life because the advanced engineers used the same highly adaptive set of programmable building blocks to construct the bodies of each species. Whether the organisms appeared strictly through emergence from a single ancestor or were physically brought and placed in turn as an already developed species, that kinship would be apparent.

Spiritual Underpinnings

The Creation story mentions several points at which God and those involved in the preparation of the new world initiate new phases in the Creation sequence. We can imagine advanced celestial engineers periodically visiting the new world to take samples of the atmosphere, water, soil, and variety of organisms and determining that the planet is ready for the next step. We can see in our mind's eye advanced celestial biologists selectively engineering certain organisms and releasing them into the environment where they take over the older generations, and slowly bring the biosphere up to a new level of readiness. This is not mere speculation; this is an engineering plan—and in some ways it's happening already. Astronomer Martin Beech provides a serious technical discussion on how we could change Mars or other worlds to be more habitable,[50] and the aerospace community is starting to see more and more credible proposals in peer-reviewed technical conferences for how we might do this. In other recent NASA proposals with which we are familiar, it has been seriously proposed to capture a small 8m diameter asteroid and bring it to earth's orbit as a practice for various technologies, such as asteroid capture, propulsion, mining, and other tasks that would be needed on larger bodies. The will, hope, faith, and causal means to move planets is being inspired in the minds of those around us already.

As we begin to prepare for a lunar outpost or visit to an asteroid and make our first tentative steps beyond the earth's moon, the solar system appears to be an ideal location to train a planet-bound civilization to become a space-faring civilization. From the moon, to Mars, to asteroids, to more remote planets and extreme environments, the stepping stones are there to guide us from simple outposts to large colonies to altering entire environments; there's enough to keep us busy for thousands of years at least, until we have gained the knowledge and self-discipline needed to join the Lord's celestial civilization. If we were allowed to join His civilization without going through the growth and experience phase, we would not be sufficiently knowledgeable and self-disciplined to handle the technologies and powers He enjoys. God will not allow us to pose a risk to His civilization. If we cannot abide the law, we cannot live in the kingdom. The thousand-year Millennium may (among other such activities as genealogy and temple work) be required as a growth and a testing period for us as individuals to see if we can actually live as a Zion society. There should be plenty of time for planetary exploration and technological development if that is what God wants us to do. This is where we feel that space technology de-

---

50. Martin Beech, *Terraforming: The Creating of Habitable Worlds* (New York: Springer, 2009).

velopment will eventually fit into the four-fold mission of the Church, by helping to perfect the Saints, and provide limitless resources for the needy.

Some critics say that emphasis on space development, particularly a panspermic space program, may be similar to the Tower of Babel. "Panspermia" refers to the spreading of the seed of life through space from planet to planet.[51] If indeed the current work is inspired as a result of the pouring out of the Spirit in the dispensation of the fulness of times, the timing is right for this technology, and the Lord is conscious of where it will be needed in the building up of His kingdom. It is not for us to say whether the technology and knowledge will be applied in our mortal sojourn or later in our progression, only that we should prepare ourselves and be ready to make the advancements when the inspiration is made available to us.

In conclusion, we suspect that Heavenly Father, as an advanced celestial engineer interested in propagating His civilization, may be pouring out his Spirit on all who will listen for the purpose of establishing a foundation to prepare us with the necessary tools and technologies that will eventually lead to the creation and colonization of other worlds. We have prepared this paper for discussion purposes and believe that the LDS community, and, indeed, all of humanity, should consider this possibility in all seriousness. The weight of public opinion on matters relating to space exploration may depend on this discussion—to our blessing or to our condemnation.

---

51. Brig Klyce, "Cosmic Ancestry: The Modern Version of Panspermia," n.d., http://www.panspermia.org (accessed February 1, 2009).

11
Welcome to the Twenty-First Century: The Uncharted Future Ahead

David H. Bailey

Abstract

The past few decades have been a time of breathtaking advances in science and technology. Our daily living patterns, social institutions, and religious institutions have all been affected. Unfortunately for those who dislike change, the forecast is for more of the same—unrelenting, even accelerating, change for decades to come. Nanotechnology, biotechnology, information technology, and medical technology are all poised for dramatic advances. These developments will challenge our social and religious institutions as never before. What are the dangers ahead? How can we direct these developments for good and not evil? Such questions have particular import for Latter-day Saints, who have had a rich tradition of progress, as exemplified by the law of eternal progression. To what extent are we (or should we be) discovering the fundamental facts of the universe and building the kingdom of God with our efforts?

Introduction

It is not unusual to hear, both in academic and religious circles, people questioning the very notion of human progress. For instance, respected historian-philosophers Will and Ariel Durant, in a book written at the conclusion of their monumental eleven-volume *Story of Civilization*, devoted one chapter to the question "Is Progress Real?"[1] Prominent scholar

---

1. Will and Ariel Durant, *The Lessons of History* (New York: Simon and Schuster, 1968), 95–102.

Thomas S. Kuhn questioned whether "successive scientific theories grow ever closer to, or approximate more and more closely, the truth."[2] More recently, other postmodern scholars have extended this skepticism much more broadly, to question any notion of scientific progress.[3] Even within the LDS Church, it is not uncommon to hear woeful talk of society "going down the tubes," and questions about whether scientific or technological advances have any eternal significance.[4]

To a researcher of science and/or technology such as myself, such talk is incomprehensible. Of course, progress is real. In spite of continuing (and very real) problems with crime, pollution, and moral disintegration, real progress is being made in a broad range of pure and applied science. To a scientist or technologist who is also a religious believer—and particularly one in the Latter-day Saint tradition—such developments raise intriguing questions. For example, to what extent is this progress ordained and even directed by God? To what extent are we (or should we be) discovering the fundamental facts of the universe and building the kingdom of God in our efforts?

A Brief History of the Past Fifty Years

The past fifty years have been quite unlike any other fifty-year period in human history. Radio and television brought instant news and entertainment from around the world to our homes. Computers emerged from the laboratory, were deployed in large corporations and universities, then came into the home, and most recently arrived in the palm of our hands in the form of smartphones. The internet and the worldwide web sprang upon us in the closing decade of the twentieth century, and already a sizable fraction of the U.S. workforce could not perform their jobs without them. Pharmaceuticals, vaccinations, and advanced medical technologies have banished many diseases and causes of premature death from much (though, sadly, not all) of the world. And scientific research has continued its relentless advance, unveiling the secrets of subatomic particles, the extent of the universe, and the digital code of life.

Needless to say, these developments have had profound impact on our social, governmental, and religious institutions. Television and the auto-

---

2. Thomas S. Kuhn, *The Structure of Scientific Revolutions* (Chicago: University of Chicago Press, 1970), 206.

3 Alan D. Sokal and Jean Bricmont, *Fashionable Nonsense: Postmodern Intellectuals' Abuse of Science* (New York: Picador, 1998), 1–17.

4 Joseph Fielding McConkie, *Answers: Straightforward Answers to Tough Gospel Questions* (Salt Lake City: Deseret Book, 1998), 223.

mobile substantially changed our daily lifestyle. Now home computers, cell phones, and telecommuting are changing our lifestyle again, except much more rapidly than before. Numerous institutions and customs, ranging from racial segregation and male-only institutions of higher learning to smoking in the workplace, have not been able to withstand the scrutiny of our modern age and have largely disappeared. National governments have been toppled in part because modern information technology exposed to their citizens the indisputable fact that economic conditions and civil freedoms were significantly better elsewhere. Although regional conflicts continue, large-scale war has disappeared, certainly not because the technology to wage war is no longer available, but instead because the modern global economic system has made armed conflicts among major trading partners unthinkable.[5]

Obviously many problems have arisen along with the good. Our global high-tech economy has greatly increased overall wealth (the U.S. gross domestic product, adjusted for inflation, has increased by a factor of 6.5 since 1950[6]), but millions have been left behind in poverty and ignorance. Millions more now fear being displaced in the rapidly changing world of global commerce. Our global economy has produced trash and pollution as prolifically as it produces goods and services—indeed, it is now widely recognized that our heavy usage of fossil-based energy is threatening our very existence on this planet.[7] The internet has created millions of new jobs and has enabled millions of others to work at home and to collaborate with others in distant lands, but it has also launched epidemics of fraud, spam, and pornography; some 90 percent of all email is now spam.[8] Cell phones have facilitated an increasingly mobile and dispersed workforce and have saved many a marriage, but they have also been used by terrorists to detonate bombs. And numerous (mostly conservative) religious traditions have been challenged by the findings of modern science, spawning a major backlash, as exemplified by the recent campaign to replace conventional geology and biology with "scientific creationism" and "intelligent

---

5. Thomas L. Friedman, *The World Is Flat: A Brief History of the Twenty-First Century* (New York: Farrar, Straus and Giroux, 2005), 414–48.

6. Bureau of Economic Analysis, U.S. Department of Commerce, "Current-Dollar and Real GDP," http://www.bea.gov/national/index.htm#gdp (accessed October 25, 2011).

7. Gabrielle Walker and David King, *The Hot Topic: What We Can Do about Global Warming* (New York: Mariner Books, 2008), 47–64.

8. "Effective Spam Filtering," http://www.spamhaus.org/effective_filtering.html (accessed October 25, 2011).

design" in U.S. public schools.[9] To many Christians, these developments echo the biblical prophecies of "wars and commotions" and "men's hearts failing them for fear" in the last days (Luke 21:9, 26).

What will the future hold? First of all, the current pace of scientific and technological advancement shows no sign of slowing down and, in fact, is likely to accelerate in the coming years.[10] For example, even during the recent economic downturn, Moore's Law (the doubling in aggregate power and capacity of computer chips every eighteen months or so) continues unabated. It recently passed the forty-five-year milestone, and experts say that it is almost certain to continue for at least another ten years.[11] Indeed, given some of the recent developments in the field of nanotechnology (the science of constructing materials and devices at or near the atomic scale), it is quite possible that Moore's Law will continue for another twenty or thirty years, yielding computers and "smart" devices millions of times more powerful and capacious than current state-of-the-art units. And there is no shortage of suggestions of what to do with all that power—scientists and technologists are brimming with ideas for useful products and services, and venture capitalists are investing, not only in North America but also in Europe, India, and China.

Meanwhile, the field of biotechnology is taking off, promising an explosion of new advances in medical technology during the next few decades. These include effective treatments for a wide range of ailments and diseases, promising treatments for various forms of cancer, remarkable prostheses for numerous handicaps, and a trend toward individually targeted medication. Many common physical handicaps, including deafness, blindness, motor impairment, and others, will be mitigated or overcome. Finally, significant extensions of human life will be achieved. In the United States, we are currently adding roughly three years to life expectancy every ten years; medical innovations and a slowing of the aging process are expected to accelerate this trend. Within a few decades, even some relatively conservative observers in this arena are saying that 120-year lifespans will become common. Others are predicting much longer lifespans by the end of the twenty-first century.

---

9. Lauri Lebo, *The Devil in Dover: An Insider's Story of Dogma v. Darwin in Small-Town America* (New York: New Press, 2008).

10. Ray Kurzweil, *The Singularity Is Near* (New York: Viking Penguin, 2005), 7–30.

11. Michael Kanellos, "Moore's Law to Roll On for Another Decade," http://news.cnet.com/2100-1001-984051.html (accessed October 25, 2011).

Welcome to the Twenty-First Century

Did you feel flat-footed with the advent of personal computers, the worldwide web, cellular telephones, DNA sequencing, or sheep cloning? Are you afraid to ask your friends what a blog, Facebook page, JPEG, MP3, GPS, Ethernet, multicore, terabyte, podcast, nanotube, stem cell, or telomere is, because this might betray your ignorance of changing times? Unfortunately, no relief is in sight. Many more new and bewildering innovations are in store. Indeed, the acceleration of change is likely to be the defining characteristic of the twenty-first century, and managing this change for good rather than evil and social mayhem is likely to be the defining task of the twenty-first century. (By the way, these terms and many others are explained lucidly at http://www.wikipedia.com, a volunteer-produced, internet-based encyclopedia—another remarkable innovation of our times.)

At present, there is grave concern about the future outlook for energy, not only because of tightening supplies (on July 11, 2008, average U.S. gasoline prices peaked at $4.11 per gallon[12]), but also because of the growing consensus that our unbridled consumption of carbon-based fuels has warmed our planet, and that even more warming will occur in the future.[13] One of many potential adverse consequences would be the melting of the Greenland and Antarctic ice sheets, which would raise sea levels worldwide, inundating coastal land in poverty-stricken nations that can ill afford the necessary countermeasures. Fortunately, this concern has spurred a new ethic of conservation, as well as additional research and development in the field. One particularly promising prospect is solar energy, which is clean, renewable, and ample; only 1/100 of 1 percent of the daily influx of sunlight on the earth is sufficient to meet all current worldwide energy needs.[14]

Overview of Recent and Future Developments

Here is a sampler of some of the amazing developments already in the works:

---

12. "U.S. Gasoline Prices Continue Steady Rise: Survey," http://www.reuters.com/article/domesticNews/idUSTRE5271QR20090308 (accessed October 25, 2011).

13. Walker and King, *The Hot Topic*, 91.

14. Ray Kurzweil, "The Near-Term Inevitability of Radical Life Extension and Expansion," in John Brockman, ed., *What Is Your Dangerous Idea? Today's Leading Thinkers on the Unthinkable* (New York: Harper Perennial, 2007); also available at http://www.edge.org/q2006/q06_index.html (accessed October 25, 2011).

1. Advances in the field of nanotechnology (the design of devices and materials at or near the atomic scale) continue to confound skeptics who just a few years ago ridiculed the field as "cargo-cult" pseudoscience.[15] In just one of many recent developments, researchers at Hewlett-Packard have fabricated "nano-imprint crossbar" devices with features significantly smaller than the current semiconductor industry state-of-the-art. HP researchers are confident they can reduce these devices even more.[16]

2. A start-up company called Nantero soon hopes to market commercial memory devices based on nanotubes (cylindrical arrays of carbon atoms). Equally amazing are recent demonstrations of nanotube-based circuitry, which has the potential of speeds and densities hundreds of times greater than silicon devices.[17] In a related development, ultra-thin sheets of nanotubes, produced by a process as simple as pulling tape off a dispenser, are 2,000 times thinner than paper and much stronger per unit mass than steel, while other potential applications of nanotubes range from strong, flexible, lightweight auto bodies to "sky hooks" for space travel.[18]

3. Scientific supercomputers, which are used for a wide range of applications ranging from supernova simulations to solar cell design, continue to advance steadily in power. In November 2008, an IBM supercomputer at the Los Alamos Laboratory in New Mexico achieved 1.105 Pflop/s (i.e., 1.105 quadrillion or 1.105×10^{15} floating-point arithmetic operations per second) on a standard benchmark test. This system currently has 129,600 individual processor cores and 103 Tbyte (i.e. 103 trillion or 103×10^{12} bytes) of main memory.

Figure 1 contains performance data from the Top 500 list, an updated ranking of the world's most powerful scientific computer systems. The Number 1-rated system is advancing at a fairly steady rate of a factor of 1,000 every twelve years or so. Although many daunting future challenges must be addressed, it is likely that this overall rate of progress will continue indefinitely.

4. Quantum computing, a futuristic computing technology based on quantum superposition, one of the most eerie effects of quantum phys-

---

15. Gary Stix, "Trends in Nanotechnology: Waiting for Breakthroughs," *Scientific American*, April 1996, 94–99.

16. Philip J. Kuekes, Gregory S. Snider, and R. Stanley Williams, "Crossbar Nanocomputers," *Scientific American*, November 2005, 72–80.

17. Kurzweil, *The Singularity Is Near*, 114.

18. Mark Peplow, "Nanotube Sheets Come of Age," *Nature News*, August 18, 2005, also available at http://www.k8science.org/news/news.cfm?art=1976 (accessed October 25, 2011).

Welcome to the Twenty-First Century

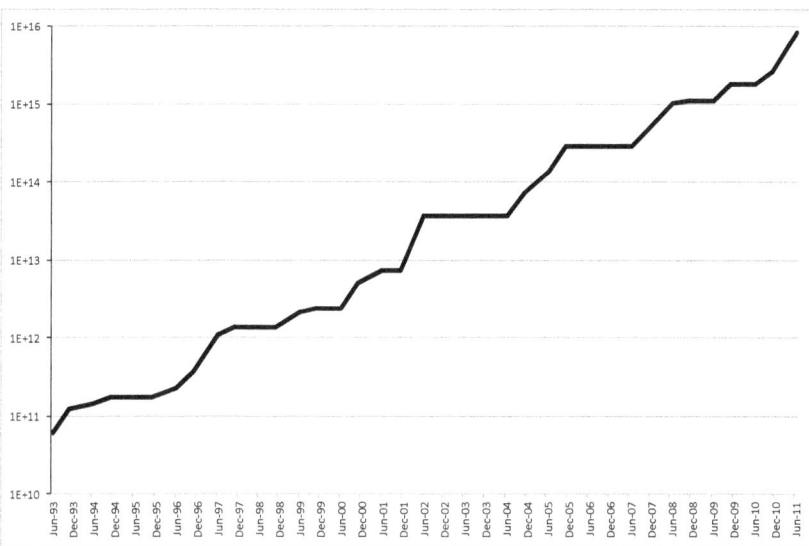

Figure 1. Performance rate of the world's most powerful supercomputer, from June 1993 to June 2011. The vertical scale is "floating-point operations per second," displayed in scientific notation: "1E+16" means 10^{16}, or in other words 10,000,000,000,000,000. Figure constructed by author, based on data from http://www.top500.org (accessed October 26, 2011).

ics, is steadily becoming more of a solid possibility for future computer technology. Scientists have already demonstrated integer factorization and image matching using a quantum computer, and are now trying to extend the capability of these systems beyond tiny laboratory demonstrations.[19]

5. Micro-electro-mechanical systems (MEMS) devices are rapidly shrinking in size and cost. They are already being widely used for air-bag systems in autos. Future uses include unobtrusive monitors for a wide range of environmental, transportation, and safety systems.[20]

6. The field of artificial intelligence (AI) has been energized by the 1997 defeat of world champion chess player Garry Kasparov by an IBM computer system and by the 2005 successful completion of a 132-mile ob-

---

19. Susan Hassler, "Prototype Commercial Quantum Computer Demonstrated," *IEEE Spectrum*, February 13, 2007, http://spectrum.ieee.org/tech-talk/semiconductors/devices/prototype_commercial_quantum_c (accessed October 25, 2011).

20. "About Citris: Mission Statement," http://www.citris-uc.org/about/mission (accessed October 25, 2011).

stacle course by several computer-controlled robotic vehicles.[21] Although many are still skeptical, some scientists are now predicting that computers will meet or exceed human intelligence (say, as defined by the "Turing test") in the 2030s or 2040s.[22] Will we then be obliged to recognize these machine intelligences as "human"?

7. Scientists now understand the structure of several major sections of the brain and are now pushing forward to model in detail the operation of some of these features. In one effort, Swiss researchers are employing an IBM BlueGene system to simulate a 10,000-neuron section of the brain. They estimate that simulating the entire brain will require perhaps a thousand times this much computing power, a level that should be available at a reasonable cost in ten to fifteen years.[23]

8. There is grave concern at present about energy consumption and global warming. But with this concern has come a new focus on energy efficiency. In January 2009 Toyota announced that in early 2012 it will offer to U.S. customers a plug-in hybrid vehicle, which will be able to run exclusively on its batteries for at least twenty miles per day; other auto companies have similar plans.[24] Numerous high-tech alternatives to fossil fuels are being developed, including nanotech-produced solar panels, and improvements in battery technology.[25] First Solar, a start-up firm in Tempe, Arizona, has recently installed a forty-megawatt solar plant in Germany and is ramping up its manufacturing capacity.[26]

9. Researchers doing work on technology for the handicapped now see a future in which physically impaired persons can regain much of their lost facility through high-tech, mentally controlled prostheses. Scientists have

---

21. John Markoff, "Behind Artificial Intelligence, a Squadron of Bright Real People," *New York Times*, October 14, 2005, http://www.nytimes.com/2005/10/14/technology/14artificial.html (accessed October 25, 2011).

22. Kurzweil, *The Singularity Is Near*, 259–97.

23. "Blue Gene Super to Simulate Key Part of the Human Brain," *Computer Business Review*, June 9, 2005, http://www.cbronline.com/news/blue_gene_super_to_simulate_key_part_of_the_human_brain (accessed October 25, 2011).

24. Michelle Maynard, "Toyota Will Offer a Plug-In Hybrid by 2010," *New York Times*, January 14, 2009, http://www.nytimes.com/2008/01/14/business/14plug.html (accessed October 25, 2011).

25. Lynn Yarris, "Sunny Future for Nanocrystal Solar Cells," October 20 2005, http://www.lbl.gov/Science-Articles/Archive/MSD-nanocrystal-solar-cells.html (accessed October 25, 2011).

26. Richard Stevenson, "First Solar: Quest for the $1 Watt," IEEE *Spectrum*, August 2008, http://spectrum.ieee.org/energy/renewables/first-solar-quest-for-the-1-watt (accessed October 25, 2011).

already succeeded in training a monkey to manipulate a robotic arm by thought alone.[27] What's more, it has been shown that long-term amputees still use patterns of mental signals to control their missing "limbs" that are entirely similar to those with real limbs, giving hope that this type of technology will be effective for them.[28]

10. Large-scale computer simulations are now being developed to test drugs "in silico," or in other words to model the effectiveness of drug agents using a supercomputer. Some researchers believe that within ten years we will be able to eliminate the need for many of the tests and clinical trials now required, yet produce drugs with fewer side effects.[29]

11. Several remarkable discoveries have been recently made in the use of stem cells. In a recent test, conducted jointly in the United States and Brazil, patients who were candidates for a heart transplant had stem cells from their bone marrow injected into the left ventricle of their hearts. In many cases, the damaged tissue regenerated itself, eliminating the need for the transplant.[30] In January 2009, Geron Corporation announced that it had received a federal go-ahead to launch clinical trials for its stem-cell-based therapy for spinal cord victims.[31]

12. Virus-induced expression of a human growth factor has reversed age-related changes in the skeletal muscle of mice. Increases of almost 30 percent in strength were witnessed in aged animals, compared with control subjects.[32] Along this line, mice at the Wistar Institute in Pennsylvania have the seemingly miraculous ability to regenerate limbs and regrow vital

---

27. "Monkey Brain Operates Machine," *BBC News*, http://news.bbc.co.uk/1/hi/sci/tech/1025471.stm (accessed October 25, 2011); see also Joel Garreau, (2005), *Radical Evolution: The Promise and Peril of Enhancing Our Minds, Our Bodies—and What It Means to Be Human* (New York: Doubleday, 2005), 19–20; and Kurzweil, *The Singularity Is Near*, 194–95.

28. Kurzweil, *The Singularity Is Near*, 308.

29. Ray Kurzweil and Terry Grossman, *Fantastic Voyage* (New York: Rodale Books, 2004), 27.

30. Ibid., 222.

31. Rob Stein (2009). "Government Approves Study Using Human Embryonic Stem Cells," *Washington Post*, January 24, 2009), http://www.washingtonpost.com/wp-dyn/content/story/2009/01/26/ST2009012601250.html (accessed October 25, 2011).

32. J. Pedro de Magalhaes, "The Dream of Elixir Vitae," in Immortality Institute, *The Scientific Conquest of Death: Essays on Infinite Lifespans* (Buenos Aires, Brazil: Libros en Red Publishers, 2004), 47–62; also E. R. Barton-Davis, D. I. Shoturma, A. Musaro, N. Rosenthal, and H. L. Sweeney (1998), "Viral Mediated Expression of Insulin-Like Growth Factor I Blocks the Aging-

organs.[33] Even more intriguing is the recent discovery that, by genetically engineering mice to "overexpress" a certain gene, scientists were able to extend the lifespan of these mice by 20 to 30 percent.[34]

13. Some remarkable cancer therapies are in development. In 2006, the drug manufacturer Merck launched a vaccine against human papilloma virus (HPV), thought to be the cause of 75 percent of all cervical cancer. Vaccines are in the works for other forms of cancer as well.[35] Another approach that may be broadly effective against many types of cancer is through the use of "angiogenesis inhibitors," namely agents that inhibit the creation of new blood vessels critical to tumor growth.[36] Great strides are also being made in the early detection of cancer. A Harvard team has developed a chip to detect prostate cancer, using silicon wires just 10 nanometers wide. When as few as three or four prostate-specific antigen (PSA) molecules are detected, the device generates a signal.[37]

14. Some remarkable advances have been achieved recently in "nanomedicine," namely the application of submicroscopic, custom-designed particles for medical diagnosis and drug delivery. For instance, submicroscopic "nanomachines" can be used to gain entry to tumor cells and then destroy them. A 2009 article in *Scientific American* described this and several other nanomedicine developments.[38]

15. In the diabetes arena, researchers at the Children's Hospital in Boston have discovered that two particular genes are changed when diabetes develops, thus suggesting effective treatment for child-onset dia-

---

Related Loss of Skeletal Muscle Function," in *Proceedings of the National Academy of Sciences* 95 (1998): 15603–7.

33. Kirsten Philipkoski, "Mighty Mice Regrow Organs," *Wired*, September 29, 2005, http://www.wired.com/news/print/0,1294,68962,00.html (accessed October 25, 2011).

34. H. Kurosu, M, Yamamoto, J. D. Clark, J. V. Pastor, A. Nandi, P. Gurnani, O. P. McGuinness, H. Chikuda, M. Yamaguchi, H. Kawaguchi, I. Shimomura, Y. Takayama, J. Herz, C. R. Kahn, K. P. Rosenblatt, and M. Kuro-o, "Suppression of Aging in Mice by the Hormone Klotho," *Science* 309 (September 16, 2005): 1829–33.

35. "FDA Approves First Drug Treatment for Late-Stage Cervical Cancer," http://www.fda.gov/NewsEvents/Newsroom/PressAnnouncements/2006/ucm108672.htm (accessed October 25, 2011).

36. Kurzweil and Grossman, *Fantastic Voyage*, 240.

37. Ibid., 154.

38. James R. Heath, Mark E. Davis, and Leroy Hood, "Nanomedicine Targets Cancer," *Scientific American*, February 2009, 44–51.

betes.[39] In a related development, researchers have successfully attached insulin-producing cells to a microchip that can be implanted in the body to provide an adequate supply of insulin and is regulated by a device that automatically monitors blood glucose levels.[40]

16. University of Michigan researchers are developing a bio-artificial kidney for cleaning blood. In a clinical trial, six out of ten critically ill patients, all but one of whom had been judged to have no more than a 10 to 20 percent chance of survival, were successfully treated.[41]

17. Scientists have identified seven broad categories of molecular and cellular difference between older and younger people (now termed the "seven deadly things"), which researchers are now actively attempting to understand and ultimately defeat: (1) a decline in the number of cells in certain tissues; (2) an accumulation of unwanted cells of certain types; (3) mutations in chromosomes; (4) mutations in mitochondria; (5) random cross-links between long-lived extracellular proteins; (6) an accumulation of chemically inert but bulky "junk" in our lysosomes; and (7) similar "junk" in extracellular spaces. Progress has been made in understanding each of these seven items.[42]

Ethical, Moral, and Social Issues

Recent discussion of future technological wonders frightens many people, and not just social conservatives, religious fundamentalists, and anti-technology "Luddites." Many scientists see vast potential for trouble, such as genetic experiments that go awry, nanotech "gray goo" that multiplies without bounds, robots running amok, computers smarter than their human masters, biotech experiments creating and destroying human life, etc. (insert your favorite science fiction scenario here). Computer technologist Bill Joy has written perhaps the gravest warning of the dangers ahead in his widely publicized essay "Why the Future Doesn't Need Us."[43] He emphasizes not only the many dangers of technology running amok, but also the possibility that future intelligent systems may increasingly deal with humans as mere "pets"—amusing companions, but no longer a vital, decision-making part of the operating world. Even inventor Ray Kurzweil,

---

39. Kurzweil and Grossman, *Fantastic Voyage*, 130.
40. Ibid., 130.
41. Ibid., 193.
42. Aubrey de Grey, "The War on Aging," in Immortality Institute, *The Scientific Conquest of Death*, 29–46.
43. Bill Joy, "Why the Future Doesn't Need Us," *Wired*, April 2000, http://www.wired.com/wired/archive/8.04/joy_pr.html (accessed October 25, 2011).

one of the more optimistic observers in this arena, soberly acknowledges these dangers.[44]

Even if major disasters can be avoided, there will be many difficult issues to confront, notably the potential for social, economic, and international strife, and the continual challenge to make these advances available to society in a reasonably democratic way. But some argue that only by aggressively exploiting these and other advanced technologies can we hope to overcome the daunting challenges we now face worldwide, where hundreds of millions lack sufficient food, clean water, decent housing, health care, adequate energy, education, and a livable environment. Observers of widely disparate political stripes can be found on both sides of the debate.[45]

If there is one thing that these observers agree on, it is that many of these developments are largely unstoppable. For example, how will anyone be able to convince some handicapped person that he and she cannot take advantage of some promising new thought-controlled prosthesis, just because a few nonhandicapped bluenoses are concerned about the "ethical issues" of such technology? Also, how can anyone convince poor farmers in rural China that they should not use a new strain of nutrient-enhanced rice that will enhance the health of millions, just because some amply fed Americans and Europeans are nervous (without much scientific basis) about potential dangers? You can't. So the best we can do is to manage these changes: thoughtfully consider the dangers, insist on thorough testing, and then carefully monitor the results. At the very least, we need to judiciously pick our battles; a knee-jerk opposition to everything new will only be seen as Luddite obstruction of progress.

We have already seen ethical concerns expressed in the area of stem cell research, with critics asserting that destroying a collection of stem cells is tantamount to destroying a human life. As a result, the U.S. Congress blocked most federal funding for stem cell research, although the Obama administration reversed that position.[46] The Catholic Church, among other groups, has opposed stem cell research for the same reason. In response, some states, such as California, have initiated and funded their own stem cell research programs. Fortunately, scientists have now demonstrated a

---

44. Kurzweil, "The Singularity Is Near," 391–424.

45. James Hughes, *Citizen Cyborg* (Boulder, Colo.: Westview Press, 2004), 107–84.

46. Rob Stein, "Government Approves Study Using Human Embryonic Stem Cells," *Washington Post*, January 24, 2009, http://www.washingtonpost.com/wp-dyn/content/story/2009/01/26/ST2009012601250.html (accessed October 25, 2011).

way to derive embryonic stem cells without destroying the embryo.[47] In any event, it is clear that this sort of issue will be thrust on society over and over again in the coming years.

Writers such as Joel Garreau and James Hughes have examined a number of these issues, including the following: (1) How can we prevent advanced technologies from falling into the hands of those who might use them for evil purposes? (2) How can we encourage constructive uses of new technology, and yet discourage unethical uses (such as "designing" a deaf child), without severe restrictions on individual freedom? (3) How are we going to handle the economic divide between those who can afford exotic technology and those who cannot? (4) How are we going to finance the medical and pension costs of an increasingly aged population, even if many of these people will be able to continue doing productive work? (5) How can we avoid the development that society will become so risk-averse (due in part to the many older citizens) that any substantive changes or new initiatives are not democratically possible? (6) How will "enhanced humans" and "conventional humans" peacefully and respectfully co-exist? (7) What type of governmental system will be best in this environment? (8) How will religious movements adapt to these changes?[48]

It is abundantly clear that education must become a top priority—not just for youth but for adults as well. Sadly, education in the United States, while somewhat improved over past years, is still mired in mediocrity. In an international study, 44 percent of eighth-graders in Singapore scored at the most advanced level in mathematics, as did 38 percent in Taiwan; only 7 percent of American eighth-graders did. American fifteen-year-olds are also below the international average when it comes to applying math to real-life tasks.[49] The United States cannot continue to rely on a steady stream of bright students from Asia to make up this education deficit; many of those talented young people now see comparable opportunities in their own booming economies. What's more, we now face the reality that, in the dynamic global economy, workers will have to reeducate themselves several times in their careers, and careers will last longer due to longer life spans.

---

47. Y. Chung, I. Klimanskaya, S. Becker, T. Li, M. Maserati, S. J. Lu, T. Zdravkovic, D. Ilic, O. Genbacev, S. Fisher, A. Krtolica, and R. Lanza, "Human Embryonic Stem Cell Lines Generated without Embryo Destruction," *Cell: Stem Cell* 2, no. 2 (February 7, 2008): 113–17.

48. Garreau, *Radical Evolution*, 229–65; see also Hughes, *Citizen Cyborg*, 187–266.

49. Friedman, *The World Is Flat*, 272.

I should mention here that the LDS Church has always had a strong tradition of education, with a particularly strong showing in science and technology, and thus is well positioned to play a leadership role in reversing the decline in science and technology. In one study in the 1970s, Utah led all other states in the percentage of home-grown students who went on to achieve advanced degrees in science.[50] But LDS leadership is this arena is dependent on LDS students and others being well-versed, not only in their particular disciplines, but in many of these broader arenas as well.

Along this line, many are concerned with the ethical and environment problems of a worldwide population that will be living significantly longer, due to progressively improved medical care. However, writers such as Max More point out that attempting to limit population by opposing available medical technology is not only unethical, it is also largely ineffective, since, in mathematical terms, longer life has no effect on the exponential growth rate. It matters little how long we live after we have reproduced.[51] What's more, one consequence of our increasing wealth and educational opportunities is that the world fertility rate has dropped dramatically since 1950, from five children per woman down to about three, with even steeper declines in developed nations.[52] As a result, the latest United Nations estimates are for the world population to level out at approximately 9.5 billion, a significantly lower figure than feared just a decade or two ago.[53]

Joel Garreau argues that the single most significant issue we will have to face in the coming century is the fundamental question of what it means to be human.[54] Will we define "humanity" based on our current (early twenty-first century) biology and psychology? If not, what aspects of our bodies, minds, emotions, art, religion, and aspirations constitute being human? If we gain power to change human personality, are there some aspects of human personality that should be moderated or cast aside, such as our tendencies toward violence, domination, and mental illness? At what point will computers and robots merit civil rights and legal protection? Will we baptize our computers and robots (provided they are waterproof)?

---

50. Kenneth R. Hardy, "Social Origins of American Scientists and Scholars," *Science* 185 (August 9, 1974): 497–506.

51. Max More, "Superlongevity without Overpopulation," in Immortality Institute, *The Scientific Conquest of Death*, 169–86.

52. Jeffrey Sachs, *The End of Poverty: Economic Possibilities for Our Time* (New York: Penguin, 2006), 12–14, 64–66, 323–26.

53. More, "Superlongevity without Overpopulation."

54. Garreau, *Radical Longevity*, 229–65.

Such questions may seem amusingly futuristic at the present time, but in the not-too-distant future they may be major items of public discourse.

The Idea of Progress in LDS Thought

Mormonism, from its founding, has been a progressive movement, in the sense of identifying with and promoting human progress. A central tenet of Mormonism is modern revelation, which affirms that progress in religious knowledge continues forward just as in the secular world: "We believe all that God has revealed, all that He does now reveal, and we believe He will yet reveal many great and important things pertaining to the Kingdom of God," states the Ninth Article of Faith. This language is strikingly similar to the definition of the idea of progress as given by Robert Nisbet: "Mankind has advanced in the past, . . . is now advancing, and will continue to advance through the foreseeable future."[55]

Closely connected with these principles is the "law of eternal progression," namely that mortal life is but an interlude between a preparatory premortal existence and an eternal postmortal existence, where the righteous will advance in knowledge and glory without limit. This doctrine was taught most clearly in Joseph Smith's King Follett Discourse,[56] although it is also suggested in scriptural passages such as "whatever principle of intelligence we attain unto in this life, it will rise with us in the resurrection," and the "more knowledge and intelligence" one gains in this life through . . . diligence and obedience," the greater the "advantage" we will have "in the world to come" (D&C 130:18–19).

After Joseph Smith's death, subsequent LDS presidents and authorities further developed these unique doctrines of progress. Brigham Young asserted that the "first great principle," the "main spring of all action," is the "principle of improvement."[57] "We have the principle within us, and so has every being on this earth, to increase and to continue to increase, to enlarge and receive and treasure up truth, until we become perfect."[58] "When we have lived millions of years in the presence of God and angels . . . shall we then cease learning? No, or eternity ceases."[59]

---

55. Robert Nisbet, *History of the Idea of Progress* (1980; rpt., Piscataway, N.J.: Transaction Publishers, 1993), 4–5.

56. Stan Larson, "The King Follett Discourse: A Newly Amalgamated Text," *BYU Studies* 18 (Winter 1978): 198–208.

57. Brigham Young, February 6, 1853, *Journal of Discourses*, 26 vols. (London and Liverpool: LDS Booksellers Depot, 1854–86), 2:91.

58. Brigham Young, July 19, 1857, *Journal of Discourses*, 5:54.

59. Brigham Young, July 31, 1859, *Journal of Discourses*, 6:344.

Brigham Young went even further than Joseph Smith in embracing progress in the secular and scientific world: "Our religion measures, weighs and circumscribes all the wisdom in the world—all that God has ever revealed to man. God has revealed all the truth that is now in the possession of the world, whether it be scientific or religious."[60]

Brigham H. Roberts, arguably Mormonism's greatest theologian, taught: "The world's best hope is the world's continued progress in knowledge of the truth."[61] While commenting on the impact of the Restoration, he declared, "By those collateral rays of light men have been led to those great discoveries in the arts and sciences and in mechanics, which make our age so wonderful as an age of progress and enlightenment."[62] Roberts was also an eloquent advocate for a progressive approach to science and religion, in the sense of championing, rather than battling, progress achieved in the scientific world. He wrote, "To pay attention to and give reasonable credence to [scientific] research is to link the church of God with the highest increase of human thought and effort."[63]

More recently, Hugh B. Brown wrote, "We should be in the forefront of learning in all fields, for revelation does not come only through the prophet of God nor only directly from heaven in visions or dreams. Revelation may come in the laboratory, out of the test tube, out of the thinking mind and the inquiring soul, out of search and research and prayer and inspiration."[64]

Conclusion

In spite of the future's many dangers and challenges, there are numerous reasons to be optimistic about it. Certainly one reason is the possibility of significant life extension, living in an environment when worldwide knowledge (both of our own world and the universe as a whole) is growing without bounds. As modern scripture promises, "Then shall they be gods,

---

60. Brigham Young, September 2, 1860, *Journal of Discourses*, 8:162.

61. B. H. Roberts, *The Truth, the Way, the Life: An Elementary Treatise on Theology* (1931), edited by Stan Larson (Salt Lake City: Smith Research Associates, 1994), 16.

62. B. H. Roberts, October 6, 1903, *Report of the Annual Conference of the Church of Jesus Christ of Latter-day Saints* (Salt Lake City: Church of Jesus Christ of Latter day Saints, semi-annual), 73.

63. Roberts, *The Truth, the Way, the Life*, 364.

64. Hugh B. Brown, "A Final Testimony," in Edwin B. Firmage, ed., *An Abundant Life: The Memoirs of Hugh B. Brown* (Salt Lake City: Signature Books, 1988), 139.

Welcome to the Twenty-First Century 173

because they have no end; therefore shall they be from everlasting to everlasting, because they continue; then shall they be above all, because all things are subject unto them" (D&C 132:20).

Along this line, Marc Geddes has observed that the desire for immortality "is one of the deepest, most enduring dreams of humanity." Not only is the quest for immortality morally good, he argues, but it is, in fact, the very foundation of morality: "Rational people understand that actions have consequences. A life of crime may help a person in the short term, but in the long run it may get you killed or imprisoned.... People are more likely to be moral when they understand they will have to face the consequences of their actions in the future. It follows that the further into the future one plans for, the more moral one's behavior should become."[65]

Albert Schweitzer once wrote:

> Affirmation of life is the spiritual act by which man ceases to live unreflectively and begins to devote himself to his life with reverence in order to raise it to its true value. To affirm life is to deepen, to make more inward, and to exalt the will to live. At the same time the man who has become a thinking being feels a compulsion to give to every will-to-live the same reverence for life that he gives to his own. He experiences that other life in his own. He accepts as being good: to preserve life, to promote life, to raise to its highest value life which is capable of development; and as being evil: to destroy life, to injure life, to repress life which is capable of development. This is the absolute, fundamental principle of the moral, and it is a necessity of thought.[66]

The hope for a better future has been a driving force for humankind from its inception. French theologian Pierre Teilhard de Chardin argued that human progress was inexorable, virtually mandated by the laws of the universe. He further saw the idea of progress as the one theme that could reunify science and religion: "To incorporate the progress of the world in our picture of the kingdom of God . . . would immediately and radically put an end to the internal conflict from which we are suffering."[67]

One way or another, the future is coming. Whether it will be hellish or heavenly will largely be up to us. Welcome to the twenty-first century.

---

65. Marc Geddes, "An Introduction to Immortality Morality," In Immortality Institute, *The Scientific Conquest of Death*, 239–56.

66. Albert Schweitzer, *Out of My Life and Thought* (Baltimore, Md.: Johns Hopkins University Press, 1953), 157.

67. Pierre Teilhard de Chardin, *Toward the Future*, translated by Rene Hague (London: Collins Press, 1975), 96.

CONTRIBUTORS

BRENT ALLSOP {brent.allsop@canonizer.com} is Senior Software Engineer at 3M Health Information Systems and founder of Canonizer.com. A founding board member of the Mormon Transhumanist Association, he served an LDS mission to Japan (1978–80). He is the author of "Representational Qualia Theory," *Journal of Consciousness Exploration & Research* 1, no. 2 (2010), available at http://www.jcer.com/index.php/jcj/article/view/18). He and his wife, Malia Fairbanks Allsop, have three adult children.

DAVID H. BAILEY {david@dhbailey.com} is the Chief Technologist of the Computational Research Department at Lawrence Berkeley National Lab in Berkeley, California. He received his B.S. in mathematics from Brigham Young University and his Ph.D. from Stanford University. Bailey is descended from several lines of LDS pioneer stock, including Henry Clegg, who "lost" the race to the River Ribble to be the first British convert, and Mary Murray Murdoch ("Wee Granny"), who was featured on the back cover of the August 2005 *Ensign*.

CHRISTOPHER BRADFORD {cbgrasshopper@gmail.com} is a software development manager, a lifelong LDS Church member, and vice-president and a co-founder of the Mormon Transhumanist Association. His degree in linguistics illustrates a combined love of technical subjects, philosophy, and the humanities. He and his wife are the parents of eight children.

RICHARD LYMAN BUSHMAN {rlb7@columbia.edu} is Gouverneur Morris Professor of History Emeritus at Columbia University in New York City and is currently visiting Howard W. Hunter Chair of Mormon Studies at Claremont Graduate University in California. Educated at Harvard College, he earned an A.M. in history and a Ph.D. in the history of American civilization from Harvard University. His first book, *From Puritan to Yankee: Character and the Social Order in Connecticut, 1690-1765* (Cambridge, Mass.: Harvard University Press, 1967), was awarded the Bancroft Prize. He has also published *Joseph Smith and the Beginnings of Mormonism* (Urbana: University of Illinois Press, 1984), *King and People in Provincial Massachusetts* (Chapel Hill: University of North Carolina Press, 1985); *The Refinement of America: Persons, Houses, Cities* (New York: Alfred A. Knopf, 1992); and *Joseph Smith: Rough Stone Rolling* (New York: Alfred A. Knopf, 2005).

LINCOLN CANNON {lincoln@metacannon.net} is a professional software engineer, internet marketer, and information technologist. In his spare time, he promotes awareness of the philosophical implications of emerging technology and serves as president of the Mormon Transhumanist Association. He holds a master's degree in business and a bachelor's degree in philosophy from Brigham Young University. Lincoln served a mission to France for the Church of Jesus Christ of Latter-day Saints, is married to Dorothée Vankrieckenge, a French national, and is father to three bilingual children.

ADAM N. DAVIS {addavis1@wsc.edu} has a doctorate in physics from Case Western Reserve University with an emphasis in cosmology. Working in the Department of Physics at a small school, Wayne State College, he pursues his interests in cosmology and philosophy of mind.

ROGER D. HANSEN {rhansen@uc.usbr.gov} is currently the Planning Group Chief for a federal water resource agency in Provo, Utah. He has an undergraduate degree in history from Brigham Young University and graduate degrees in civil and environmental engineering from Utah State University, plus minors in other subjects, including chemistry, economics, and French. From this educational background, Roger writes on diverse topics including: Mormonism, technology and ethics, history of water development, Native American issues, organizational dynamics, and travel. He enjoys foreign adventures and has lived in and/or visited and/or worked on five continents and more than forty countries. He currently divides his time between Provo, the Navajo Nation, and Uganda. Roger is a member of the Mormon Transhumanist Association and is on the local board of Engineers Without Borders. Additionally, he is the principal writer for the blog "Tired Road Warrior," He and his wife, Dona, have three children and eleven grandchildren.

A. SCOTT HOWE {Scott.Howe@jpl.nasa.gov} is a Senior Systems Engineer for NASA Jet Propulsion Laboratory, specializing in robotic construction for space environments. A licensed architect with a Ph.D. in architecture from University of Michigan, he has a second Ph.D. in industrial and manufacturing engineering (modular robotics) from Hong Kong University. After serving an LDS mission in Fukuoka, Japan, he practiced architecture in Japan for ten years and taught architecture and mechanical engineering for six years at Hong Kong University. In addition to numerous peer-reviewed journal and technical papers on robotics, he is the editor, with Brent Sherwood, of *Out of This World: The New Field of Space Architecture*, in the AIAA History of Spaceflight series (Reston, Va.: American Institute of Aeronautics and Astronautics, 2009). He is currently serving as Venture Coach/Assistant Scoutmaster (teachers' quorum) in the Wrightwood Ward, Victorville California Stake, which he describes as his "favorite calling." He has six adult children from a previous marriage and is married to Ing Ping Chia.

TERRYL L. GIVENS is the author of several books, including *By the Hand of Mormon: The American Scripture that Launched a New World Religion* (New York: Oxford University Press, 2002), *When Souls had Wings: Premortal Life in Western Thought* (New York: Oxford University Press, 2010), and (with Matthew Grow) *Parley P. Pratt: The Apostle Paul of Mormonism* (New York: Oxford University Press, 2011). He is currently at work on a two-volume history of Mormon theology for Oxford University Press. Dr. Givens is Professor of Literature and Religion and holds the James Bostwick Chair of English at the University of Richmond.

ALLEN W. LEIGH (engineer@bergstedt.org) is a retired software engineer and adjunct instructor. He has B.S. and M.S. degrees in electrical engineering from Utah State University and an M.S. degree in computer information systems from Boston University. He is the author or co-author of the following books: *One Mormon's View of the Science-Religion Debate* (Baltimore, Md.: Publish America, 2005); *Quest for Eternity* (Salt Lake City: Self-published, 1988, 2008), http://www.lulu.com/spotlight/allenleigh; *Generations of Websters,* with Amy L. Van Cott (Cedar City, Utah/Salt Lake City: Self-published, 1960, 2008), http://www.lulu.com/spotlight/allenleigh. He is the webmaster of several religious, family history, running, and political blogs.

WILLIAM R. PICKETT {zither@prodigy.net} is a Senior Hardware Engineer and Antenna Range Master at the Jet Propulsion Laboratory (1969–retired 2011). His specialty is spacecraft antenna systems starting with Mariner 8, Viking, Voyager, Galileo, GRACE, GRAIL, the Mars rovers, and the Mars Science Laboratory spacecrafts among others and various classified programs. Before 1969, he worked on the Apollo Program command and service module antenna systems with North American Aviation/Rockwell. He graduated from Fullerton Junior College and California State College Fullerton. A former member of the Association for Computing Machinery and a member of the Antenna Measurement Techniques Association, he is an amateur radio operator. He has served as a teacher in LDS classes, as high priests' group leader, as high councilor, and in family history positions. He and his wife, Judy, are the parents of four and grandparents of eleven.

ANDREW WEST {andybwest@gmail.com} is an aspiring chef at a high end-restaurant in Salt Lake City. He and his wife, Cherie Merrell West, recently welcomed their first child, a daughter. Andrew enjoys movies, television, books, and spending time with close friends and family.

A. JOSEPH WEST {ajosephwest@gmail.com} is a fourth-year graduate student at the Department of Sociology at the University of Arizona. His research interests include religion, culture, and science and technology, while his personal interests span running, camping, biking, reading, and watching movies.. He and his wife, Jessica Jones West, are the parents of two children.

JAMES W. YOUNG { retired in 2009 as the Resident Astronomer and Astronomy Team Leader at Table Mountain Observatory. He served on the Senior Staff in the Space Science Division of NASA's Jet Propulsion Laboratory from 1962 to 2009. He is the co-author or author of more than forty refereed papers on asteroid physical properties and rotational rates published between 1969 and 2009. He also co-authored or authored more than 1,500 Minor Planet Center (MPC) and International Astronomical Union (IAU) electronic circulars (2002-9), and discovered more than 400 asteroids (174 currently numbered), two Near-Earth Objects (NEOs), and an extra-galactic supernova. He and his wife, Karen, now live in Seaside. Among his Church callings are elders' quorum president, seventy's president (stake), stake mission president, and high priests group instructor.

CARL A. YOUNGBLOOD {carl@youngbloods.org} is a director of the Mormon Transhumanist Association. He holds a bachelor's degree in Portuguese from Brigham Young University and a master's degree in computer science from the University of Washington. Currently employed as a senior software engineer at Cisco Systems, he is an active participant in the open source software community. He is also an active member of the Sandvika Ward near Oslo, Norway, where he currently serves as a counselor in the elders' quorum.

Scripture Index

Note: To prevent confusion with continued verse numbers and page numbers, a colon separates the scriptural reference from the page number.

OLD TESTAMENT

Genesis 1: 150 note 41
Genesis 2:6: 154
Proverbs 8:22–31: 32
Proverbs 29:18: 148
Song of Solomon 4:15: 128
Jeremiah 2:13: 128
Jeremiah 17:13: 128
Jonah 3: 92
Zechariah 14:8: 128

NEW TESTAMENT

Mark 13:19–20: 69
Luke 21:9: 160
Luke 21:26: 160
John 4:10–14: 128
John 7:37–38: 128
John 14:9: 65
Matthew 17:20: 31
Romans 4:18–13: 117
1 Corinthians 15:51–54: 33
2 Corinthians 5:1: 24
James 2:14–22: 32
Revelation 8:8: 149

BOOK OF MORMON

1 Nephi 17:36: 151
2 Nephi 2:11–12: 64
2 Nephi 2:14: 23
2 Nephi 2:27: 46
2 Nephi 9:10: 41
2 Nephi 29:30: 18
Mosiah 5:9: 35
Mosiah 16:7: 35
Alma 11:44: 10
Alma 32: 37
Alma 32:28: 31
Alma 32:32: 31
Alma 32:33: 31, 32
Alma 32:34: 31
Alma 32:35: 32
Alma 32:39: 31
Alma 36:3: 65
Alma 42:13: 32, 63–64
Alma 42:22: 63–64
Alma 42:25: 63–64
Alma 60:11: 41
Alma 60:11–12: 149
3 Nephi 27:33: 108
3 Nephi 28:2: 41
Mormon 9:16: 32
Ether 2:15: 152
Ether 2:24: 152
Ether 3:16: 4, 24

DOCTRINE AND COVENANTS

Doctrine and Covenants 29:31–33: 31
Doctrine and Covenants 33:37: 33
Doctrine and Covenants 50:24: 18
Doctrine and Covenants 52:11: 136
Doctrine and Covenants 63:20–21: 33, 80
Doctrine and Covenants 63:49–52: 33
Doctrine and Covenants 76: 35
Doctrine and Covenants 76:7–10: 32
Doctrine and Covenants 76:24: 22, 151

Doctrine and Covenants 76:36–39: 64
Doctrine and Covenants 76:55–56: 59
Doctrine and Covenants 76:98: 35
Doctrine and Covenants 77:2: 4, 24
Doctrine and Covenants 84:33: 85
Doctrine and Covenants 84:45: 17
Doctrine and Covenants 88:1–13: 98
Doctrine and Covenants 88:6–13: 61
Doctrine and Covenants 88:6–19: 37
Doctrine and Covenants 88:7–13: 31
Doctrine and Covenants 88:11–13: 19
Doctrine and Covenants 88:13: 23
Doctrine and Covenants 88:14–41: 35
Doctrine and Covenants 88:18–19: 132–33
Doctrine and Covenants 88:25: 66
Doctrine and Covenants 88:27–33: 85, 91
Doctrine and Covenants 88:34–35: 37
Doctrine and Covenants 88:36: 32
Doctrine and Covenants 88:38: 32
Doctrine and Covenants 88:111: 70
Doctrine and Covenants 93:24: 20, 32
Doctrine and Covenants 93:29: 17, 31, 47
Doctrine and Covenants 93:30: 17, 20, 32
Doctrine and Covenants 93:33: 23, 31, 45, 58, 108
Doctrine and Covenants 93:36: 17
Doctrine and Covenants 101:26–34: 41, 81
Doctrine and Covenants 101:29–31: 33
Doctrine and Covenants 103:9: 35
Doctrine and Covenants 104:17: 139
Doctrine and Covenants 109:7: 70
Doctrine and Covenants 121:26–30: 32
Doctrine and Covenants 121:26–32: 68
Doctrine and Covenants 128:18: 80
Doctrine and Covenants 130:9–11: 83
Doctrine and Covenants 130:18–19: 18, 171
Doctrine and Covenants 130:20–21: 88
Doctrine and Covenants 130:21: 32
Doctrine and Covenants 130:22: 31, 60
Doctrine and Covenants 131:7: 1, 31, 33, 58
Doctrine and Covenants 131:7–8: 3, 24, 44
Doctrine and Covenants 131:8: 1
Doctrine and Covenants 132:20: 172–73
Doctrine and Covenants 132:22: 109

PEARL OF GREAT PRICE

Moses 1:11: 58
Moses 1:29: 151
Moses 1:33: 32, 65, 151
Moses 1:38–39: 109, 151
Moses 1:39: 66, 94
Moses 2: 151
Moses 3:5: 59
Moses 3:6: 154
Moses 3:7: 12
Moses 7:32: 21
Abraham 3:1–19: 60 note 1
Abraham 3:2–19: 32
Abraham 3:22: 18
Abraham 3:22–24: 22
Abraham 3:23: 19
Abraham 3:24: 31
Abraham 4:1: 59
Abraham 4:3: 151 note 41
Abraham 4:7: 151 note 41
Abraham 4–5: 151 note 41
Abraham 5:4: 151 note 41
JS—History 1:43: 148
Articles of Faith 3: 35
Articles of Faith 9: 30, 87, 171
Articles of Faith 13: 70

Index

A

Abraham, vision of cosmos, 60–61 note 1
actuators, spiritual analogue of, 25
advanced beings. *See* posthumans.
agency. *See* free will.
aging, in Mormon theology, 40–41; mitigation of, 160, 165, 167
Alexander, Thomas G., 126, 134
Allsop, Brent, 55
"angel argument" for posthumans, 113–14, 120
"Are You Living in a Computer Simulation?", 77
artificial intelligence, 2, 54, 76, 163
artificial kidney, 167
asteroid 203 QQ47, 145
asteroid 3554 Amun, 142
asteroid 29075–1950 DA, 145
asteroid 69230 Hermes, 145–46
asteroid 99942 Apophis, 145
asteroids
    and precious metals, 141–42
    classifications of, 146
    list of, 145
    numbers of, 146–47
    potential impact on earth, 145–47
atonement
    effect on physical world, xi
    Mormon interpretation of, 91
Autino, Adriano, 142
automobile, development of, 158

B

Bailey, David H., 124
"Basic Argument, The," 43, 45–51
Bednar, David A., 108
Beech, Martin, 155
"benevolence argument" for posthumans, 115, 120
Big Bang, 66
Binzel, Robert, 142
biosphere, as entropy reduction, 101
biotechnology, accelerating changes in, 157, 160. *See also* change.
birth, entropy calculations for, 103–4
"black box" problem, of information processing, 51–53
black holes, 115
bodies. *See also* medical technology *and* spirit bodies.
    and spirit, 5, 23–28
    seen as a burden, 108
    communication with spirit, 11
    enhanced and healed, 36, 76–77. *See also* aging.
    glorified, characteristics of, 60
bosons. *See* light.
Bostrom, Nick, 71, 77–78, 116
Bradford, Christopher, 55
"brain in the vat," 10
brain modeling, 164
Brown, Hugh B., 87–88, 172

C

CAD model, 25–26
Calvinism, 37–38
cancer therapy, 166
Cannon, George Q., 69, 80
Cannon, Lincoln, 2, 55–56
Catholic Church, 130, 168
causality, compatible with Mormonism, 32, 41
celestial order, and technology, 56
cell phones, 159
change
  accelerating, 157, 160
  as unstoppable, 168
  ethical issues, 169
  in past fifty years, 158–61
  management of, 161, 168
  rate of in computer power, 162
charity
  and entropy, 56
  and faith, 91
  increases choice, 110
chess, computer, 163
Chesterton, C. K., vii, xvii
Chicxulub, Mexico, asteroid, 143
Children's Hospital, Boston, 166
choice. *See* free will.
Claremont Graduate University, v
Clarke, Randolfe, 50
Coleridge, Samuel Taylor, x
Collins, Patrick, 142
colonizers, in scripture and Church history, 123, 154
Columbia River Basin, 130–31
Columbia River Watershed: Caring for Creation and the Common Good, The, 130
Comet P/Shoemaker–Levi 9, 144, 147
communities
  encapsulate individual members, 110
  pooling resources, to decrease entropy, 105
  required for God's work, 107
compatibilism, 49
complacency, and undesired experience, 113
computational model
  death in, 10
  described, 24–25
  of spirit/matter, 9–12
  problems with, 10–12, 15
computers, 136, 158–59
configurational entropy. *See* entropy.
consistency, compatible with Mormonism, 32, 41
Conway, John, 20–21
cosmetics industry, 139
creatio ex nihilo, denied in Mormonism, 48
"creation argument" for posthumans, 116, 121
creation. *See also* terraforming.
  of earth, 58–59, 62, 150
  of other worlds, 69–70, 86
  spiritual precedes physical, 58–59
creationism, 159
creativity
  and engineering, increase of order from, 110
  and entropy, 56
  entropy calculations for, 104–5
Crutzen, Paul, 129

D

Dante, ix
Darwinism, vii, xiv, xvi, 119
Davis, Adam N., 1–2, 33
Dawkins, Richard, 119–20
de Laplace, Pierre–Simon, xi
death, entropy calculations for, 103
decision tree, applied to morality, 94, 97
design cycle
  and God, 55, 57, 62–63
  stages in, 57–58
desire, at root of morality, 113
destructive capacity, exponential rate of increase, 115
determinism, 49–51
diabetes, 166
Dick, Thomas, ix–x
digital code of life, 158

Parallels and Convergences

Dijkstra, Edsger W., xi–xii
dinosaur extinction, 143
disciples
　moral obligation of, 40
　Nephite, 40–41
dispensation of the fulness of times. *See* fulness of times.
divorce, entropy calculations for, 105–6
DNA decoding, 34, 75–76
Drexler, Eric, 76
drug testing, 165
dualism, not required by Mormonism, 45
Durant, Will, and Ariel, 157

E

earth
　as sentient, 123
　evolving in complexity, 127
　progress on, 125
education
　LDS tradition of, 170
　mediocre state in USA, 169
　stimulated by space research, 142
element, as matter, 33
elements, not created, 58
emergence, defined, 53–54
energy
　consumption, 161, 164
　interactions with environment, 98, 100
　space-based, 140
engineering
　ability to manage complexity, 110
　and terraforming earth, 154–55
　as assisting God in His work, 123
　as maximizing order, 101
　connections to divine knowledge, vi
　defined, 1
Engines of Creation, 76
Enlightenment, Mormonism compatible with, 39–40
entanglement, 27
entropy, as measure of order, 98–100
environment, and space research, 142–43
environmentalism, and Mormonism, 132, 134

Epicurus, 49
Esfandiary, Fereidoun M., 71 and note 4
"eternal lives," as Mormon goal, 109
eternal progression, 86–87, 132
ethical imperatives, in simulations, 78
Everlasting Man, The, vii
evil, problem of, 48
evolution
　accelerated rate of, 113
　of earth, 133
Extropy Institute, 72

F

faith
　Alma's sermon and scientific method, 31
　and Transhumanist concepts, 88–89
Fermi, Enrico, 114
First Epoch, 73
First Solar, 164
FM–2030, 71, 90
Foresight Institute, 72
four-fold mission, 136, 156
Fourth Epoch, 72–73, 84–85
free will
　and individual particles, 20–21
　and materialism, 43–56
　increases future choices, 95
　possibly engineered, 21
　relation of body and core, 51
freedom, 94, 96
fulness of times, accelerated knowledge during, 36–42, 56, 67–68, 73, 80, 85
Fyodorov, Nikolai, 71

G

Gaia, 125
Galilei, Galileo, 70–71
Garden of Eden, as terraforming colony, 154
Garreau, Joel, 169–70
Geddes, Marc, 95, 173
genetics, parallels with Mormon thought, 85
genocide, 115

geo-engineering, 129
Geron Corporation, 165
global economy, 159, 169
global warming, 161, 164
glories, degrees of, 35–37
God the Father
    and failure, 55, 63–66
    anthropomorphic, x
    as celestial engineer, 150
    as "perfect engineer," 55, 57
    creation of other worlds, 65–66, 151
    eternal progression of, 150
    glorified body of, 60–61
    obedience to law, 55, 59–61, 93–94, 118–19
    Old Testament view of, xiv
    plan for this earth, 66
    power of, xv–xvi
    vulnerability of, xv
God Delusion, The, 119
godhood
    and progressive development, 150
    and Transhumanist analogue, 86
    as full manifestation of love, 90
    as heresy, xv
    in Mormon theology, 83–85, 131
gods, plurality of, 82–83
Grand Teton National Park, meteor near–miss, 144
Grant, Jedediah M., 4
Gross, Neil, 127

H

Hansen, Roger D., 123
Hanson, Robin, 114
heavy metals, available on asteroids, 141–42
Hegel, G. W. F., xvi
Heinlein, Robert, 141
Hewlett–Packard, nano–imprint crossbars, 162
Hinckley, Gordon B., 30
Howe, A. Scott, v, 1–2, 56, 123
Hughes, James, 169

human responsibility
    as co–creators/participants in God's work, 132–34, 149–51
    dignity, ethic of, 112
    meaning of, 170
Human Genome Project, speed of, 76
Humanity+, 71

I

IBM BlueGene system, 164
ideology as information systems, 39–40
idleness, entropy calculations for, 107
"If You Could Hie to Kolob," 82
immortality
    and morality, 173
    and Transhumanism, 85–86
    as priesthood ordinance, 81–82
    defined, 81–82
    in Mormon theology, 35–37, 80–82
    prophecies of, 69–70
Immortality Institute, 72
information density, limitations of, 12, 15
information technology, accelerating changes in, 157
inspiration, not limited to Mormons, 87–88, 136, 147. *See also* Brigham Young.
Institute for Ethics and Emerging Technologies, 72
insulin by microchip, 167
integrated systems, to leverage strengths, 39
Intel Corporation, 73
intelligence
    and agency, 21
    and light, 17, 22–23
    and personality, 18–19
    as uncreated, 53
    defined, 21
    in matter, 22
intelligent design, 159
intelligent matter, 2, 43–56
    and free will, 46
    and spirit, 58
    and Strawson's Basic Argument, 50–51

Parallels and Convergences

defined, 47–49
internet
  as earth's nervous system, 127
  development of, 158–59
  involuntary servitude, entropy calculations for, 106, 107, 108

J

James, William, xiv
Jeffrey, Duane E., 126
Jesus Christ
  anthropomorphic, x
  as creator, 61–62
  atonement and entropy, 56
  disciples assume identity of, 35
  embodies qualities of the Father, 65
  role in resurrection, 35
jewelry, spending on, 139
joy, 23, 28
Joy, Bill, 167
justice
  and preserving structure, 98
  as cause and effect, 107

K

Kane, Robert, 50
Kasparov, Garry, 163
Key to the Science of Theology, x
Kimball, Heber C., 4, 153
Kimball, Spencer W., 22, 153
kindness, entropy calculations for, 106
king, mathematician, and grain of rice, 74
King Follett Discourse, x, xv, 30, 131, 171
knowledge, acceleration of, 36–42, 73, 85. *See also* change.
Kochen, Simon, 20–21
Kolob, 61 note 1
Kuhn, Thomas S., 158
Kurzweil, Ray
  on atomic/electromagnetic motion, 20
  on dangers of technology, 167–68
  on "fourth epoch," 73
  on genetics, 75
  on the Singularity, 74–75
  predictions of, 67

L

LASIK eye surgery, 76
law. *See also* God the Father.
  as eternal, 32, 59–63, 93–94
  as light of Christ, 61
Law of Acceleration Returns, 73
Leigh, Allen, 55
leptons. *See* light.
Lewis, John, 142
life expectancy, 34
light
  and interactions with environment, 98, 100
  as spirit matter, 17–28. *See also* spirit.
  of Christ, 61
  physical/spiritual matter, 7, 13, 19–20, 23–24
  speed of, and remote storage, 11, 15
liquid propane, and cloud seeding, 129
Lovelock, James, 125
Lugo, Italy, meteroid over, 144

M

Malthus, Thomas, xvi
man. *See* human.
Mankins, John, 140
Marquis de Condorcet, 71
marriage, entropy calculations for, 105
massively multiplayer games, 9
materialism, 43–56. *See also* spirit.
Matrix, The, 78
matter, 31–32. *See also* intelligent matter *and* spirit.
Maxwell, Neal A., 153
McConkie, Bruce R., 22
McKay, David O., 136
McMurrin, Sterling M., 118
McTaggart, John, xiii–xiv
medical technology, accelerating changes in, 157–58
memory, 20, 23, 51
Merck Laboratories, 166
meteorites. *See also* asteroids.
  list of recent impacts, 144

potential dangers to earth, 143–47
micro-electro-mechanical systems (MEMS), 163
microtubules, and brain function, 26
Millennium
   and Transhumanism, 55
   destruction to precede, 89
   in Mormon theology, 80–82
   parallels with the Singularity, 85
   renewal of earth, 69–70
   space technology development during, 155–56
Milton, John, viii
miracles, in accordance with law, 32
mirror model
   problems of, 7–8, 14
   spirit and physical properties, 5–8
   synchronization and separation in, 8
Mormon cosmology, vii–xvii
Mormon physics, characteristics of, 32
Mormon theology, and engineering, vi
molecular assemblers, 76
"Moon Is a Harsh Mistress, The," 141
Moore, Gordon, 73
Moore's Law, 73, 160
morality
   and order, 94
   benefit/harm to community, 102
   impossible in randomness, 51
   in Transhumanism, 89
   in water management, 129–30
   mathematical model of, 93–110
   reversible/irreversible consequences as measure of, 102
More, Max, 71, 170
Mormon Studies conference, Claremont, v
Mormon Transhumanist Affirmation, 72, 75, 134
Mormonism
   and Transhumanism, 80–87, 89
   as integration between Judeo-Christianity and Enlightenment, 39–40
   beyond traditional thought, 117
   in secular world, 118
   traditional values in, 90
mortality, and manipulating matter, 108
Moses, vision of, 58
motes, defined, 129 note 15

N

Nagel, Thomas, xiv–xv
nanobots, self-replicating, 115
nanotechnology
   accelerating changes in, 157
   and Mormon thought, 85
   and water management, 129
   defined, 76, 160–61
nanotube circuitry, 162
Nantero, 162
NASA
   economic benefits of, 137–39
   proposals for asteroid capture, 155
   spacecraft, 25
NASA Jet Propulsion Laboratory, v
NASA, Jet Propulsion Laboratory Table Mountain Observatory, 146
National Aeronautics and Space Administration. *See* NASA.
natural law. *See* law.
Nature, 137
near earth objects, 141–42, 146
Near Earth Asteroid Rendezvous (NEAR) project, 144–45
near-death experiences, in Mormon thought, 5
negentropy, 105
Nelson, Russell M., 147
neohumans. *See* Transhumanism *and* posthumans.
neurophysics, and body information systems, 53
New God argument, 112–20
   summary of syllogisms, 120–21
Newton, Isaac, xi
Nibley, Hugh, 132
Nisbet, Robert, 171

Parallels and Convergences

O

objectivity, compatible with Mormonism, 32, 41
Omega Point, 127, 130
optimism, about future, 89, 172–73
ordered states, and entropy, 56
ordinances, 33, 86
Origen, vii, xvi
Ostler, Blake T., 48

P

"Panspermia," 156
Paradise Lost, viii
Paulsen, David L., 48
Pearce, David, 71
Pelagianism, role of works in, 37–38
perceptual information, required for free will, 51
perpetual revelation, 30
Petersen, Morris S., 132
phase model, 13–14
Philo of Alexandria, xvi
philosophy of mind, 44
Philosophy of a Future State, ix–x
physical salvation, Mormon obligation of, 40–41
physical world as simulated reality, 10
physicalism. *See* materialism.
physics
   defined, 1
   Mormon interpretation of, 29–42
physiology
   merged with information systems, 36–37
   Mormon interpretation of, 29–42. *See also* bodies.
Pickett, William, 123
Plato, xv, xvii
polytheism, Mormonism as, xii–xiii
posthumans. *See also* Transhumanism.
   as gods, 119
   characteristics of, 78–79
   created earth, 56
potentiality test, of morality, 93–95
potentially hazardous objects, 146
poverty, solution to, 139
Powell, John Wesley, 128
power
   and desire to do good, 89–90
   God achieves by obedience, 93–94
   positive and negative, 92–93
pragmatism, as extension of faith, 113
Pratt, Orson, on science, xii
Pratt, Parley P., 1
   as systematizing theologian, ix–xi
   on characteristics of God, xvii
   on godhood, xii–xiii
   on mirror model of spirit/matter, 5–6
   optimistic theology, xvi–xvii
   science as encompassing theology, xi
   spirit as form of matter, 9
prayer, as wireless coupling, 25
prehumans and posthumans, improbability of, 114
"Principles of Extropy," 71
process theology, and Mormonism, 132
progress. *See also* eternal progression.
   cynicism about, 157
   in Mormon theology, 171–72.
prostheses, mentally controlled, 164. *See also* medical technology.

Q

quantum computing, 162
quantum foam, 21, 23, 27
quantum mechanics, and simultaneous information, 52
quantum tunneling, 26–27

R

radio, development of, 158
randomness, 49–51
recreation, spending on, 139
religion, and respect for science, 131
remote functioning, 26–27
remote storage, of spirit matter coding, 11, 15
resources, of universe, 139–40

resurrection
  and technology, 55
  as applied to worlds, 82
  as physiological process, 33–35
  prophecies of, 69–70
reverence for life, 173
river basin sentience, 128–30
Roberts, Brigham Henry, on progress, 132, 172
robotics
  parallels with Mormon thought, 85
  revolution in, 76
  vehicles, 164
Romney, Marion G., 22
Russell, Peter, 127

S

salvation, definitions of, 38
Satan's plan, 106–7
Schweitzer, Albert, 173
science and technology, 70, 111
scientific method, 31
Scientific American, 166
scriptural inerrancy, not Mormon doctrine, 30
Second Coming, preparation for, 134
Second Epoch, and biological systems, 73
Second Life, 9, 77
secularism, as source of religious understanding, 87
self-replication and control of entropy, 109
sensors, spiritual analogue of, 25
sentience of earth, 127–28, 133
sentient races, 56
service
  entropy calculations for, 106
  produces greater choices, 110
SimCity, 77
simplicity (irreducibility) of intelligent matter, 49, 51
Simulation Argument, 77–78
simulations
  and water management, 129
  in the Singularity, 77
  increasing sophistication of, 116
sin, and entropy, 56, 97
Singularity
  and Omega Point, 127–28
  defined, 74
Singularity Institute for Artificial Intelligence, 72
sins of commission/omission, 56, 94
Smith, George Albert, 136
Smith, Joseph. *See also* King Follett Discourse.
  as religious humanist, 71
  defines salvation, 110
  on degrees of glory, 35
  on dispensation of the fulness of times, 80
  on God's progression, 150
  on matter, 44–45
  on millennium, 81
  on progression to godhood, 36, 84, 86, 117, 131
  on progressions of heavenly worlds, 82–83
  on responsibility to earth, 134
  on restoration of knowledge, 68–69
  on spirit as co-eternal with God, 47
  on transfiguration, 33
  on truth, 40
  rejects biblical infallibility, 30
  unity of all living things, 126
Smith, Joseph F., 134
Smith, Joseph Fielding
  divine law in universe, 150
  humans on other planets, 153
  on technology as inspired, 88, 148
Snow, Lorenzo, 117, 131, 150
solar energy, 161, 164
space program
  and economy, 137–40
  and Millennium, 136
  critique of, 135–36
  inspiration regarding, 135–36
  solar system as stepping stones, 155
  theological significance of, 135–56
space research

Parallels and Convergences 189

and technology, 147–49
 testimony of, 151
spam, 159
speed of light constraints, 26, 148–49
Spinoff, 137
spirit and matter, continuity of, x–xi, xiv
spirit, as light, 17–28. *See also* light and intelligence.
spirit bodies
 and spirit world, 5, 14
 creation of, 47–48
 and physical bodies, 4–5
spirit matter
 and physical world, 12
 as elementary particles, 28
 as light, 1
 characteristics of, 3–15
 discernible, 28–29, 33
 location, 10–11, 15
 physics of, 17–28
spirit world, descriptions of, 4
Stegner, Wallace, 133
stem cell research, 165, 168
stewardship, and ecological systems, 130
Story of Civilization, 157
Strawson, Galen, 43, 45–46
subatomic particles, 158
substance abuse, entropy calculations for, 106
Sudan, 2008 TC3 asteroid, 144
suicide bombers, 115
sulfurous debris, and cloud seeding, 129
Sunstone, 134
supercomputers, 162–63
supernaturalism. *See* spirit.
survival, and maximizing number of opportunities, 100–101
syntropy, 105

T

Taylor, John, 150
technical interpretations, compatible with Mormon theology, 37–42
technical language, as mode of gospel expression, 1

technology
 fears of, 167–69
 list of recent developments in, 161–67
 preparation for Millennium, 124
Teilhard de Chardin, Pierre, 127, 133, 173
television, development of, 158
temple ceremonies, 35
terraforming, 150, 154
Tertullian, xv
theft, entropy calculations for, 104
theology, defined, viii–ix
theosis. *See* godhood.
thermodynamic entropy. *See* entropy.
Third Epoch, and intelligent systems, 73
Thomas, Christina, 142
Thorne, Kip, 149
Timaeus, xvii
Tipler, Frank, 34, 79
tobacco and alcohol, spending on, 139
tradition, respect for, 90
transfiguration
 and technology, 55
 and worlds, 82
 as physiological process, 33–35, 41
 in Mormon theology, 80–81, 85
 prophecies of, 69–70
transgression. *See* sin.
Transhumanism
 and creation of earth, 111, 116
 and human evolution, 112
 and Mormonism, 55, 67–92, 132
 defined, 70–71
 history of, 71
 posthumans as gods, 79, 111–12, 118
 view of the future, 72–80
Transhumanist Declaration, 71
truth
 calculation of, 20
 essential unity of, 37
Tunguska (Siberia) meteor impact, 144, 146
Turing Machines, 52
Turing test, 164

U–V

Uchtdorf, Dieter F., 38
uniformity, compatible with Mormonism, 32, 41
University of Michigan, 167
unselfishness, and greater choices, 110
Urim and Thummim, 60 note 1
vandalism, entropy calculations for, 104
Vinge, Vernor, 74–75
virtual worlds, 108

W

warfare, reduced by global trade, 159
West, Andrew, 55
West, Joseph, 55, 56
Western Water Policy Review Advisory Commission, 129
Whitehead, Alfred North, 132
"Why the Future Doesn't Need Us," 167
Widtsoe, John A., 125, 132, 134
Wikipedia, 161
Wistar Institute, 165–66
Woodruff, Wilford, 117
works, moral choice of, 37–38
world fertility rate, 170
World Transhumanist Association, 71–72, 90
"World Turned Upside Down, The," xi
worlds
 innumerable, 82
 Mormon and Transhumanist beliefs in, 86
worldwide web, development of, 158
wormholes, 27, 148–49
Worster, Donald, 128

Y–Z

Young, Brigham
 on becoming gods, 117
 on Book of Mormon, 30
 on chemistry, xii
 on earth, 125–26, 134
 on eternity, 82, 92
 on God's progression, 132, 152
 on human origins as another planet, 152–53
 on location of spirit world, 5
 on Millennium, 81
 on progress, 171
 on resurrection, 82
 on revelation and science, 31, 147, 172
 on transfiguration, 33
Young, James W., 123, 146
Youngblood, Carl, 55
zeroeth law of thermodynamics, 97–98

Also available from
GREG KOFFORD BOOKS

Discourses in Mormon Theology: Philosophical and Theological Possibilities

Edited by
James M. McLachlan and Loyd Ericson

Hardcover, ISBN: 978-1-58958-103-6

A mere two hundred years old, Mormonism is still in its infancy compared to other theological disciplines (Judaism, Catholicism, Buddhism, etc.). This volume will introduce its reader to the rich blend of theological viewpoints that exist within Mormonism. The essays break new ground in Mormon studies by exploring the vast expanse of philosophical territory left largely untouched by traditional approaches to Mormon theology. It presents philosophical and theological essays by many of the finest minds associated with Mormonism in an organized and easy-to-understand manner and provides the reader with a window into the fascinating diversity amongst Mormon philosophers. Open-minded students of pure religion will appreciate this volume's thoughtful inquiries.

These essays were delivered at the first conference of the Society for Mormon Philosophy and Theology. Authors include Grant Underwood, Blake T. Ostler, Dennis Potter, Margaret Merrill Toscano, James E. Faulconer, and Robert L. Millet

Praise for *Discourses in Mormon Theology*:

"In short, *Discourses in Mormon Theology* is an excellent compilation of essays that are sure to feed both the mind and soul. It reminds all of us that beyond the white shirts and ties there exists a universe of theological and moral sensitivity that cries out for study and acclamation."
    -Jeff Needle, Association for Mormon Letters

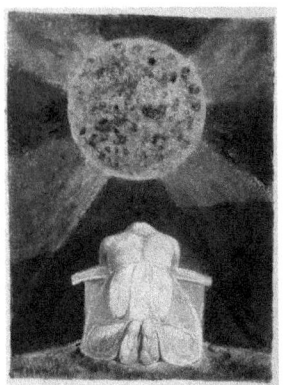

Perspectives on Mormon Theology Series

Brian D. Birch and Loyd Ericson,
series editors

(forthcoming)

This series will feature multiple volumes published on particular theological topics of interest in Latter-day Saint thought. Volumes will be co-edited by leading scholars and graduate students whose interests and knowledge will ensure that the essays in each volume represent quality scholarship and acknowledge the diversity of thought found and expressed in Mormon theological studies. Topics for the first few volumes include: revelation, apostasy, atonement, scripture, and grace.

The *Perspectives on Mormon Theology* series will bring together the best of new and previously published essays on various theological subjects. Each volume will be both a valued resource for academics in Mormon Studies and an illuminating introduction to the broad and sophisticated approaches to Mormon theology.

Mormonism and Evolution: The Authoritative LDS Statements

Edited by William E. Evenson
and Duane E. Jeffrey

Paperback, ISBN: 978-1-58958-093-0

The Church of Jesus Christ of Latter-day Saints (the Mormon Church) has generally been viewed by the public as anti-evolutionary in its doctrine and teachings. But official statements on the subject by the Church's highest governing quorum and/or president have been considerably more open and diverse than is popularly believed.

This book compiles in full all known authoritative statements (either authored or formally approved for publication) by the Church's highest leaders on the topics of evolution and the origin of human beings. The editors provide historical context for these statements that allows the reader to see what stimulated the issuing of each particular document and how they stand in relation to one another.

"This is My Doctrine": The Development of Mormon Theology

Charles R. Harrell

Hardcover, ISBN: 978-1-58958-103-6

The principal doctrines defining Mormonism today often bear little resemblance to those it started out with in the early 1830s. This book shows that these doctrines did not originate in a vacuum but were rather prompted and informed by the religious culture from which Mormonism arose. Early Mormons, like their early Christian and even earlier Israelite predecessors, brought with them their own varied culturally conditioned theological presuppositions (a process of convergence) and only later acquired a more distinctive theological outlook (a process of differentiation).

In this first-of-its-kind comprehensive treatment of the development of Mormon theology, Charles Harrell traces the history of Latter-day Saint doctrines from the times of the Old Testament to the present. He describes how Mormonism has carried on the tradition of the biblical authors, early Christians, and later Protestants in reinterpreting scripture to accommodate new theological ideas while attempting to uphold the integrity and authority of the scriptures. In the process, he probes three questions: How did Mormon doctrines develop? What are the scriptural underpinnings of these doctrines? And what do critical scholars make of these same scriptures? In this enlightening study, Harrell systematically peels back the doctrinal accretions of time to provide a fresh new look at Mormon theology.

"*This Is My Doctrine*" will provide those already versed in Mormonism's theological tradition with a new and richer perspective of Mormon theology. Those unacquainted with Mormonism will gain an appreciation for how Mormon theology fits into the larger Jewish and Christian theological traditions.

Exploring Mormon Thought Series

Blake T. Ostler

IN VOLUME ONE, *The Attributes of God*, Blake T. Ostler explores Christian and Mormon notions about God. ISBN: 978-1-58958-003-9

IN VOLUME TWO, *The Problems of Theism and the Love of God*, Blake Ostler explores issues related to soteriology, or the theory of salvation. ISBN: 978-1-58958-095-4

IN VOLUME THREE, *Of God and Gods*, Ostler analyzes and responds to the arguments of contemporary international theologians, reconstructs and interprets Joseph Smith's important King Follett Discourse and Sermon in the Grove, and argues persuasively for the Mormon doctrine of "robust deification." ISBN: 978-1-58958-107-4

Praise for the *Exploring Mormon Thought* series:

"These books are the most important works on Mormon theology ever written. There is nothing currently available that is even close to the rigor and sophistication of these volumes. B. H. Roberts and John A. Widtsoe may have had interesting insights in the early part of the twentieth century, but they had neither the temperament nor the training to give a rigorous defense of their views in dialogue with a wider stream of Christian theology. Sterling McMurrin and Truman Madsen had the capacity to engage Mormon theology at this level, but neither one did."
 —Neal A. Maxwell Institute, Brigham Young University

"Let the Earth Bring Forth"
Evolution and Scripture

Howard C. Stutz

Paperback, ISBN: 978-1-58958-126-5

A century ago in 1809, Charles Darwin was born. Fifty years later, he published a scientific treatise describing the process of speciation that launched what appeared to be a challenge to the traditional religious interpretation of how life was created on earth. The controversy has erupted anew in the last decade as Creationists and Young Earth adherents challenge school curricula and try to displace "the theory of evolution."

This book is filled with fascinating examples of speciation by the well-known process of mutation but also by the less well-known processes of sexual recombination and polyploidy. In addition to the fossil record, Howard Stutz examines the evidence from the embryo stages of human beings and other creatures to show how selection and differentiation moved development in certain favored directions while leaving behind evidence of earlier, discarded developments. Anatomy, biochemistry, and genetics are all examined in their turn.

With rigorously scientific clarity but in language accessible to a popular audience, the book proceeds to its conclusion, reached after a lifetime of study: the divine map of creation is one supported by both scientific evidence and the scriptures. This is a book to be read, not only for its fascinating scientific insights, but also for a new appreciation of well-known scriptures.

Who Are the Children of Lehi? DNA and the Book of Mormon

D. Jeffrey Meldrum
and Trent D. Stephens

Hardcover, ISBN: 978-1-58958-048-0
Paperback, ISBN: 978-1-58958-129-6

How does the Book of Mormon, keystone of the LDS faith, stand up to data about DNA sequencing that puts the ancestors of modern Native Americans in northeast Asia instead of Palestine?

In *Who Are the Children of Lehi?* Meldrum and Stephens examine the merits and the fallacies of DNA-based interpretations that challenge the Book of Mormon's historicity. They provide clear guides to the science, summarize the studies, illuminate technical points with easy-to-grasp examples, and spell out the data's implications.

The results? There is no straight-line conclusion between DNA evidence and "Lamanites." The Book of Mormon's validity lies beyond the purview of scientific empiricism—as it always has. And finally, inspiringly, they affirm Lehi's kinship as one of covenant, not genes.

The Gift and Power: Translating the Book of Mormon

Brant A. Gardner

Hardcover, ISBN: 978-1-58958-131-9

From Brant A. Gardner, the author of the highly praised *Second Witness* commentaries on the Book of Mormon, comes *The Gift and Power: Translating the Book of Mormon*. In this first book-length treatment of the translation process, Gardner closely examines the accounts surrounding Joseph Smith's translation of the Book of Mormon to answer a wide spectrum of questions about the process, including: Did the Prophet use seerstones common to folk magicians of his time? How did he use them? And, what is the relationship to the golden plates and the printed text?

Approaching the topic in three sections, part 1 examines the stories told about Joseph, folk magic, and the translation. Part 2 examines the available evidence to determine how closely the English text replicates the original plate text. And part 3 seeks to explain how seer stones worked, why they no longer work, and how Joseph Smith could have produced a translation with them.

Second Witness: Analytical and Contextual Commentatry on the Book of Mormon

Brant A. Gardner

Second Witness, a new six-volume series from Greg Kofford Books, takes a detailed, verse-by-verse look at the Book of Mormon. It marshals the best of modern scholarship and new insights into a consistent picture of the Book of Mormon as a historical document. Taking a faithful but scholarly approach to the text and reading it through the insights of linguistics, anthropology, and ethnohistory, the commentary approaches the text from a variety of perspectives: how it was created, how it relates to history and culture, and what religious insights it provides.

The commentary accepts the best modern scholarship, which focuses on a particular region of Mesoamerica as the most plausible location for the Book of Mormon's setting. For the first time, that location—its peoples, cultures, and historical trends—are used as the backdrop for reading the text. The historical background is not presented as proof, but rather as an explanatory context.

The commentary does not forget Mormon's purpose in writing. It discusses the doctrinal and theological aspects of the text and highlights the way in which Mormon created it to meet his goal of "convincing . . . the Jew and Gentile that Jesus is the Christ, the Eternal God."

Praise for the *Second Witness* series:

"Gardner not only provides a unique tool for understanding the Book of Mormon as an ancient document written by real, living prophets, but he sets a standard for Latter-day Saint thinking and writing about scripture, providing a model for all who follow. . . . No other reference source will prove as thorough and valuable for serious readers of the Book of Mormon."
    -Neal A. Maxwell Institute, Brigham Young University

1. 1st Nephi: 978-1-58958-041-1
2. 2nd Nephi–Jacob: 978-1-58958-042-8
3. Enos–Mosiah: 978-1-58958-043-5
4. Alma: 978-1-58958-044-2
5. Helaman–3rd Nephi: 978-1-58958-045-9
6. 4th Nephi–Moroni: 978-1-58958-046-6

On the Road with Joseph Smith: An Author's Diary

Richard L. Bushman

Paperback, ISBN 978-1-58958-102-9

After living with Joseph Smith for seven years and delivering the final proofs of his landmark study, *Joseph Smith: Rough Stone Rolling* to Knopf in July 2005, biographer Richard Lyman Bushman went "on the road" for a year, crisscrossing the country from coast to coast, delivering addresses on Joseph Smith and attending book-signings for the new biography.

Bushman confesses to hope and humility as he awaits reviews. He frets at the polarization that dismissed the book as either too hard on Joseph Smith or too easy. He yields to a very human compulsion to check sales figures on Amazon.com, but partway through the process stepped back with the recognition, "The book seems to be cutting its own path now, just as [I] hoped."

For readers coming to grips with the ongoing puzzle of the Prophet and the troublesome dimensions of their own faith, Richard Bushman, openly but not insistently presents himself as a believer. "I believe enough to take Joseph Smith seriously," he says. He draws comfort both from what he calls his "mantra" ("Today I will be a follower of Jesus Christ") and also from ongoing engagement with the intellectual challenges of explaining Joseph Smith.

Praise for *On the Road With Joseph Smith*:

"The diary is possibly unparalleled—an author of a recent book candidly dissecting his experiences with both Mormon and non-Mormon audiences ... certainly deserves wider distribution—in part because it shows a talented historian laying open his vulnerabilities, and also because it shows how much any historian lays on the line when he writes about Joseph Smith."
-Dennis Lythgoe, *Deseret News*

"By turns humorous and poignant, this behind-the-scenes look at Richard Bushman's public and private ruminations about Joseph Smith reveals a great deal—not only about the inner life of one of our greatest scholars, but about Mormonism at the dawn of the 21st century."
-Jana Riess, co-author of *Mormonism for Dummies*

Saints of Valor: Mormon Medal of Honor Recipients

Sherman L. Fleek

Hardcover, ISBN: 978-1-58958-171-5

Since 1861 when the US Congress approved the concept of a Medal of Honor for combat valor, 3,457 individuals have received this highest military decoration that the nation can bestow. Nine of those have been Latter-day Saints. The military and personal stories of these LDS recipients are compelling, inspiring, and tragic. The men who appear in this book are tied by two common threads: the Medal of Honor and their Mormon heritage.

The purpose of this book is to highlight the valor of a special class of LDS servicemen who served and sacrificed "above and beyond the call of duty." Four of these nine Mormons gave their "last full measure" for their country, never seeing the high award they richly deserved. All four branches of the service are represented: five were Army (one was a pilot with the Army Air Forces during WWII), two Navy, and one each of the Marine Corps and Air Force. Four were military professionals who made the service their careers; five were not career-minded; three died at an early age and never married. This book captures these harrowing historical narratives from personal accounts.

Hugh Nibley: A Consecrated Life

Boyd Jay Petersen

Hardcover, ISBN: 978-1-58958-019-0

Winner of the Mormon History Association's Best Biography Award

As one of the LDS Church's most widely recognized scholars, Hugh Nibley is both an icon and an enigma. Through complete access to Nibley's correspondence, journals, notes, and papers, Petersen has painted a portrait that reveals the man behind the legend.

Starting with a foreword written by Zina Nibley Petersen and finishing with appendices that include some of the best of Nibley's personal correspondence, the biography reveals aspects of the tapestry of the life of one who has truly consecrated his life to the service of the Lord.

Praise for *A Consecrated Life*:

"Hugh Nibley is generally touted as one of Mormonism's greatest minds and perhaps its most prolific scholarly apologist. Just as hefty as some of Nibley's largest tomes, this authorized biography is delightfully accessible and full of the scholar's delicious wordplay and wit, not to mention some astonishing war stories and insights into Nibley's phenomenal acquisition of languages. Introduced by a personable foreword from the author's wife (who is Nibley's daughter), the book is written with enthusiasm, respect and insight.... On the whole, Petersen is a careful scholar who provides helpful historical context.... This project is far from hagiography. It fills an important gap in LDS history and will appeal to a wide Mormon audience."
    —Publishers Weekly

"Well written and thoroughly researched, Petersen's biography is a must-have for anyone struggling to reconcile faith and reason."
    —Greg Taggart, Association for Mormon Letters

www.ingramcontent.com/pod-product-compliance
Lightning Source LLC
Chambersburg PA
CBHW071714160426
43195CB00012B/1679